SEE HOW THEY RUN

See How They Run

The Administration of
Venerable Institutions

EDWIN SAMUEL

THE WOBURN PRESS – LONDON

First published in 1976 *in Great Britain by*
THE WOBURN PRESS
11 Gainsborough Road, London E11 1HT,
England

and in United States of America by
THE WOBURN PRESS
c/o International Scholarly Book Services, Inc.
P.O. Box 555, Forest Grove, Oregon 97116

ISBN 0 7130 0131 3

Printed in Great Britain by
T. J. Press (Padstow) Ltd., Padstow, Cornwall

Contents

Foreword

I personally find an absorbing interest in the administration of venerable institutions. That an administrative organisation has been able to survive for centuries is proof enough of its viability. During the years, its administration has been altered to meet changing circumstances and refined to keep down increasing costs. New equipment has often been introduced behind the scenes when the economic advantages have been tested elsewhere and proved.

As a former colonial administrator and university lecturer on institutions and administration for much of my working life I have naturally been interested in such developments. But it was not until 1963 that I began a close study of the administration of venerable institutions. In that year I succeeded my father, took my seat in the House of Lords and began trying to find my bearings in that 700 year old institution. Everyone concerned with its administration helped to explain the workings of the offices of the Lord Chancellor, of the Clerk of the Parliaments, the Printed Paper Office, the Post Office, the Police Force and the Maintenance Staff. It all seemed to me to work as smoothly as silk; so I decided to write an article on *The Administration of the House of Lords*. While so doing, I was somewhat surprised to find that it was the first time in seven centuries that such an attempt had ever been made. My facts were checked by every department concerned and the study appeared in the 1963 issue of *Public Administration in Israel and Abroad*. An off-print, in a red leather cover, is now available in the House of Lords Library for all new Peers who want to find out, in their turn, how the House of Lords is run.

Three years later, in 1966, I decided to write an article on the administration of another ancient institution. I looked around and found one, not only far more venerable but one that was spread world-wide – the Catholic Church. This involved much study in the British Museum Library, especially of Canon Law. The results were checked by the Apostolic Delegate to Great Britain, then Archbishop Cardinale. They were published in the annual. A South American journal of public administration subsequently asked for (and was given) permission to translate it into Spanish and reprint it there for its Catholic readers.

For this study I needed three management audits (prepared by the American Institute of Management) of the administrative efficiency of the Vatican. The Library of the British Museum was so disordered in getting copies of the audits for me that, the following year, I turned my little searchlight on the Library. The present Library buildings were erected between 1826 and 1852, to contain several collections of books and manuscripts, one of which had been acquired as far back as 1700. The British Museum Library thus qualified as a venerable institution and, with the help of Lord Radcliffe (then chairman of the board of trustees), Sir Frank Francis (director of the British Museum and principal librarian) and his staff, the study was completed. Again, it was the first administrative study of the Library that had been published and it aroused some interest.

In 1970, I did a study of *The Administration of the Royal Opera House, Covent Garden*, which dates back to 1662. There I had the support of a friend – Sir Leon Bagrit, a former director of the company that now manages the Opera House. I also was helped by Mr John Tooley, then the general administrator-designate, and his staff. Here again, it was the first time such a study had been made.

I then decided to publish annual monographs and only about venerable *British* institutions (the Catholic Church is international). As I am now in London during May, June and July every year to attend debátes in the House of Lords as a Labour Peer, it was not difficult to get permission one summer to do a study of some venerable institution the following summer, within the three months at my disposal. Each study was checked for accuracy by the staff of the institution and corrected accordingly. I was not concerned with criticising the institution, with its personalities or with gossip. I merely tried to present an objective and well-balanced picture of the management concerned.

After the Royal Opera House, I did a study of *The Administration of Balliol College, Oxford.* Five members of my family (my father, a brother, two sons and I) had attended it over half a century. The College had celebrated its 700th anniversary in 1964 and hence qualified well for my purpose. The Master, Mr Christopher Hill, and leading members of the College staff gave me every help.

That next was on *The Administration of Westminster Abbey* which is even more venerable; it had recently celebrated its 900th anniversary. To understand today's administration, a historical preface was essential; consequently the study was much longer. Again, it was the first that had ever been published. Here I was helped by the then Dean (the Very Reverend Dr Eric S. Abbott, KCVO), the then Sub-Dean (the Reverend Canon M. A. C. Warren) and the Chapter Clerk (Mr W. R. J. Pullen).

The last in the present series of seven studies is that of *The Administration of The Times,* the London daily. It has been in continuous publication for 186 years, but no one had previously enquired how it was managed. I am indebted for much patient assistance by Mr William Rees-Mogg (the Editor), by Mr John Grant (the Managing Editor), by the heads of all editorial departments, and by the chairman and directors of the Board.

All these studies were intended to be primarily of interest to professional administrators as well as to the staffs of these venerable institutions themselves. My historical approach may also have made them of some interest to historians. I, personally, learned a great deal from my own enquiries.

Meanwhile, I am continuing to make other studies. The next, with the backing of Lord Carrington, then Secretary of State for Defence, will be on the historical development of British Naval Manning and Supply since Pepys.

I also have permission from the Governor of the Tower of London to make a study of the administration of that very venerable institution indeed.

In this process, I have already developed into a venerable institution myself.

SAMUEL

The House of Lords

In February, 1963, I inherited a viscountcy on the death of my father. I took my seat as a Labour peer in June and attended every sitting of the House till the session closed at the very end of July. I was much struck, as a newcomer, by the remarkably smooth running of the parliamentary machine, all the more surprising in view of the great antiquity of Parliament—nearly seven hundred years. The smooth operation is no less surprising in view of the large number of separate authorities that share in the management of the Palace of Westminster, where the House of Lords and the House of Commons are both accommodated. I am grateful to all the representatives of those authorities with whom I spoke for the information that they supplied, especially to those connected with the House of Lords, with which this article is primarily concerned.

For readers not familiar with London, I must explain that the Palace of Westminster is on the west bank of the River Thames, at a point where it makes a bend and flows from south to north. Although the present Palace is in Gothic style, it was built between 1835 and 1855, following a fire in 1834 that destroyed the greater part of the former Royal Palace of Westminster, where many of the Kings of England had lived and where the House of Lords and the House of Commons had been accommodated as the guests of the Crown. The present building has a river front of 940 feet (with a terrace 700 feet long) and a depth of 400 feet. The total cost of administering the Palace and providing all the necessary services is in the order of £3,000,000 sterling a year.

The actual Chambers of the two Houses are situated one floor above street level on the so-called principal floor. With the basement, there are two floors below the principal floor and two floors above, making five in all. Both Chambers are comparatively small; that for the House of Commons was destroyed by German air-attack in 1941 but has been rebuilt almost on the former lines, which does not allow seats for all members. The House of Lords provides only 200 seats for peers (at a pinch, 300 can squeeze in) although, on March 1st, 1963, there were 930 Peers of the Realm, six being minors, three bankrupt, 72 had not applied for a writ of summons, and 80 had obtained writs but never taken the oath of allegiance. That is to say, 161 peers were not entitled to sit in the House. Of those so qualified, 220 had been given leave of absence. So the number of those actually eligible to sit was about 550. Many of these did not, however, attend regularly. The average daily attendance during the 1961–62 session was under 150, and not all were ever in the Chamber at any one moment. So there is, in practice, little overcrowding.

The members in both Houses sit facing each other, perhaps a relic, so far as the Commons are concerned, of the days when Parliament met in the choir stalls of St Stephen's Chapel in the earlier Palace. The acoustics in the present House of Lords are imperfect: microphones hang suspended over the red leather benches, and amplifiers are let into the backs of the benches for each seat, in addition to the provision of earphones that can be plugged in.

I will not give figures of the categories or the several ranks of peers and peeresses. Nor will I describe much of the legislative procedure, except to complete the verbal picture by stating that at one end of the Lords' Chamber is the Throne, used once a year when the Queen formally opens Parliament. (It is on the steps of the Throne that, on many occasions during the last 25 years, I have sat as the eldest son of a peer to listen when my late father was speaking.) In front of the Throne is the Woolsack[1] on which, except when the House is in Committee, the Lord Chancellor sits as Speaker, in full-bottomed wig and black silk 18th century costume, the Mace behind him. Facing him is the Table, at which sit the three clerks of the House— the Clerk of the Parliaments, the Clerk Assistant of the Parliaments and the Reading Clerk. On either side of the Table are the front Government Bench and the front Opposition Bench where the leading members of each party sit. Behind the Clerks are the shorthand writers: behind them again are the Cross Benches for peers who are not affiliated to any party, and behind *them* is the Bar of the House beyond which no stranger may advance. Members of the House of Commons are entitled to listen to the proceedings of the

---

[1] The Woolsack—a red couch—was originally placed in the House of Lords as a mark of defiance when England and Holland were rivals in the wool trade.

House from the Bar as well as from a special gallery provided for their use. When the Royal Assent is given to Bills, the Speaker comes with the Commons to the Bar of the House to hear it pronounced. Counsel plead from the Bar when the House sits judicially. Beyond the Bar are also the Black Rod's[2] box, seats for distinguished visitors and for wives and eldest sons of peers. Above, are the press gallery, more seats for distinguished visitors and the general public. Along the sides and above the Throne are galleries for peeresses and other special visitors.

Westminster is a Royal Palace, of which the custody and control are entrusted to the Lord Great Chamberlain, at present the Marquess of Cholmondeley. One of his most important duties is to maintain the security of the Palace, which includes fire precautions. It is he who allocates the rooms in the Palace and spaces in the car parks outside. He also licenses the 120 authorized guides who show visitors round parts of the Palace and controls the taking of photographs.

The Metropolitan Police are responsible for maintaining free access to Parliament for peers, MP's and, incidentally, all those working in the Palace. Fifteen constables from the Cannon Row Police Station of Whitehall are engaged on Parliamentary Crossing Duty, as it is called, when the House is meeting. A further 60 constables, two sergeants and a Police Inspector are employed *inside* the building from 2 p.m. until the House rises. Three are plain-clothes men, one being always in the Strangers' Gallery in the House of Commons in case of attempts at disturbance. Special precautions are taken to control access by day or night, to the residences and offices of the Lord Chancellor and the Speaker of the House of Commons within the building and to the offices of Ministers and Lords of Appeal. These sixty-three police on duty *inside* the Palace cost £56,000 a year and are paid for from parliamentary funds (£40,000 from the House of Commons vote and £16,000 from the House of Lords vote).

In addition to the Metropolitan Police, both outside and inside the Palace, Parliament has its own force of Custodians. They wear blue uniforms with flat peaked caps and Parliament's own insignia—a fortress portcullis flanked by chains. The force has a strength of 50 men in all—a Senior Inspector, three Inspectors, 42 regular Custodians and four Custodian Firemen. The Custodians cost Parliament

---

2 The equivalent of a Serjeant-at-Arms. He carries a gold-mounted black wand of office.

a further £42,000 a year (including £7,000 for shift pay). The House of Lords share is £25,000.

The daily exercise of these custodial functions is supervised on behalf of the Lord Great Chamberlain by the Staff Superintendent, a retired naval officer with a residence in the building. He also supervises the head cleaner and 25 part-time women cleaners employed in the building as well as the five attendants allotted to the House of Lords.

The Secretary to the Lord Great Chamberlain has a staff of two clerks, and it is in his office that applications from strangers (made before the House is sitting) for seats in galleries and elsewhere are handled. Once the House is sitting, the admission of visitors is controlled by Black Rod, an Officer of the House.

* * *

The postal services in the Palace come under another authority, ultimately the Postmaster-General. There are two post offices, one in the central and the other in the members' lobby. (The former includes a telegraph office.) These post offices are managed by a Parliamentary Postmaster, assisted by an Overseer, 16 counter staff, seven messengers and six postmen. They deal with the mail of both Houses. The volume of business is heavy, as MP's receive much mail from their constituents. They are allowed to send a few letters daily postage free: some post large numbers of additional letters at their own expense. (One MP recently despatched 5,000 letters to his constituents in one day!) About 8–10,000 incoming and 12–13,000 outgoing letters are handled daily. As an example of the efficiency of the Parliamentary services I will mention that, one day, I placed an oral request in the House of Lords Printed Paper Office at 11 a.m. for a particular document and received it *by ordinary post* at my flat in Westminster at 3 p.m. the same day!

The Parliamentary Telegraph Office works in two shifts and may handle up to 500 incoming telegrams a day when some crisis occurs which prompts constituents and public bodies to telegraph to their MPs.

The telephone exchange in the building is operated by a Superviser, an Assistant Supervisor and 15 operators, who also look after the 851 internal staff telephones. There is also a Members' telephone room, run by two Assistant Supervisors and twelve operators, where messages for Members are taken. Four Post Office engineering staff are also employed for maintenance duties. The rental of switchboards and the cost of official calls and telephone operators come to some £50,000 a year, of which the House of Lords share is £10,000.

The maintenance of the fabric of the building and the engineering service in the Palace are carried out by the Ministry of Public Building and Works, at a cost of £550,000 a year, of which the House of Lords share is £161,000. The fabric is under the supervision of a Resident Surveyor with 65 architectural, building and clerical staff. The Resident Engineer has an engineering staff of 110, of whom 17 are technicians and 15 clerical. The rest are engineering or electrical fitters and mates and lift attendants. (And even include three men who cook for the rest.) The supplies staff comes to fifty, making a total Ministry staff of 225 in the Palace. The value of the engineering plant alone for which they are responsible is £2,300,000.

The Palace is enormous. It has 1,200 rooms, including 12 complete apartments for resident officials. There are eleven courtyards, 100 staircases, two miles of passages, 37 lifts and hoists and no less than thirteen acres of floor area. Even so, there is not enough space for the 640 members of Parliament and their secretaries, for those peers who attend the House of Lords, for the members of the Cabinet and their secretaries, for the 270 members of the press and for the 700 permanent staff. Together with visitors, (including tourists, and constituents coming to see their MPs) there may be up to 3,000 people in the Palace at any one moment. Hence, the roof of the Palace along the eastern edge is now to be raised to provide more office accommodation, including rooms for fifty-one MPs and 25 secretaries, at a cost of £500,000. Across the way, facing Whitehall, a whole block covering six acres is to be redeveloped at a cost of £11,000,000. One big building and an underground car park will be reserved for parliamentary needs. The parliamentary building will have a floor space of 50,000 square feet, enough for some 280 rooms, but will not be completed till 1968. Even so, there will be no space for the recreation and relaxation of MPs, many of whom normally have to stay in the House till late at night.

During the winter, 160 tons of oil fuel a week (costing £3,400 a month) are needed to heat the existing 9,250,000 cubic feet of air space through 1,200 radiators. Some 25,000 gallons of hot water must be provided daily through 520 hot taps. A few gas and electric fires are still in use.

The Chamber of the House of Commons is air-conditioned; but the system has not yet been extended to other parts of the building, including the House of Lords. Humidity control has been introduced for the book and document stores.

Cold water in quantities must be supplied for domestic use and for fire-fighting (through 89 hydrants). Water under pressure is also needed for those lifts that are hydraulic; and a water-softening plant has been installed for tap-water. A sewerage system and incinerators have to be maintained, and refuse disposal has to be organised. Power vacuum machines are used for floor-cleaning.

Within the Palace are fifteen dining-rooms, tea rooms and cafeterias, with their attendant kitchens. There is seating for 1,130; and 2,500 main meals can be supplied daily for peers, members of Parliament and their guests, the press, the permanent staff and visitors. In the kitchens are refrigerators and deep-freeze cabinets, including three beer-cooling cabinets, with over 1,550 cubic feet of space. But there are not enough restrooms for the staffs concerned.

Large quantities of electricity are supplied from the external mains. The load is 3,000 kilowatts, and four transformers are in use. There are 7,700 lights, both bulb and fluorescent, to be serviced. Three hundred electric motors drive the fans, air-compressors, pumps, refrigerators and the lifts. The electricians are also responsible for the lightning conductors on the roof, the electric bell systems, and the 47 annunciators that print or announce, from time to time, the stage reached in debate in both Houses. (The 14 microphones in each House and the 960 amplifiers, of which 360 are in the House of Lords, are looked after by the firm that installed them.) Lastly, the Ministry of Public Building and Works operates the cinema projection room and the television set available for MPs and maintains the Big Ben clock and its chimes.

* * *

The Press Gallery in the House of Lords is operated on a system similar to that in the Commons. The Commons have 254 accredited British newspaper correspondents, of whom 177 work both in the Press Gallery and in the lobbies, the remainder in the Gallery only. There are also 27 accredited Commonwealth and 67 foreign press correspondents. They all receive annual permits from the Serjeant-at-Arms in the House of Commons and the Lord Great Chamberlain in the House of Lords. Day permits can be issued to casual and visiting press correspondents. Each regular press correspondent has a desk in one of the rooms behind each Press Gallery, several sharing one room. Separate rooms are allotted to the parliamentary staff of the Press Association, Reuters, the BBC, the 'Times' and the 'Daily Telegraph'. The 'Times' and Reuters have their own teleprinters; that of the 'Times' sets the linotype machines in the 'Times' head office by remote control. All British national morning and evening newspapers and news agencies have direct telephone lines from the parliamentary press rooms to their offices; there are call-boxes for other press correspondents. The accredited press correspondents have their own small reference library, a lounge, dining-room, cafeteria and bar. They elect their own chairman, treasurer and secretary annually, the last tending to be re-elected. This committee looks after the needs of all the parliamentary press correspondents.

The House of Lords and the House of Commons each have an extensive library. That of the House of Commons has larger demands to meet and is the bigger. But the House of Lords library alone has some 70,000 titles, and receives nearly 200 periodicals. It occupies four large rooms along the River front, in one of which—the Queen's Room—ancient documents are displayed for visitors to see. It is particularly rich in legal books for use in appellate cases: some are very rare. Peers may also use the House of Commons reference library. The House of Lords Librarian and his assistant aid peers needing information or references for their speeches. (Many MPs now demand a large increase in the research staff provided in the House of Commons library, as in the United States Library of Congress.) To the House of Lords library vote of £5,500 a year is added a further £4,400 from H.M. Stationery Office for new books and for binding. There is a bindery on the top floor of the Palace.

* * *

Several other specialised authorities are concerned with the House of Lords itself. One is the Gentleman Usher of the Black Rod, who is usually a distinguished retired army, navy or air force officer, appointed by the Crown, the present incumbent being Air Chief Marshal Sir George Mills, G.C.B., D.F.C. He sits in a box 'below the Bar' of the House of Lords and controls all the doorkeepers. He is assisted by a Yeoman Usher; this post at present is held, along with the post of Serjeant-at-Arms, by the Secretary to the Lord Great Chamberlain. Black Rod has been officially responsible for 'Keeping the Doors' of the House since 1523(!) and in that capacity supervises the door-keepers. Today there are two principal doorkeepers and 17 door-keepers or assistant doorkeepers. They are mostly men who have re-tired from the armed forces as Chief Petty Officers, Warrant Officers or NCOs and they are resplendently attired in white ties and tail coats provided at public expense. Those with over seven years' service wear gold badges of office across their waist-coats; the others wear broad blue ribands round their necks. The cost of the doorkeepers comes to about £17,000 a year. One of them, in top hat and red frock coat, with rows of medal ribbons, stands outside the Peers' Entrance to the Palace: two are inside the Peers' Entrance; four in the Peers' Lobby (one controlling tickets for visitors to the galleries); four are 'below the Bar' and act as messengers for the Clerks at the Table: one of them operates the loudspeaker that notifies the oc-cupants of public rooms in the Palace of the state of the proceedings in the Chamber, and the Division bells. Four doorkeepers are on duty in the Princes' Chamber[1] (the ante-room behind the Throne). They distribute letters received for individual peers (for whose faces the doorkeepers have an unfailing memory). Of the remaining three, one is the Bishops' messenger, one looks after the Press Gallery and the other looks after the Strangers' Gallery.

The most ancient office in the House of Lords, dating from 1280, is that of the Clerk of the Parliaments (the plural dates from the earliest times when Parliaments were of short duration and implies that the same Clerk continued in office from one Parliament to an-other). He is appointed by the Crown (by Letters Patent) on the advice of the Prime Minister of the day; and is removable only on an Address of the House to the Sovereign. He sits at the Table of the House, facing the Lord Chancellor on the Woolsack, together with two colleagues, the Clerk Assistant and the Reading Clerk. All three wear legal uniform—white ties, Q.C.s' coats, black silk gowns and wigs. The Clerk of the Parliaments wears a short Judge's wig; the other two Clerks, barristers' wigs.

The Clerk Assistant is responsible, under the general authority of the Clerk of the Parliaments, for the preparation of the Minutes of Proceedings of the House. These are sent for printing at the end of each day's sitting, are printed overnight and distributed by first post on

[1] So called because one of the rooms in the old Palace was used as a nursery for the Royal princes.

8

the following day. It is from these Minutes that the printed and bound Journals of the House of Lords are prepared by the Clerk of the Journals. In these Journals the titles of the peers who attend* each sitting of the House still appear in Latin. The Order Papers—the agenda for each sitting—are also prepared by the Clerk Assistant and printed daily.

Public Bills may originate in either House, unless they deal primarily with finance or representation, when they are always introduced in the Commons. Usually, however, Bills likely to raise strong political controversy go through the Commons before the Lords, while those of an intricate but uncontroversial nature are frequently introduced in the Lords before being sent to the Commons. The process of passing a Bill is basically the same in the Lords as in the Commons. The Bill receives a formal First Reading on introduction; it is then printed. On Second Reading the general merits or principles of the Bill are debated. In Committee of the whole House, detailed amendments are moved and there is a further opportunity for moving amendments on Report. Finally, on Third Reading (when there is a limited opportunity for making further amendments) the Bill is passed.

Public Bills are drafted by the Parliamentary Counsel who sit in a Treasury building in Whitehall. The printed copy of each Bill originating in the House of Commons comes eventually to the House of Lords, bound in blue and interleaved with blue paper sheets. It is handed over formally at the Bar of the Upper House by one of the Commons clerks in wig and gown to the Clerk of the Parliaments, with formal bows. As amendments are passed in the House of Lords, the text of each amendment is pasted in on the blank pages by the Reading Clerk and the Bill reprinted for each reading. The Bill, as finally passed, is reprinted and returned to the Lower House interleaved in white. Eventually, when both Houses are agreed on the text, the Royal Assent is signified by a Royal Commission of Peers and pronounced in Norman French by the Clerk of the Parliaments, as each short title is successively read out by the Clerk of the Crown. This formal ceremony is attended by members of the House of Commons who are summoned to the House of Lords by Black Rod and come to the Bar of the House, led by their Speaker. Clerks at the Table are assisted in their work by the staff of the Public Bill Office.

* The Reading Clerk and the doorkeepers take note of the peers who enter the Chamber.

Private Bills are dealt with in a separate office. These are more limited in scope than Public Bills and are subject to a different procedure. They originate in Petitions to the Crown and either provide for exemptions from the general law or confer special authority for particular purposes.

All the printing for both Houses is undertaken by Her Majesty's Stationery Office, founded in 1786. Each order is given a serial number and the script placed in one of several special boxes scattered throughout the Palace that are cleared every half hour by a messenger. The material is then taken by motor van to the Parliamentary Printing Press (blitzed but rebuilt in 1961) across the River near Waterloo Station. The last collection is at 11 p.m. if the House is still then sitting. The Press employs over 500 men and a few women out of the 7,000 employees of H.M.S.O. at other printing works and at headquarters; 230 of the printers work all night. Twenty-one linotype machines are used and four more are in reserve. Proofs of the Minutes of Proceedings are corrected at the Press and queries telephoned at any time of the night to the house of the Clerk Assistant.

In both Houses, an hour of debate produces about nine pages or 18 columns of printed report: in the year, the Press turns out some 65,000 columns. In addition, it prints reports of Select Committees; House of Commons Votes and Proceedings and Order Papers and their House of Lords equivalents; reports of nationalised industries and reports of the Estimates Committee. It despatches by post copies of each publication to all persons on its distribution lists. Small additional quantities are sent to the Printed Papers and Vote Offices in each House, where peers and MPs can get copies on request. The House of Lords Printed Paper Office has one clerk and two assistants.

The verbatim reports of the proceedings of each House were started first by Mr. T. C. Hansard in 1811: they are now produced directly by Parliament. In the Upper House nine expert reporters work in turns of ten minutes each. After his turn each dictates from his shorthand notes to a typist, and checks the typescript, which is worked over by the Editor of Debates or one of his two assistants. The proceedings of the House are also recorded on tape through the amplifying system. But a tape-recording cannot take the place of a Shorthand Writer sitting in the House. In particular, one cannot reliably identify from a tape-recording each speaker at times of animated exchanges—if, for example, there is noise and excitement and interruption and two or three Members of the House are on their feet trying to speak at the same time. Within seventy-five minutes of utterance in the Chamber, the edited text is placed in the box for dispatch to the Stationery Office for printing. Material that is not ready by 11 p.m. is printed in the following day's issue. The daily parts of Hansard are also available in a weekly edition. Peers who take part in a debate have the opportunity of correcting the reports of their speeches for the bound volumes of Hansard, which are prepared and issued every few weeks, each issue containing some twelve to fifteen hundred columns. Rotary presses are used for the Commons Hansard, as so many copies are needed. The copies of the Lords Hansard are produced on a flat-bed press. The quantities of Hansard usually printed are as follows: House of Commons: 6,000 daily edition (average issue 125 pages) plus 3,000 weekly edition; House of Lords: 3,000 daily edition (average issue 60 pages) plus 1,000 weekly edition.

Of the 3,000 copies of the daily House of Lords Hansards, 360 are sent to peers, 250 to House of Commons and House of Lords offices, 1,220 to other public offices, 400 to subscribers (chiefly libraries in Britain and abroad), and 60 to British Embassies abroad, and 750 are for sale by H.M.S.O. Of the 1,000 copies of the weekly edition of the House of Lords Hansards, 170 are sent to peers, 500 to public offices and 350 to subscribers or for sale. The whole Stationery Office vote for Parliamentary printing and stationery is nearly £600,000, of which £ 104,000 is for the House of Lords alone.

The Clerk of the Parliaments is assisted in his duty of 'keeping true Records of the things done and passed' in the House by the Clerk of the Records. The Clerk of the Records and his five assistants keep the documents of both Houses. The total number of these documents now reaches some 2,000,000. Among them are some 80,000 parchment rolls of original Acts of Parliament dating back to 1497, but incomplete. All these records are now stored in the reconditioned and massive Victoria Tower at the south end of the Palace. Some 32,400 square feet of floor space have recently been fitted up by the Ministry of Public Building and Works at a cost of £ 330,000.*

The Clerk of the Parliaments is the Accounting Officer for the

---

* Incidentally, I have arranged for my late father's political and literary papers to be deposited in these parliamentary archives, with the exception of his "Palestine" papers. These are now in the Israel Government Archives so that they may be together with those Mandatory Government documents that survived in Palestine and have been inherited by the Government of Israel.

House of Lords Vote and is assisted in that capacity by the Accountant and his staff of three Assistants. They prepare in October and November the annual Estimate for the succeeding financial year beginning from the following 1st April. The Estimate is prepared in accordance with Treasury regulations and contains provision only for salaries and expenses previously agreed with the Treasury and authorised by the House of Lords Offices Committee. The Estimate is then considered by the Finance Committee of the Offices Committee before being submitted to the Offices Committee itself for approval. When approved, it goes to the Treasury at the beginning of December and is published as Class I Government and Exchequer, Vote 1, of the Civil Estimates early in the New Year.

The Accountant is responsible for the financial and accounting arrangements of all Departments borne on the Vote, including reimbursement of travelling and other expenses of peers, the calculation and payment of salaries, wages and superannuation benefits of the staff, the assessment and collection of all fees on proceedings of the House, and maintains the staff records.

Salary lists with income tax and national insurance deductions are prepared monthly, and payable orders (cheques) are given to each member of the staff or are sent direct to his bank at his request. Weekly-paid staff are paid in cash by the Staff Superintendent from a bank imprest.

Peers receive no salaries: nor are they entitled to office accommodation and secretarial assistance at public expense. They are, however, entitled to repayment of their expenses up to a maximum of three guineas for each day on which they attend a sitting of the House, or a Committee of the House. In addition, provided they attend at least a third of the sittings of the House, they can obtain a refund of their travelling expenses between place of residence and London. Provision is made in the estimates for £60,000 for peers' travelling and other expenses.

The House of Lords accounts are audited in accordance with the provisions of the Exchequer and Audit Department Act, 1921, by Auditors of the Department of the Comptroller and Auditor General.

The total staff of the Parliament Office numbers 59 and the estimated amount required to meet the cost of it in the Estimate for

A micro-film of my father's "Palestine" papers is being made in Israel for presentation to the Clerk of the Records in London.

12

1963–64 is £ 92,000. The staff includes an Examiner of Acts, a registry clerk (for non-staff files), four secretaries (one of whom acts as private secretary to the Clerk of the Parliaments) and thirteen office assistants, senior office assistants and messengers.

* * *

We now come to the last and perhaps the most imposing of the great Officers of State concerned with the House of Lords—the Lord Chancellor or, more fully, the Lord High Chancellor. This office has existed for 900 years and the holder was originally the King's principal adviser and kept the Great Seal. As such, the Lord Chancellor is still a senior member of the Cabinet, as well as Speaker of the House of Lords. As Speaker, he receives a salary of £ 4,000 a year and an official residence within the Palace. But the Lord Chancellor is also President of the Supreme Court and recommends judges and recorders for appointment by the Queen. As such, he receives a judicial salary of a further £ 8,000 a year. He is responsible for the Official Solicitor's Office; the Public Trustee's Office; the Public Record Office; the Land Registry and the office of Judge Advocate-General. The present Lord Chancellor is Lord Dilhorne*. He proceeds daily from his residence in the Palace of Westminster to the Woolsack at the time of the sitting of the House, preceded by the Serjeant-at-Arms carrying the Mace (a duty also fulfilled by the Deputy Serjeant-at-Arms, who is also the Lord Chancellor's Private Secretary) and by his purse bearer** and followed by his train bearer, all in black silk breeches. The Serjeant-at-Arms and purse bearer wear swords. (For the rest of the day, his purse bearer and train bearer act as his messengers.)

The Permanent Secretary of the Lord Chancellor, Sir George Coldstream, is also Clerk of the Crown in Chancery (see below). There are as well in the Palace a Deputy Secretary, a Secretary of Commissions, an Establishment Officer (for the Supreme Court in general), three Assistant Solicitors, four Senior Legal Assistants (of whom one acts as private secretary to the Lord Chancellor); and a

* As Reginald Manningham-Buller, he came to Palestine as counsel representing the Crown before the Royal Commission of Enquiry into the Wailing Wall riots of 1929.
**The purse, a flat oblong cloth bag wholly embroidered on one side with the royal arms, originally carried the moulds for the Great Seal with which the Lord Chancellor was entrusted.

13

secretary for Ecclesiastical Patronage (as the appointment to 525 benefices is made by the Lord Chancellor on behalf of the Crown).

The Clerk of the Crown in Chancery is a senior official on the establishment of the Supreme Court. All Writs of Summons to Parliament (including my own) bear his name on behalf of the Queen. By long tradition, he signs with his surname alone, a style usually reserved for peers. The Clerk of the Crown also calls on the sheriffs to hold general elections and, when Parliament opens, presents the electoral rolls to the House of Commons. He is assisted by a Deputy Clerk of the Crown (who is also Deputy Secretary to the Lord Chancellor) and by a Clerk of the Chamber who actually prepares the writs and patents. The Great Seal affixed to patents is kept by the Lord Chancellor in a green leather box and consists of two deeply engraved silver moulds from which the wax seal is cast, to be attached to the patent by embedded cords. When a new Sovereign comes to the throne and new seal moulds have been made, the old seal moulds are defaced by the new Sovereign, in person, with a hammer blow.

Apart from the Lord Chancellor, the only other paid officer of the House of Lords who is himself a peer is the Chairman of Committees, appointed for each Session. This post is held at present by Lord Merthyr. He is assisted by a Legal Adviser with the title of 'Counsel to the Chairman of Committees', who considers all Private Bills before they are referred to Private Bill Committees; and by the Principal Clerk of Private Bills. He has his own office in the Palace. For his work in the House he is assisted by about eight unpaid Deputy Chairmen of Committees. These are peers, drawn from the different Parties and appointed for the Session. Not only does Lord Merthyr himself sit on the Woolsack from time to time as one of the Deputy Speakers of the House of Lords, but he is also responsible for the operation of all the Standing Committees of the House. There are no Standing Committees to which Public Bills are referred outside the Chamber, as in the House of Commons (or as in the *Knesset* in Israel): Public Bills are discussed only in the Committee of the whole House. There are some Standing Committees which meet infrequently, such as the Committee of Privileges (that deals largely with claims to peerages); the Committee of Selection (that meets when necessary to choose members of a Select Committee set up to consider an opposed Private Bill*); the Procedure of the House Committee

* In practice, the selection is done largely by the Committee Office.

(that meets once or twice a year to consider procedural questions); the Private Bills Standing Orders Committee and the Personal Bills Committee.

The Standing Committees that meet regularly are the Offices Committee (which has some forty members and deals with accommodation and staff); the Special Orders Committee (that keeps a watch on all delegated legislation); the Leave of Absence Committee (composed of the Whips of the three Parties); and the Joint Committee on Consolidation Bills (composed of six or seven legally-trained members from each House).

The Offices Committee has three sub-committees dealing with the Library (meeting only once a year); with the Refreshment Department; and with the Estimate (mentioned above and composed of Lord Merthyr and the Whips of the three Parties). Most of the Committee rooms are on the floor above the principal floor. But one is on the principal floor itself, the so-called Moses Room, from one of the frescoes on the wall.

* * *

The House of Lords not only has legislative functions but is also the final court of appeal for the United Kingdom. The same Lords who sit in the Appellate Committee of the House of Lords are also eligible to sit in the Judicial Committee of the Privy Council (which, however, may include some Privy Councillors who are *not* peers). The Appellate Committee of the House of Lords consists of:

(a) Nine Lords of Appeal in Ordinary, appointed by the Queen on the recommendation of the Prime Minister, largely from the Judiciary, but occasionally from the Bar. These are full-time paid appointments, terminable on reaching pensionable age.

(b) All peers who hold or have held high judicial office, who may sit from time to time to assist. This includes the Lord Chancellor (who is too busy to sit frequently himself); all ex-Lord Chancellors; all ex-Lords of Appeals in Ordinary; and the existing and all former Lord Chief Justices (if peers).

Five of these Law Lords normally sit at a time. Till 1948, they sat in the Chamber itself: now they sit in one of the Committee rooms. But judgement is delivered in the Chamber at a sitting which is technically a sitting of the House, opening as all sittings do with the Mace being placed on the Woolsack and with Prayers as the first business. (In future, the Opinions will not normally be read out in

15

the House but will be delivered in writing.) Each of the Lords of Appeal in Ordinary has a room in the Law Lords' Corridor, with, collectively, a personal assistant and two typists. Each writes his own judgement—or concurs in one of the others'. The judgements are circulated among the other four Lords of Appeal in case one wishes to change his opinion. The final opinions are printed and then delivered in the Chamber, as already mentioned.

The judicial business of the House of Lords is handled by a Principal Clerk and two other clerks.

* * *

I would like finally to describe, from my own personal experience, a typical day in the life of an ordinary peer. There are several ways to the House of Lords, the usual entrance being under a portico leading from the Old Palace Yard.* This is an open space at the side of a public street and is used as a car park for both the cars of peers and the overflow of cars of MPs, who normally use the New Palace Yard at the other end of the building for parking. Parking is controlled by the police constable on duty and by 'Red Coat', one of the doorkeepers. Both have phenomenal memories for peers' faces, even new ones'. Within the revolving doors is a small lobby (with writing tables and telephones) from which you enter the peers' cloak room. Another doorkeeper, in white tie, full evening dress and a gold badge of office, takes your hat and umbrella and hangs them on a peg, labelled with your name, in alphabetical order. (I use my father's old peg.) But the red tape loops for swords (still hanging in the House of Commons cloak rooms and changed periodically) have disappeared from the House of Lords cloak room. There is a dressing room and washroom nearby, where you can also dust your shoes. A specimen of the printed Orders of the Day (the agenda) lies on a table. You go up to the principal floor by a broad staircase; the more elderly peers use a tiny lift. At the top of the stairs is a Custodian or a policeman in his blue uniform. On one side are the offices of the Clerk of the Parliaments and the other Clerks at the Table. Along the corridor is the Printed Paper Office where you can pick up any document you need for the debate. In the Princes' Chamber—the ante-room to the Chamber itself—another doorkeeper recognises you and takes out from a rack any letters that have come for you. All the

* This has not really been a 'yard' for over a century; nor has the 'Palace' served as a royal residence for over 350 years.

16

usual reference books are set out on a table below the rack. In the middle, there are two large writing tables for four persons each, with supplies of stationery, and side tables on which brief-cases can be laid. On either side of the Princes' Chamber is a big fireplace, with padded leather chimney seats. The Government peers tend to gather on one side near their own benches inside the Chamber, the Labour and Liberal peers on the other. There you meet your friends before Prayers are read at the beginning of each sitting. The doors of the Chamber are closed during Prayers. Once Prayers (which you need not attend unless you wish) are over, you go into the Chamber and take your place on the benches used by your Party. I usually sit near the back of the Labour benches.

Further along the corridor are a news teleprinter, and dressing rooms for the Archbishops and Bishops. Twenty-one Diocesan Bishops take it in turns, each taking duty for a week at a time, to read Prayers. The peers' dining room is at the end of the corridor, with small tables in the outer room for peers with guests. In the inner room there are tables for Law Lords and for the Officers of the House—the Clerks at the Table, the Librarian, the Clerk of the Records, and so on. At a very long table in the inner room the other peers sit along both sides, as in a college refectory. There you may sit next to different peers at lunch or tea daily, and get to know your colleagues. Meals can be had at almost half the cost outside, as no rent, electricity or heating charges are paid. The Refreshment Department is run by a manageress appointed by the Refreshment Committee, instead of being run by a firm of caterers. When the House sits late, a cold buffet supper is available. New dining rooms are below, looking out on the Terrace and the River. Beyond the dining room on the principal floor is a guest room and bar and, beyond that, the House of Commons dining rooms. Near the peers' dining room are the four large rooms of the House of Lords library with books—many leather-bound—along the walls from floor to ceiling. In the inner room, silence is observed and the deep red leather arm chairs invite a nap after lunch. In two rooms smoking is allowed. In all the library rooms are writing tables, with House of Lords stationery and plain paper for speech notes. There are numerous reference books, daily papers, the current periodicals—all the facilities of a first-class London club. From time to time, a loudspeaker announces who is speaking in a debate or what clause of a Bill has been reached. When the division bell rings, all the peers in the library troop back to the Chamber to vote.

If you go along the corridor on the east side of the Palace, on the principal floor, your will find rooms for the Leader of the House. It is his Secretary who accepts the names of peers who wish to speak in any debate. *All* who wish to speak, may—unlike the procedure in the House of Commons, where you have to "catch the Speaker's eye". The Secretary closes the list at 1 p.m. and has it duplicated (so that you can pick it up at a table in the Princes' Chamber with pigeon holes, in which are also to be found printed copies of all the Bills and amendments to be discussed). Beyond his office are the rooms of the Government Whips, of the Lord Great Chamberlain's staff; of the Leader of the Opposition (Lord Alexander of Hillsborough) and of the Chief Opposition Whip (Lord Lucan), as well as the room of the Leader of the Liberal Party, which, for many years, my father used to use, now occupied by Lord Rea. The order of business of the House is arranged between the three Party Whips, the so-called 'usual channel'.

As I take the Labour Party whip, every Friday I receive by post from the Labour Party office in the Palace a duplicated programme of the business arranged for the following week. Important debates are underlined once, twice or three times, a three line whip implying that your attendance is highly desirable if at all possible. There is a meeting of the regular attenders among the Labour peers (about a third of the sixty or so) in one of the Committee Rooms upstairs every Thursday for three quarters of an hour before the House meets. The chairman is Lord Alexander of Hillsborough, and Lord Lucan, the Party Whip, discusses the business for the following week. Sometimes a peer will be invited to address his colleagues on some matter of general interest for half an hour. (I was invited to speak on Israel and the Middle East.) Those peers who will participate in one of the policy debates, usually held on Wednesdays, will meet in the Chief Whip's room a few days earlier to coordinate their speeches. (I attended such a meeting before the education debate on July 24th in which I made my maiden speech.) The front bench members of the Labour Party in the House of Lords meet in Lord Alexander's room every Tuesday to settle party policy.

Downstairs there are rooms for those peers who are Ministers, in addition to their rooms in their own Ministries, as well as a room for the Opposition peers. There are also rooms for the life peeresses. Upstairs are the accountants, the Editor of Debates, the Clerk of the Records, the Principal Clerk to the Appellate Committee and, on the other side, facing the River, there is a whole range of Committee rooms.

This, then, is the way the Palace of Westminster looks to a new-comer. Everywhere one goes, especially at the House of Lords end, there is a spirit of quiet efficiency, high morale and exquisite courtesy. It is a fascinating, if arduous, existence for a new peer who attends daily.

The Catholic Church

If one excludes national States such as China and India, the Catholic Church is one of the oldest and is certainly the biggest organization in the world today, dating back to the first century. Its growth in the past four hundred years has been phenomenal—from under fifty million adherents in the sixteenth century to over five hundred and fifty million today. (There has, of course, been a simultaneous increase in world population over this period.) At the same time we have a current decrease in the temporal power of the Catholic Church. It now has temporal jurisdiction only over Vatican City. But it still faces the innumerable administrative problems that arise from the management of 420,000 churches in 180,000 parishes, employing 406,000 priests (with a further 65,000 seminarians); the education of 23,300,000 children in 160,000 schools; the provision of assistance to 16,000,000 people a year in 33,000 charitable institutions and the employment of a total staff of some five million.

Hence it is of great interest to administrators everywhere to know how this vast Invisible Empire is governed. What matters, for example, can be decided locally and which must be referred to the Centre?

I have attempted to present the administrative system and the administrative problems of the Catholic Church as objectively as possible, without touching on dogma. I trust that nothing I have written will give offence to any Catholic who may read this article.

I am grateful to the British Museum for bringing over for me from the United States a copy of three management audits, dated 1956, 1960 and 1962, on the efficiency of the Catholic Chuch: I was able to study them while recently in London. These audits were

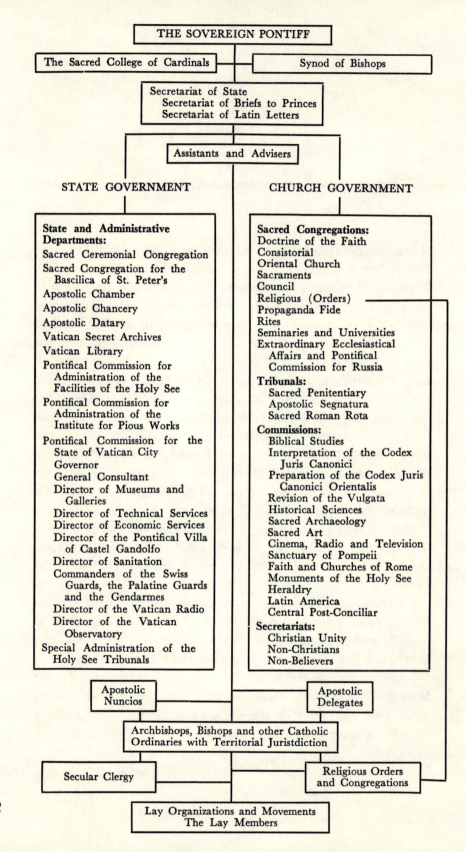

THE SOVEREIGN PONTIFF

The Sacred College of Cardinals

Synod of Bishops

Secretariat of State
Secretariat of Briefs to Princes
Secretariat of Latin Letters

Assistants and Advisers

STATE GOVERNMENT

CHURCH GOVERNMENT

State and Administrative Departments:
Sacred Ceremonial Congregation
Sacred Congregation for the Bascilica of St. Peter's
Apostolic Chamber
Apostolic Chancery
Apostolic Datary
Vatican Secret Archives
Vatican Library
Pontifical Commission for Administration of the Facilities of the Holy See
Pontifical Commission for Administration of the Institute for Pious Works
Pontifical Commission for the State of Vatican City
Governor
General Consultant
Director of Museums and Galleries
Director of Technical Services
Director of Economic Services
Director of the Pontifical Villa of Castel Gandolfo
Director of Sanitation
Commanders of the Swiss Guards, the Palatine Guards and the Gendarmes
Director of the Vatican Radio
Director of the Vatican Observatory
Special Administration of the Holy See Tribunals

Sacred Congregations:
Doctrine of the Faith
Consistorial
Oriental Church
Sacraments
Council
Religious (Orders)
Propaganda Fide
Rites
Seminaries and Universities
Extraordinary Ecclesiastical Affairs and Pontifical Commission for Russia
Tribunals:
Sacred Penitentiary
Apostolic Segnatura
Sacred Roman Rota
Commissions:
Biblical Studies
Interpretation of the Codex Juris Canonici
Preparation of the Codex Juris Canonici Orientalis
Revision of the Vulgata
Historical Sciences
Sacred Archaeology
Sacred Art
Cinema, Radio and Television
Sanctuary of Pompeii
Faith and Churches of Rome
Monuments of the Holy See
Heraldry
Latin America
Central Post-Conciliar
Secretariats:
Christian Unity
Non-Christians
Non-Believers

Apostolic Nuncios

Apostolic Delegates

Archbishops, Bishops and other Catholic Ordinaries with Territorial Juristdiction

Secular Clergy

Religious Orders and Congregations

Lay Organizations and Movements
The Lay Members

prepared by the American Institute of Management, as part of an efficiency study of the principal religious organizations, started in 1948, for the benefit of the Institute's own fifteen thousand members, the great majority, presumably, being American business-men. I am grateful to the Institute for permission to reprint the chart shown opposite. I am also grateful to the Apostolic Delegation in London for its assistance.

Among other sources of information have been the 1966 issue of the *Annuario Pontifico,* published in Vatican City; Addis and Arnold's Catholic Dictionary, published by Routledge and Kegan Paul, London, sixteenth edition (revised), 1967; the Catholic Encyclopedia, published by Robert Appleton, New York, 1907–22; the French-language Dictionary of the Canon Law (*Codex Juris Canonici*) of the Catholic Church, which has been appearing in parts in Paris since 1919 and, by 1963, had reached the letter V. (Till the Second Lateran Council of 1139 AD, general ecclesiastical legislation in the Western Church was based on decrees of General Councils and Papal letters. The best known source of early Canon Law was formulated by Gratian, an Italian monk of the 12th century. Further progress in formulating the Faith and the structure of the Church was made at the Council of Trent in 1565. The present code was compiled by a commission of Cardinals appointed by Pope Pius X in 1904. It was brought into effect in 1919 and is at present being revised by a Commission whose final report is not expected for several years.)

* * *

Supreme control over the Catholic Church—legislative, judicial and administrative—is, of course, vested in the person of the Pope. The local ecclesiastical authority in each of the nearly 2,000 dioceses throughout the world is the Bishop. Of these dioceses, 700 are in Europe, 400 in Asia, 350 in Latin America, 250 each in North America and Africa, and 50 in Oceania.

The dioceses are grouped into provinces, over each of which presides an Archbishop (in the Oriental Rite provinces, he is called a Patriarch). The Archbishop is also Bishop of the diocese in which his archiepiscopal residence is situated. In Rome, the Pope himself is also Archbishop of the Roman Province as well as Bishop of the diocese of Rome.

The Bishops, as members of the College of Bishops which will meet in future in periodic Synods, share with the Pope responsibility for the whole Church.

Like the Pope, each Bishop has joint legislative, judicial and administrative powers within his diocese, as laid down in the Code of Canon Law. The Canons of the Chapter of his Cathedral act as a consultative council. As with the Executive Council in British colonial administrations, a Bishop is bound, in certain matters, to seek the Chapter's advice; but he is normally not bound to follow that advice. Where, as for example, in many dioceses in the United States, there is no Chapter of Canons, there are twelve Diocesan Consultors.

As far as legislation is concerned, each diocese has its own code of local ecclesiastical laws, promulgated in Diocesan Synods by former Bishops. This code is subordinate to the Canon Law of the Catholic Church as a whole, based largely on Edicts from the Popes throughout the ages. Where there is due cause, a Bishop may issue dispensations from certain ecclesiastical laws to Catholics in his diocese.

In judicial matters, the Bishop is the judge of first instance in all cases affecting the discipline of ecclesiastics in his own diocese (canon no. 1572). There is a right of appeal to the Archbishop's Provincial Court and, in certain cases, to the Sacred Rota in Rome (canon no. 1594). The Bishop has power to enforce his judicial decisions by a variety of penalties, the severest among them being excommunication (2241); but this is rarely used.

As far as administration is concerned, the Bishop has authority in both doctrinal and secular matters. He creates and abolishes churches* and benefices (152, 1162, 1187, 1414 et seq), ordains clergy (111, 955 et seq), appoints clergy to ecclesiastical offices, transfers them and may remove them (2157 et seq). Permanent rectors of parishes are in some cases selected by competitive examina-

* The establishment of *Cathedral* Churches requires approval by the Pope, as does also the constitution of new Religious Orders.

24

tion, for which priests may sit who have served in the diocese for at least ten years and who have had at least three years' experience of parish work. The Bishop also licenses Catholics to preach and to teach theology and the catechism. He has power of censorship over religious and moral books published by Catholics. He fixes the rates of the diocesan dues (canon 1504) and supervises the administration of all Church property.

For the administration of general Church property, the Bishop is assisted by a board of trustees. Each institution—for example a Catholic school or hospital—has its own administrator or committee of administration (canon 1358). In some cases, the commitee may have a lay majority, but it is still subject to Church discipline. In the event of a breakdown in the administration of such an institution, the Bishop appoints a committee of investigation (1359). Property belonging to Religious Orders is administered by the Superior of the Order concerned, under the general supervision of the Congregation of the Religious in Rome.

* * *

In view of the wide spiritual and secular powers vested in a Bishop, he is required to have certain qualifications, in addition to the obvious moral qualities of piety, integrity and zeal. To be eligible for appointment as Bishop, a priest must be over thirty years of age and legitimate by birth. Five years at least must have passed since his ordination; and he must have a University doctorate in theology or Canon Law or some other academic equivalent.

In the early centuries of the Catholic Church, Bishops were elected by their flock: now they are appointed by the Pope after local consultation. In certain countries—for example, Spain— concordats have been reached between Church and the State whereby, among other things, the civil authorities are consulted before the appointment of Bishops by the Pope.

After appointment, the Bishop has four months within which he must take up his new post (canon 430). Till then, the management of the diocesan property is in the hands of the Vicar Capitular, an administrator appointed by the Canons of the Cathedral Chapter (432).

The Bishop may not be absent from his diocese for more than three months in any one year. He must visit each church in his diocese at least once a year (343), and all other Catholic institutions at least once in three years. Hospitals, seminaries and schools belonging to monastic Orders are controlled by the Superiors of the Orders and not subject to inspection by the Bishop (512, 344 and 1261).

Every five years, each Bishop must send a written report on his diocese to Rome. A different group of provinces reports each year. During the same period of five years, each Bishop must come to Rome in person to visit the tombs of the Apostles Peter and Paul and for an audience of the Pope.

A Bishop's appointment is terminated by death in office, or resignation (186–191), or transfer (430) or deposition (2303). It cannot be terminated by the action of any secular authority.

* * *

In certain countries, the Pope is represented by an Apostolic Nuncio, Pro-Nuncio or Internuncio, who has diplomatic status. There are other Papal representatives, without diplomatic status, known as Apostolic Delegates, who watch over the conditions of the Church generally within a specified area. They act as the eyes of the Holy See in the same way that General Montgomery employed staff officers in the field to report to him directly on the course of the battle.

Episcopal administration is also supervised generally by the Archbishop of the Province in which each diocese lies. In this respect he is the Metropolitan and the Bishops are his Suffragans. At least once in every twenty years, the Archbishop must convene a Provincial Council of his Bishops (canon 283). In practice, the Bishops of each country meet at least annually in an Episcopal Conference.

Ultimate supervision of episcopal administration is vested in the Curia in Rome—the administrative headquarters of the Catholic Church. The Curia consists basically of the following eleven Sacred Congregations of Cardinals, each Congregation acting as a departmental board of management and provided with a staff of officials.

The Supreme Congregation of the Doctrine of the Faith, founded in 1542 and reorganised in 1965. It now deals with faith and morals, and mixed marriages, and keeps watch on all books and publications. Its proceedings are strictly secret.

The Sacred Consistorial Congregation, an ancient institution, was organized in stable form in 1588. It deals with the establishment of new dioceses, the supervision of episcopal administration (with the exception of that of the Oriental Churches and of Mission territories) and the appointment of Bishops. It examines the Bishops' five-yearly reports (248).

The Sacred Congregation of the Oriental Church became autonomous only in 1917. The Oriental Church includes those Churches that broke away but subsequently returned to Rome, such as the Maronites, Melchites (Greek Catholics), Chaldeans, Copts, Syrians and Armenian Catholics. This Congregation has exclusive jurisdiction over the Middle East, Greece, Bulgaria, Southern Albania, Northern Ethiopia and Afghanistan, and over Oriental Rite Catholics in other lands.

The Sacred Congregation of Sacramental Discipline, set up in 1908.

The Sacred Congregation of the Council, established in 1564, today deals with the discipline of the clergy and the faithful, catechetical instruction, pious legacies, and ecclesiastical property and taxes (250).

The Sacred Congregation of the Religious, founded in 1586, deals with the Religious Orders, both for men and for women. The twenty principal Orders for men have between them 185,000 members, the two largest being the Jesuit Order with 31,000 and the Franciscan with 26,000. The seventeen principal women's Orders have over a million members between them, the largest being that of St. Vincent de Paul, with 43,000.

The Sacred Congregation for the Propagation of the Faith became a permanent body in 1622 and deals with all the missionary activities of the Catholic Church. Its jurisdiction reaches to all portions of the world where the Catholic hierarchy has not yet been regularly established. As new dioceses are set up, they pass under the jurisdiction of the Sacred Consistorial and other Congregations. Even in Mission territories, the Congregation of the Doctrine of the Faith and the Congregation of the Oriental Church have certain jurisdiction.

In 1955, the Mission territories (principally in Asia and Africa) had 31,500,000 Catholic adherents, or 2.5 per cent of the total population there of 1,200,000,000. Those Catholics were grouped in 11,600 parishes, with 74,000 churches, 30,000 priests, 92,000 monks and nuns, 66,000 schools and 127,000 teachers for 5,700,000 children. Through 5,900 charitable institutions, aid was given to 7,000,000 people, while 58,000,000 visited Catholic hospitals and clinics during the year.

The Sacred Congregation of Rites was set up in 1588 and has competence over all the ceremonies of the Latin rite Church.

The Sacred Congregation of Ceremonial, founded in the same year, deals with all the liturgical and non-liturgical ceremonies of the Curia in Rome.

The Sacred Congregation for Extraordinary Ecclesiastical Affairs, established in 1814, deals with the relations between the Church and civil Governments.

Lastly, *the Sacred Congregation on Seminaries and Universities,* founded in 1588, has jurisdiction over all Catholic seminaries except those of the Oriental Church or of the Missions, as well as over all Catholic Universities (there are more than forty) and Faculties.

There are many Commissions attached to these Congregations, as shown in the chart on page 22.

The Bishop's administration of his diocese is thus supervised by a variety of Congregations in Rome. Basically, if he is not in territory which comes under the Congregation for the Propagation of the Faith or of the Oriental Church, it is to the Sacred Consistorial Congregation that he is primarily responsible for his administration. But, on certain matters, for example the management of Church property, his reports are passed on by the Consistorial Congregation to the Congregation of the Council (canon 251). Those reports concerning churches within his diocese that follow an Oriental rite are passed to that Congregation (257); similarly with a Seminary or University (256), a missionary establishment (252) or a monastic Order.

All appeals from a Provincial Ecclesiastical Court are passed to the Rota in Rome. There is the right of further appeal to a still higher Ecclesiastical Court in Rome, the Segnatura.

Each of the eleven Congregations or Boards of Cardinals is presided over by one of the senior Cardinals, who becomes the Prefect of the Congregation. Eight of the eleven Prefects holding office at present are Italian; the others are French, Spanish and Armenian. All are over seventy years old, for it takes many years for them to reach such eminence in the College of Cardinals.

To each Congregation is attached a corps of consultants, all of whom are themselves ecclesiastics. Many are not Italian.

Nearly all the permanent civil servants who work for each Congregation are also ecclesiastics. A few laymen are employed, but there are no women among them It is entirely a man's world, and basically ecclesiastical at that.

The central offices of the Holy See also include the Apostolic Chancery, which issues Pontifical Bulls, and the Apostolic Datary, that deals with benefices. Each is headed by a Cardinal. The Apostolic Camera, under the Cardinal Camerlongo, is the Treasury of the Catholic Church. The Cardinal Secretary of State is the Chief Executive Officer of the Holy See (canon 263) to whom are directly responsible the Papal Representatives overseas. There are also Secretariats for Christians, non-Christians and non-believers. The general economic administration of the Holy See is directed by two Consultative Commissions which are advised by lay officials.

The Cardinals in the Sacred College are appointed by the Pope more or less on a geographical basis. They are at the moment ninetinine in number and of thirty-three different nationalities. Italians are now in the minority but are still over-represented. Athough some able men are appointed in their forties and fifties, two thirds of the present Sacred College are over sixty. There is no retirement age, and several are very frail.

The Sacred College has no elected element and no lay element. It acts largely as an advisory body, except after the death of a Pope, when the Holy See is put in commission, as it were. The whole College then acts as the Trustee for the Catholic Church until a new

Pope is elected by the College from among the Cardinals who comprise it. The new Pope must receive the support of at least two-thirds of the Cardinals. Voting is secret.

* * *

In addition to his position as head of the Catholic Church, the Pope is also the temporal Sovereign of the Vatican City, all that now remains of the former Papal States of Italy. The Vatican City covers only 108 acres of land; but within this area are the Basilica of St. Peter, the Vatican Palace, several world-famous museums, art galleries and libraries, an astronomical observatory, and all the ancillary services required, such as a radio station broadcasting in a multiplicity of languages, a post office, a printing press and the Swiss Papal Guard. By virtue of the Lateran Treaty of 1929, the Pope also has extra-territorial jurisdiction over thirteen important buildings in the City of Rome, as well as over his own summer residence— the Villa Castel Gandolpho, fifteen miles south of Rome. There is a separate administration in Vatican City, as shown in the chart on page 22.

* * *

How efficient is the administration of the Catholic Church? According to the American Institute of Management, the percentage efficiency rating has risen and fallen throughout the centuries as follows, although it is hard to imagine how the Institute can possibly know.

Century	Rating	Century	Rating	Century	Rating	Century	Rating
1st	50	6th	80	11th	40	16th	50
2nd	60	7th	70	12th	45	17th	50
3rd	65	8th	65	13th	60	18th	60
4th	75	9th	60	14th	55	19th	70
5th	80	10th	40	15th	45	20th	88

This table would indicate a steady rise in efficiency over the first five centuries of the Church, followed by a steady decline in the Middle Ages. There was a brief increase in efficiency in the thirteenth century, during the Renaissance. But it is not until the eighteenth

30

century that efficiency began to rise systematically. Today, according to the Institute, at 88 per cent it is higher than it has ever been. This may well be true, and even to be expected.

The efficiency rating of 88 per cent in 1960 is based on the series of ten criteria given below which I have re-arranged in the ascending order of merit achieved by the Catholic Church. These criteria have been drawn from the world of business management, and it is doubtful whether they are all applicable to a venerable religious institution. In assessing the over-all efficiency rating, that given for each criterion has been weighted by an arbitrary factor shown on the right-hand side of the table. These weights add up to a total of 100. Thus, effectiveness of leadership with a factor of 21 is given three times as much weight as operating efficiency with a factor of only 7. But even leadership is only a means to an end, that end presumably being, from a Catholic point of view, the saving of souls. And as that is not shown as a criterion, the audit must be regarded as somewhat superficial. In any case, it is hard to conceive what samples the Institute

Efficiency of the Catholic Church, as assessed by the American Institute of Management in 1960

(Table reproduced from page 1 of the 1960 Audit)

Criterion	Percentage Rating	Percentage Weight of Total Rating
1. Growth of facilities	75	5
2. Development programme	81	8
3. Membership analysis	85	13
4. Organizational structure	88	8
5. Trustee analysis	88	8
6. Fiscal policies	88	8
7. Operating efficiency	93	7
8. Effectiveness of leadership	95	21
9. Administrative evaluation	97	12
10. Social function	100	10
		100

took, and where. Presumably, the prime sources of information were the United States (as the Institute is an American organization) and in Rome. But I wonder whether much of significance was obtained. The Catholic Church is reluctant to throw open its archives even to Catholic priests seeking material for their own doctoral dissertations. (I once myself went through dozens of such dissertations in the Library of Congress in Washington in search of reliable statistical information, but with little success.)

The total efficiency rating, after weighting, comes to 88 per cent. This figure need not be taken literally. What is important is that the lowest rating for any criterion was 75 per cent—for growth of facilities.

The Audits also set out under 32 heads what business management can learn from a study of the Catholic Church, as follows. (Spelling and grammar are given verbatim):

1. The value of widespread diversification to a continuing enterprise.
2. The necessity of autonomous controls geographically.
3. The benefit of long executive training and slow promotion.
4. The importance of doctrine and indoctrination in assuring continued unity of thought and action after the authority for decentralized operations has been delegated.
5. The necessity of giving top men full authority once they have been chosen.
6. The efficacy of being absolutely certain concerning each individual's integrity, ability, and industry before he is given any authority whatsoever.
7. The benefit of promotion from the ranks.
8. The wisdom of not too much obvious zeal once a position of influence has been attained.
9. The beneficial result of not too frequent reports to headquarters.
10. The advantage of haste in some directions and delay in others.
11. The requirement of constantly defensive action where authority is imperiled.
12. The need to utilize the knowledge and power of elderly men in staff capacities.

13. The advantages of an atmosphere of diplomacy in all dealings.

14. The wisdom of relieving incompetent executives of their authority.

15. The usefulness of fixed policies understood by and adhered to by everybody.

16. The importance of being slow to praise, and slower still to condemn.

17. The long-term benefit of avoiding nepotism in the hierarchy of any management.

18. The value of instilling all employees with a sense of public contribution and social values.

19. The advantage of realizing that monetary reward by itself has never been a great motivating force for man's best activities.

20. The need to abandon activities that have lost their usefulness.

21. The benefit of choosing directors that can be utilized in some manner of advisory level through their knowledge of the operation.

22. The importance of striving constantly to maintain unity of command.

23. The advantage of concentrating activities within national boundaries, to the extent possible.

24. The wisdom of publicly honoring past contributors to the undertaking.

25. Never rob Peter to pay Paul, or do not lose the returns on one activity to support the production and distribution of another.

26. The need to recognize the advantages of simple beginnings in any new enterprise.

27. The profit from the starting of an enterprise at a time of adverse conditions.

28. The importance of being willing to deviate from fixed rules when intelligent management deems such action advisable.

29. The need to maintain at all times strict discipline and an atmosphere of some struggle and humility.

30. The everlasting advantage of advancing and denying at times, while retreating and affirming at others.

31. The importance of being amenable to constructive criticism.

32. The long-term importance of selling or persuasion by demon-
stration and example rather than aggressive pressure.

On the other hand, the Audits also mention some of the major
deficiencies of the administration of the Catholic Church. Apart
from the advanced age of the Prefects of the eleven Sacred Congregations, and their overwhelming Italianate nature, the most signi-
ficant criticisms made are:

(a) *Fiscal policy.* An archaic investment policy; no depreciation
funds for the reconstruction of antiquated buildings, such as
Catholic hospitals and schools; inadequate financial planning
and an excessive secrecy over Church finance generally.

(b) *Central management.* Few meetings of heads of departments;
over-working of the Pope himself and little staff research.

(c) *Other matters.* Aesthetic insensibility in the architecture and
decoration of new buildings; inadequate public relations and
public information services; and a multiplicity of Catholic
periodicals instead of concentration on a smaller number of
higher quality.

As far as the Curia itself is concerned, the Institute considers that
its staff work very hard. Time clocks have been introduced. Salaries
were increased by 25 per cent by Pope John, which makes it un-
necessary for lay employees to moonlight. But the speed of executive
decision varies. As the first Audit says (page 18): "The hierarchy
moves quickly in administrative matters, slowly in its social customs
and not at all where dogma is concerned". This is what one might
expect.

As far as secrecy is concerned, the first Audit says (page 19):
"Conferences are seldom held in private offices, even when but two
individuals are involved. Everything, and literally everything, is kept
under lock and key. The Pope keeps the key to his own desk". But
none of this would be considered unusual in any Bank director's
suite in London.

As far as the reform of the Catholic Church is concerned, the
Institute lists the ten following aims. Those which are of particular
administrative interest are marked with an asterisk.

1. To survive, always, is the first duty of the Church.

2. To expand, continually, is the second requirement.
3. To better champion the oppressed by social reform and attract the great developing middle class.
*4. To secure needed larger contributions from members.
5. To separate the Church from any air of intrigue and Latin thinking, yet not lose its tradition.
6. To maintain a better atmosphere of propriety and yet protect itself politically.
*7. To rid itself and the world of nepotism.
*8. To increase both the zeal and the intellectual standing of its members.
*9. To incorporate the better business methods of industrial corporations into its activities and yet not become materialistic.
10. To become the champion of the family the world over in positive rather than in negative social terms.

My own personal conclusions are that the Catholic Church has developed a very remarkable and efficient system of administration. It is a venerable and world-wide institution which has to contend with problems of distance, language, national susceptibility and varying levels of culture. As an ecclesiastical organization, it must be conservative in outlook. To use contemporary American methods, for example, in public relations and publicity would be undignified. It is concerned primarily with its own adherents and not with its 'image' among non-Catholics.

I would, however, venture to suggest that a series of authoritative monographs should be written on different aspects of the administration of the Catholic Church, both in the past and today. They should be written under the direction of the Hierarchy and published officially. This would be of the greatest possible interest to professional administrators everywhere, especially in view of the thorough overhaul which the Church administration is now undertaking.

The British Museum Library

*As a user of the British Museum Library on many occasions while in London over the past forty years, I have for long been puzzled by some of the apparent complications in its administration. With the blessing of the chairman of the board of trustees, Lord Radcliffe, and the active help of the director and principal librarian of the Museum, Sir Frank Francis, I was enabled last summer to go through the whole administrative system. I am particularly indebted to the principal keeper in charge of the department of printed books, Mr Hugh Chaplin; to the assistant secretary of the Museum, Mr George Morris; to the superintendent of the reading-room, Mr Richard Bancroft; to Mr David Rodger, Mr David Paisey and others who acted as my guides. I have also been much helped by the following two books by Arundel Esdaile, a former assistant keeper in the department of printed books—*National Libraries of the World: Their History, Administration and Public Services: *published by the Library Association, London, (second edition) 1957; and* The British Museum Library: A Short History and Survey; *published by George Allen and Unwin, London, 1946. Then there is* The Reading Room of the British Museum, *by G. F. Barwick (superintendent of the reading-room from 1900 to 1915), published by Ernest Benn, London, 1925.*

The future of all large libraries, including that of the British Museum, is bound up with automation. The general problems involved are dealt with in The Brasenose Conference on the Automation of Libraries, *edited by John Harrison and Peter Laslett; published by Mansell, London, 1967.*

The British Museum Library is the national library of Great Britain, maintained by the Government from funds voted by Parliament. It is one of the six libraries of deposit under the Copyright Laws, (see page 46). It differs in many respects from the great university libraries at Oxford (the Bodleian) and at Cambridge and also from the Library of Congress in Washington, which started as a parliamentary library. The British Museum Library is not a lending library. Readers who wish to borrow books to be read off the premises have access to the network of municipal lending libraries established in every county and city in Great Britain and in each of the thirty-two boroughs of the Greater London Council. All draw from other lending libraries through the National Central Library and through regional inter-lending centres those books requested which they do not have on their own shelves. The British Museum Library is thus a library for reference and for research which cannot reasonably be carried out in any single library elsewhere in Britain.

It is situated in Bloomsbury, a district noted as one of the main intellectual centres of London.* Just to the north of the Library are some of the main buildings of the University of London. The Museum buildings in Bloomsbury also house the national museum of antiquities and ethnography and the Museum's own collection of prints and drawings. This composite collection of books and other objects owes its origin to the undiscriminating taste of Sir Hans Sloane two hundred years ago. In the eighteenth century there was none of today's differentiation. Collectors of books and manuscripts also collected paintings, antiquities, geological specimens and even shells. However, the Museum's natural history collections were hived off between 1880 and 1883 to a separate museum in South Kensington which, since a new Act was passed in 1963, is now under a separate administration.

History of the British Museum Library

The Museum library itself is truly a product of the eighteenth century—the age of enlightenment. The Royal Society—the British academy of science—had been founded in 1660. There were at that time many private libraries in Britain, but there was no national library, similar to those already established in France, Sweden,

* For many years the offices of the World Zionist Organization were just opposite, at 77 Great Russell Street.

Italy and Austria. By the eighteenth century, even the Vatican library was already two hundred years old.

Some of the component parts of a national library had, however, already become the property of the British Government. On the dissolution of the monasteries by King Henry VIII between 1525 and 1546, many manuscripts were dispersed. Some were acquired by Sir Robert Cotton, who was arrested in 1629 for political offences; he was released a year later but his library remained under control of the royal librarian. By an Act of 1700 (12–13 William IV 67), the Cotton library was acquired for £ 4,700. The Cotton mansion, in which it was housed, having decayed, the manuscripts were eventually moved to Westminster School, near the Abbey.

In 1738, Arthur Edwards left his books to the State, together with £ 7,000 for their maintenance.

In 1749, Sir Hans Sloane, secretary—and later president—of the Royal Society, bequeathed his manifold collections to the State for the nominal sum of £ 20,000, on condition that a repository be provided for them.

In 1753, the second Countess of Oxford sold to the State, for £ 10,000, some 8,000 volumes of manuscripts collected by her grandfather and father, Robert and Edward Harley: this became the Harleian collection.

The accumulation of these several diverse collections led in 1753 to the Act of Incorporation of the British Museum (26 Geo. II 22). It provided for the acquisition of accommodation for the Cottonian manuscripts and for payment for the Harleian collection. As there was no money in the Treasury for those purposes, a State lottery was authorized which raised £ 100,000. The Harleian collection was paid for and Montagu House was purchased and repaired for use as the new Museum.

Montagu House had been built in 1670 for the Dukes of Montagu. In 1759, the first reading-room, with twenty chairs, was opened in its basement. All the land to the north was then open country, and a favourite place for duelling.

Two years earlier, George II had presented to the new Museum the royal collection of manuscripts, together with the old royal library originally founded by Edward IV (1461–83). Other bequests followed: in 1759, Solomon de Castro left to the Museum his collection of Hebrew books: in 1799, it acquired the Cracherode library; in 1823, George IV presented 65,000 books (collected by George III) to form what it now called the King's Library; at his death in 1846, Thomas Grenville left the Museum his collection of over 20,000 volumes. The Museum and its library have thus been created, first, by great private collectors—such as Cotton, Sloane and the Harleys; secondly, by royal gifts; thirdly, by the proceeds of a public lottery; and, lastly, by annual Government grants.

ACCOMMODATION

After the royal gift of 1823, the need for additional library space became urgent and £ 120,000 was voted by Parliament to build it: Smirke was selected as the architect. Thus the present main Museum buildings were erected between 1826 and 1852 on the four sides of a quadrangle—one side forming the King's Library. The continuous accumulation of books, newspapers and other periodicals under the Copyright Laws has led to a constant search for additional storage space. This has limited the amount of additional space available as reading-rooms for research scholars and the general public. There is wholly inadequate room for cataloguing and for all the other services needed by a great library. In 1914 and again in 1931–36, the North Library was reconstructed as a reading-room for rare books and periodicals. In 1914, just before World War I, King Edward's wing was constructed even further to the north. It is used largely for the Museum's antiquities and ethnographical collections; but part of the ground floor serves as the State Paper library (including acquisitions by international exchange) while the basement is used for book storage, the mezzanine for music and maps, with a print room on the top floor.

During the Second World War, the Museum and its library were not only unable to enlarge their accommodation; it was even reduced by bomb damage. The Ministry of Public Buildings and Works is still engaged on a ten-year reconstruction project, due to be completed by 1970; but it is several years in arrear.

40

Meanwhile, the only solution to the relentless expansion of library stock at ever-increasing speed has been the eviction of whole classes of publications to out-of-town repositories: for example, a large part of the State papers to Woolwich. There is now a proposal to transfer further selections of the Museum's ethnographical collections for display in new Government buildings or in rented buildings elsewhere in London. This would allow more space for the State papers library, pending the construction of a new main library building (see below).

The newspaper collections were evicted as early as 1906. Then a depository was established at Colindale, near Hendon, about half an hour's drive to the north. In 1936, a newspaper reading-room was added at Colindale; in 1957, a six-storey extension was built to provide space for the next ten years' accretions. But, with the establishment of a microfilm unit, in 1949, with Rockefeller money, many issues have been photographed. Once the newspapers from abroad have been photographed, the originals will be disposed of to other libraries and there should then be enough space for future accretions, not of the next ten years but of the next twenty-five.

In 1959, it was decided to amalgamate the Museum library's science books with the Patent Office scientific library and so create a great National Reference Library of Science and Invention (NRLSI). This would have about a million volumes in all languages, which it was proposed to arrange on shelves with open access (as with the Cambridge University Library). It would have a reference section and specialised staff for each of the major scientific disciplines with a general reference library equipped with an instant photo-copying service. It was at first proposed that NRLSI should be housed, together with the Patent Office itself, on the South Bank in a new building to be completed by 1965. But the scheme has fallen on evil days. First, the original plans met with criticism both from the County Council and the Royal Fine Arts Commission. Then, the Government decided that the new Patent Office should be built *outside* London as part of the plan for the dispersal of the civil service. So the Patent Office library is still in the old Patent Office building at Holborn; the rest is housed, but without open access, in the upper floors of Whiteley's shop in Bayswater. Now, the Greater London Council has decided to use the South Bank site for other purposes. So a new site must be found and a new science library designed and built, which will take several years. This, in an age of increasingly rapid scientific and technological development, is deplorable.

But none of these developments is capable of solving the basic problem—this desperate shortage of library space in Bloomsbury itself. As early as 1928, it became apparent that a large extension of the Museum library was essential. That was nearly forty years ago. As it would be too costly to remodel the existing monolithic classical block, the only solution was to create a whole new Museum library building *south* of the present Museum, on several blocks of land at present occupied by private houses, flats, offices, shops and a hotel. But it was not until 1952 that a public inquiry was held and the new site approved. It took a further ten years to prepare the specifications and to get the architects appointed: not until 1964 was the outline scheme approved by the Government. Three years later, the Ministry of Public Buildings and Works was still engaged in buying up the plots required. It was hoped to start actual construction in the 'early 1970s'; but, in October, 1967, the Government suddenly announced that it had abandoned the whole project as a result of objections by existing occupiers of the site. The whole question of the functions and organization of the national libraries is to be reconsidered. Meanwhile, the congestion in all the existing British Museum buildings will grow worse and worse.

ORGANIZATIONAL STRUCTURE

A curious feature of the British Museum is that, two centuries after its creation, there is, by law, still a single director and principal librarian in charge both of the antiquities and other collections, and of the library. The present director, Sir Frank Francis, himself a 'library man', devotes about half his time to each side of the institution.

Until 1963, the director and principal librarian was not allowed to have a deputy. This was a relic of the 19th century fear that such a deputy would, in fact, do all the work, the chief post itself being regarded by its holder as a mere sinecure; which of course it is not.

The organizational structure of the library was largely developed by Sir Antonio Panizzi, an Italian refugee, who headed the Museum from 1856 till 1866. Today, the Museum consists of twelve administrative units, of which seven deal with the antiquities and other collections, and four with the library; the last is a joint laboratory. One of the Museum's great handicaps is that, by tradition, these administrative units are highly autonomous. The head of each department reports direct, not only to the director and principal librarian, but also annually to the board of trustees. However, several common services have been developed—photography, publications casts (Museum only) and works planning (execution is in the hands of the Ministry of Public Buildings and Works).

The Museum has no organization and methods unit of its own, which is a curious omission. A constant internal roving eye would be of great value for detecting and solving minor administrative problems. For major investigations—such as the automation feasibility study—the library consulted the Treasury's experienced management services division, which, by then, had already approved the installation of some sixty computerised systems.

Of the four library departments, the central and largest is the department of printed books, which includes sections administering the collections of printed music, maps and postage stamps. The great circular reading room is part of this department. Adjacent are the department of manuscripts (which broadly includes manuscript music and maps) and the department of oriental printed books and manuscripts. The latter does not, however, administer the collection of oriental State papers. These are acquired and made available in the department of printed books as part of a wider arrangement with Her Majesty's Stationery Office (see page 136 below). The last of the three smaller library departments is that of prints and drawings; it could equally be classified as one of the Museum's antiquities collections and not as a part of the library.

The rest of this monograph deals largely with the department of printed books, by itself the largest public library in Britain.

The Board of Trustees

Under the new British Museum Act of 1963, the director and principal librarian is responsible to a board of twenty-five trustees. One is appointed by the Queen (as the Museum embodies a royal library), four represent the Royal Society, the Royal Academy, the British Academy and the Society of Antiquaries; fifteen are appointed by the Prime Minister; the remaining five are co-opted on the recommendation of the other trustees. Each trustee may serve not more than ten years.

The trustees normally meet seven times a year. Part of their work is devolved on to committees—for buildings; investment; publications; printed books; manuscripts and oriental printed books and prints and drawings; antiquities (two committees); and the research laboratory. Each of these committees meets at least once a year and, in practice, more often. The two library committees each meet twice a year.

Any important administrative change, for example, a proposal to split an existing department, would have to be approved by the trustees.

The Ministry of Education and Science

Until 1963, the Museum used to deal directly with the Treasury, which on the whole, was sympathetic towards its needs. Public inquiries into its problems were held in 1835–36, 1847–49 and 1928–30.

Since 1963, the Museum falls within the province of the Ministry of Education and Science. Miss Jennie Lee, now joint Parliamentary Under-Secretary, has insisted on the closest liaison being maintained between her senior officials and those of the Museum, which is all to the good.

The Museum's budget is included in the civil estimates and is dealt with more fully below (page 148). It is, however, not easy to run a museum—and especially a great public library—as if it were a Government department. Some of the grades of the staff are peculiar to the Museum and other similar State institutions. Many are standard civil service grades which do not allow of adequate flexibility.

At first sight, it might seem advantageous for the Museum to become a statutory corporation with power to fix its own salary scales on the lines of, say, the BBC, or, now, the GPO. But it has little revenue of its own and would have in any case to be maintained largely from Government grants-in-aid, with little real independence. In actual fact, it is administered by the trustees, and not by the Ministry, which is perhaps the best possible arrangement.

ACQUISITION OF BOOKS

The library was founded two centuries ago with universalist ambitions—both domestic and foreign, both antiquarian and contemporary. With the publication of books at an ever-increasing rate all over the world, it is becoming harder and harder for the library to achieve those ambitions. To the extent that it does achieve them, it is faced with the almost superhuman problems involved in processing and storing the enormous annual accretions of stock.

The library obtains its stock by four methods:

(a) A deposit copy, under the Copyright Laws, of every book published in the United Kingdom and in certain colonial territories.

(b) Documents from abroad received (largely in the State Paper department) in exchange for documents published in the United Kingdom.

(c) Donations and bequests of books and other material.

(d) Purchase of books either from abroad, or if of antiquarian interest, from Britain.

A large part of the intake of the department of printed books is received by copyright deposit. The proportion varies between the categories of literature. Over 40,000 books were received in 1966 by copyright out of a total of over 112,000. On the other hand, parts of copyright serials and periodicals accounted for little more than 60,000 out of a total of over half a million, of which almost a half consisted of literature received by international exchange. Under the original 1709 legislation, enacted before the establishment of the Museum, copies of every book had to be supplied to nine institutions (the Royal Library, the Bodleian Library at Oxford, the University of Cambridge, Sion College in London, the four Scottish Universities, and the Faculty of Advocates at Edinburgh). By an Act of Parliament of 1801 (41 Geo. III, c. 107) eleven examples of the best and largest copies of each work had to be deposited at Stationers' Hall for the privileged libraries, which by this time included Trinity College, Dublin, and King's Inns, Dublin, while the Museum had taken the place of the Royal Library. Since that time the Scottish Universities, King's Inns, Dublin, and Sion College have disappeared from the list. The National Library of Scotland has taken the place of the Faculty of Advocates in Edinburgh, and the National Library of Wales has achieved the distinction of being added to the privileged few. There are thus six libraries in Great Britain which may receive books by copyright deposit, but only the Museum is obliged to take every book offered; the others may be as selective as they wish.

Most publishers in the United Kingdom send their deposit copies out with their review copies. They are allowed one month's delay, after which claims may be made by each deposit library. Difficulties arise largely with books printed privately or issued by amateur publishers.

A copy of every issue of every periodical must also be deposited; and here there is a difference in treatment between newspapers (all dailies as well as non-technical weeklies and fortnightlies) which are stored and read at Colindale, and all other periodicals, which are stored at Bloomsbury and read in the periodicals gallery in the North Library. But both categories are received at Bloomsbury, often in composite parcels. Daily newspapers usually come in daily, but the *Times* and *Telegraph* come in monthly. They are all pigeon-holed alphabetically for a month. Issues for the month are then recorded in ledgers and any missing numbers claimed. They are tied up in bundles and sent to Colindale for filing, binding and cataloguing. On the other hand, the weeklies and fortnightlies are pigeon-holed for a year before being registered.

An index is maintained of all newspapers and periodicals and a formal receipt is issued (by law) for the first issue of any new title.

46

A Colindale van takes newspapers out weekly and makes half a dozen extra trips at the end of each year. It may seem strange, half a century after Colindale was established, that newspapers are not delivered by publishers direct to Colindale, thus saving all these journeys. The reasons advanced by the Museum are the composite parcels, the economy of staff in a centralised office and the advisability of making deposit procedure as simple as possible for publishers.

The variety of periodical material received at the library under the Copyright Laws is amazing. It includes women's magazines, parish magazines, 'house' magazines, comics, firms' annual reports and even examination papers. Membership lists of learned societies and advertising matter are *not* called for. All publishers' lists are checked to see that a copy of each book is eventually received.

The receipt issued to the publisher for every item received is made out in duplicate. Much of the information recorded on these receipts has to be written out again by the cataloguers. To prevent this duplication is one of the aims of the proposed automation of the library's records.

* * *

The number of items obtained through international exchange has shown a phenomenal increase since World War II—from 18,000 in 1938 to 439,000 in 1966. Most of these documents form part of the State Paper collection; but, for lack of space at Bloomsbury, half is stored at Woolwich.

International exchange is conducted largely with national libraries and other government institutions overseas. In a few cases, the library offers valuable British publications in return for rather meagre foreign publications in the hope of a better rate of exchange later—a form of pump-priming. The Stationery Office does the actual distribution, in accordance with the library's instructions. The cost of the British publications is borne by the Stationery Office; so the library receives, in exchange, vast quantities of foreign documents without payment from its own vote. This is an additional Government contribution to the Museum (as is also the binding of its books, see p. 55).

Since 1767, duplicate books received as gifts may be sold. But unimportant books which the library does not already have, if received as gifts or bequests, must be kept for ever.

The purchase of books from abroad is limited by the size of the library vote for this purpose. It is constantly being increased. In 1832, only £ 1,000 was voted for the acquisition of books from abroad. The Government vote for *each* of the four years from 1964–68 was £ 182,000, of which £ 45,000 was earmarked for the National Reference Library of Science and Technology. The cost of books, however, has gone up considerably since 1939. Under 8,000 books were bought in 1939 compared with 27,000 in 1965. But whereas the *number* of books bought was tripled, the *expenditure* in 1966 was nine-fold what it had been in 1939.

World War II played havoc with the regular receipt of serials to which the library subscribed. Some from enemy countries were secretly stored abroad and sent on after the armistice. Many of the Museum's foreign books were destroyed in the blitz. Some were subsequently replaced by gifts; but, as an economy measure, Government refused to allow a library purchasing mission to go abroad to replace the missing books and serials. Some 100,000 books are still missing.

* * *

The ordering of new foreign books by the Museum is in the hands of language specialists, within financial allocations made by the deputy keeper in charge of acquisitions. The exception to this system is the National Reference Library of Science and Invention, which orders its books through subject specialists, who are assisted only when necessary by linguists. In the rest of the department of printed books, one specialist on each language orders books on all subjects, but the trend is towards selection by subject specialists, particularly if further specialised reading-rooms are created, with their own staffs. The purchase of any book costing over £ 50 is subject to the approval of the trustees. Such purchases are largely in the English antiquarian field.

To prevent the same book from being ordered twice, each order is card-indexed, showing the author, the title, the publisher, the date of order, the agent abroad and the date of receipt. This is another example of duplication of records to be eliminated by automation. Every few years, completed cards are weeded out and destroyed.

One of the problems of acquisition from abroad is the delay that occurs between the decision to order the book and its receipt. In countries from which few books are ordered, the agent is instructed to wait until he has enough books for a complete parcel, and so to economize on postage. As books are then sent by sea, it may take up to three months from the decision to order until receipt at the library. As the library is chronically short of funds, it may be that economy even in postage is essential, though added delay is irritating to would-be readers. Processing and cataloguing may take up to another six months (see page 50.), making up to nine months delay in some cases. Having myself had to wait for many months for a book specially ordered from the United States at my request, I was particularly interested to ascertain the reasons for such long delays.

BOOK STOCK

The library's book stock has constantly increased over the two centuries. It originally included some 9,000 books of the old Royal Library, acquired in 1757, many specially bound. George III's library was added in 1826 and a separate gallery built for it. The Museum's rare books include over 10,000 *incunabula* (books printed before 1500). Among the books printed before 1600 are 21,000 in Italian, 12,500 in French and 3,000 in Spanish and Portuguese. By 1837, the library contained nearly a quarter of a million books. By 1867, it had reached one and a half million, and, since then, the stock has doubled almost every fifty years, i.e., to about three million before World War I and to over six million today. The rate of intake each year for different classes of material has risen as follows:

	1939	1965
Printed books and pamphlets	40,000	130,000
Serials	90,000	580,000
Maps (sheets) and atlases	6,000	23,000

Only the intake of music has remained steady, at about 10,000 items a year. The intake of newspapers has reached 250,000 issues, while the total of other acquisitions now runs at about 700,000 items. To process and store such immense quantities of material is now a major problem for the library, and much processing is in arrear.

CATALOGUING

The Library of Congress in Washington has experimented with 'cataloguing-at-source'. This means cataloguing from page-proofs without waiting for a book to be actually printed, bound and delivered. It was hoped that such a system would reduce the time between receipt of the book and its indexing. But it was found, in practice, that publishers occasionally added or suppressed pages, and even amended the title before printing, which made the catalogue entry inaccurate. So the scheme—which in any case required special staff in New York to keep in constant touch with publishers—has been abandoned. The method provides no solution for the cataloguing problems of the Museum's library. Some of these problems may, however, be soluble through automation (see page 43).

Some libraries, to reduce the ever-increasing volume, and hence cost, of cataloguing, no longer index individual pamphlets. They are stored in boxes, which are handed to readers. If the reader returns the right number of pamphlets, no further check is made. The Museum library has always tried to catalogue each pamphlet separately even if, in the early years, several were bound together in the same volume. But today, many pamphlets are not separately catalogued and are stored unbound in 'dumps'. These are boxes, each containing the pamphlets published by a particular organization—for example, the Royal Society for the Prevention of Cruelty to Animals.

Separate catalogues of newspapers, maps and music are maintained at the library. I shall deal here only with the cataloguing of printed books and periodicals.

Books may be indexed in various ways:

(a) alphabetically by the name of the author;

(b) alphabetically by the title of the book;

(c) alphabetically by the subject and then by the author;

(d) numerically by the position of the book on the library shelves; or

(e) chronologically by date of acquisition.

In addition, temporary subordinate indexes are kept to prevent duplication of orders (see page 48) and to serve as a basis for payment.

Ahthors' Catalogue

Apart from an abortive single volume in 1841, the first comprehensive printed author catalogue of the department of printed books was begun in 1880 and completed, with a supplement, in 1905. It reproduced all the Museum's printed catalogue slips which had been pasted into folio volumes over the years. Copies of the new catalogue were cut up and used, as subsequent editions have been to the present day, to form the basis of new folio loose-leaf volumes for consultation on the premises by readers and staff.

Between 1931 and 1955, a second edition was attempted with extensive revisions and improvements in lay-out. It had reached the letter D when the decision was taken to abandon the project in favour of a photo-lithographic reproduction, with only minor alterations, of the first edition (or, for the letters A–D, of the second edition) and of all the slips since added to the folio volumes. This work was completed in 263 volumes, each of about 500 pages, between 1959 and 1966. While it was being planned and carried out, no new slips could be added to the catalogue, although new entries from 1956 onwards were available to readers on cards. The laborious process of converting the new editions and the accumulated printed slips into about 1,300 pasted-down folio volumes for internal use has not kept pace with the remarkable speed of the photo-lithographic process and is still in progress. A supplement is already being prepared for the press. However, the folio volumes have great advantages over cards: they occupy less space and allow the reader to glance through a double page of entries in a fraction of the time that it would take to finger the equivalent number of cards.

The preparation of the entries in the authors' catalogue is done by some thirty cataloguers (some of whom do other work as well) They are divided up by language group as follows: English 13½; French 4; German 2¾; Spanish and Portuguese 2¼; Scandinavian, Russian and other Slavonic languages 1½ each; Italian 1; and Dutch ¾. A cataloguer can prepare about 30 slips a day. Each slip is checked by a senior cataloguer to see if it complies with the standard rules for indexing.

The manuscript slips prepared in each language each day are then arranged for incorporation alphabetically by author's name and are sent to the printer each week or so. If they are sent at shorter intervals, more work is involved later in rearranging all the printed copies of each slip alphabetically.*

* For the past sixty years, Clowes, of Beccles, have been the contract printers of these slips. They have all the necessary founts in all the languages involved. Experiments have been made with Vari-typing; but too many different founts are needed for it to be economical.

The galleys are read twice, once by a less experienced cataloguer in that language, then by a more experienced one—not necessarily the same who prepared or checked the original manuscript entry. Additional sets of the galleys are kept in case extra copies of entries are needed later.

At least a dozen copies of each entry are printed on cards and three on slips. The slips are required for pasting into the three sets of loose-leaf catalogues, of which one is for public use, one for the cataloguing and purchasing staff and one for the staff incorporating new entries. The blue-covered set for public use is always kept complete by substituting volumes of the cataloguers' red set for those which are removed to be brought up to date. The incorporators' green set is always the first to receive additions since it serves to show how the entries are to be added in the other sets. Printed slips are pasted in monthly: more frequent moving of the volumes would be uneconomical.

This means that it takes at least three months for a hand-written catalogue entry to be printed and pasted into the reading-room catalogue. Meanwhile, the book is either being labelled and bound or is on its allotted shelf, but temporarily very difficult to find, which is irritating for would-be readers. A completely uncatalogued book is more accessible, because it can be traced in the acquisitions office. This problem could be overcome if a copy were kept of the manuscript entries in the hands of the printers. A new procedure is now, in fact, being introduced whereby the printers receive photocopies of the manuscript entries. The Museum can then proceed straight away to file these entries and make them accessible to the staff serving the public, which greatly reduces the time during which a book is, as it were, in limbo.

(b) *Title Index.* No index is kept by the library of books alphabetically arranged by title. As far as British books are concerned, such books can be traced—if the title alone is known—in the cumulative UK book index or in various commercial book catalogues. If the approximate date of publication is also known, a book can be traced through the British National Bibliography.

(c) *Subject Index.* The subject is written on the slip prepared for the authors' index and a more senior subject indexer checks the first indexer's work. Often, two or more subjects are named, so that as many as eight of the twelve printed catalogue cards are needed for the subject index card catalogue. Every five years this card catalogue is thoroughly checked, and produced in book form by photo-lithography. It is a relatively easy by-product of the authors' index, but it was not always so. Before 1956, the two operations were separate, with a consequent duplication of effort in bringing the books to the staff and printing the entries.

(d) *Shelf Index.* Each book is placed in that part of the library where books on similar subjects are kept. Books are first divided into serials (in which case they join previous issues) and 'monographs' (which do not). Originally, monographs were allocated to one or other of some 400 subjects between which the shelves of the library used to be divided. That classification was found to be too complex and slow and the shelves are now divided between only 21 subjects for monographs and 25 for serials. In some of the adjustable steel stands, the shelving is now arranged to accommodate books of varying heights—below nine inches, between nine to eleven inches, and between eleven to fifteen inches. This classification by height is also marked on the catalogue entry before printing. As there is no public access to shelves (except to the reference library in the reading room—see page 56), it does not matter much *where* each book is placed provided that it bears a shelf-mark which indicates on which shelf and in which position on that shelf it is to be found. Hence books on the same subject are now not always contiguous.

With the present enormous annual accretions, shelving is increasingly scarce. Experiments were made with sliding steel shelving which provided for access at any one time between only two shelves.

But apart from the load being too heavy for the existing structure, and the excessive wear on the books themselves, the sliding shelving tended to jam. There are now electrically-operated models which may be adopted in the new building.

The original manuscript slips, on return from the printer, are filed under their author headings, but for the benefit of the junior filing clerks this is done according to simpler rules that in the authors' index itself. One set of the printed cards is maintained in order of shelf-mark as a stock record. The manuscript slips are available to cataloguers so that they can order amendments in the authors' index without rewriting the whole entry. The 'stock cards' proved their worth after the blitz of 1941: they were the only means of knowing what had been destroyed.

* * *

As soon as the receipt of a new acquisition has been recorded, the book is sent for stamping. Only after stamping is it catalogued. The colour of the ink used for the stamp impression indicates the method of acquisition—blue for copyright deposit; green for a donation; black for international exchange; red for purchase, and brown for all other methods. The copyright and exchange copies are stamped in their own departments: the rest by five men in a special room. Each books is stamped in a number of specific places—on the half title, on the back of the title-page, on each plate, at the end of the text of the index and of the notes and on any *errata* slip.

If a stamped book is later discovered to be a duplicate, the official cancellation stamp must be added before disposal to another institution is possible. The Museum cannot dispose of books deposited under the Copyright Laws. They must take precedence over books acquired in any other way.

The shelf-mark is shown on the manuscript slip and, in pencil, on the title-page of the book itself: it then goes, if necessary, to the binder. Serials are bound periodically in the same form as previous volumes. Some 3–4,000 paper-backs and other soft-cover publications (for example, many of the books printed in France) are rebound in temporary hard-covers each month before being placed on the shelves to prevent disintegration through constant use.

There is also a great deal of restoration to be done, not only of the leather covers of old volumes but also of their pages. Rare books are repaired only on the premises, but some of the others are sent for binding to a second bindery at Manchester. Both binderies are run by the Stationery Office as a charge on its own vote. Including a third bindery at Colindale for newspapers, some 200 men and women are employed at a total cost of about £ 250,000 a year. This is, in fact, a direct Government subsidy to the Museum library.

Until quite recently, the ban on books ever leaving the Museum building precluded books being sent outside unless for production in a court of law by *subpoena;* but certainly not for rebinding. So there is a back-log of about 100,000 volumes, largely from the 17th and 18th centuries, now needing repair. The Treasury, however, will not allow the Stationery Office to take on temporary additional staff to deal with this back-log, quite apart from the difficulty in finding a place for them to work in. These old books will gradually fall in pieces, which is a breach of the conditions under which they were originally acquired. Perhaps the recent arrangements for sending new paper-backs to be bound in Manchester will release staff at the Museum for repairing antiquarian books.

Access to Books

The British Museum library is basically for research. Scholars may consult simultaneously any number of volumes (within reason) that they need, for months at a time. (At the *Bibliothèque Nationale* in Paris, only *two* books may be in use at the same moment by any one reader.) There is a special room for reading rare books (the North Library); periodicals and any collection of more than twelve volumes (the gallery of the North Library); Government publications, both domestic and foreign (the State Paper room); oriental books and manuscripts; other manuscripts; maps; science books (at Holborn) and newspapers (at Colindale).

But the big circular reading-room at Bloomsbury remains the hub. It has a special, civilised air about it that, in my own experience, is unrivalled by any other library in which I have ever worked, including the Library of Congress in Washington, and the great New

York public library. To begin with, the domed hall erected in 1857 within the original Museum quadrangle by Sir Antonio Panizzi, at a cost of £ 150,000 (worth at least ten times as much today) was the first specially-built reading-room. It was also one of the earliest iron-frame buildings to be constructed. circular in form, under what was then the broadest dome in Britain. Many eminent men have sat and worked in this reading-room (for example, Karl Marx and George Bernard Shaw). Many of the constant users today consider themselves to be almost a fraternity.

The main reading-room has only 390 seats, set on both sides of partitions radiating from the centre. The majority of seats are comfortably fitted with reading desks. There are a further 220 seats in the North Library, including the gallery. The main catalogues are all in the centre of the wheel; while, around the outer edge, is an excellent reference library of some 20,000 volumes with open access to anyone with a reader's ticket. No fees are charged by the library, which is conveniently open from 9 a.m. till 5 p.m. daily (except on Sunday), and, on three evenings a week, till 9 p.m. There is a great demand for tickets, which can be made valid for a whole year (renewable), or for part of a year, or even for only a few days.

A century ago, with the beginnings of mass literacy, the problem was how to restrict the library to serious users. By 1856, there were 36,000 ticket-holders. To exclude schoolchildren using up library space to prepare their lessons, the minimum age for admission had originally been fixed at eighteen; but, in 1862, it was raised to twenty-one, with occasional exceptions. By 1888, the number of ticket-holders was still 14,000 of whom many came in every day mainly to read the morning newspapers, or novels, free of charge, or merely to sit down and keep warm. The issue of tickets for the casual reading of novels was restricted the following year.

In 1966 not only were 10,400 long-term tickets renewed and 5,100 long-term tickets issued for the first time, but 13,000 temporary tickets, valid for not more than one week, were also issued. Thus there were over 15,000 long-term readers with valid tickets in addition to the temporary readers. Experience shows that a long-term ticket is generally renewed if the holder intends to use the reading-room seriously.

In Victorian days, a section of the reading-room was reserved for ladies; but that form of segregation has been abolished. Sixty years ago, only a fifth of the ticket-holders were women; today, almost half are.

In the eighteenth century, the main reading-room was a great place of daily rendezvous for persons of distinction. But, with the growth of gentlemen's clubs and private and municipal libraries, its use as a social meeting-place declined after 1830. Today, some 800 readers occupy the desks during each day: many come as soon as the library opens to be sure of getting a place, or even their accustomed place.

An enormous amount of reading is done in the main reading-room: even by 1887, 4,000 books were being brought in from the stocks or the reserved shelves daily, an average of seven books per reader, apart from those consulted on the reference library shelves.

Although, in some cases, readers are supplied with books from the stacks within a half-an-hour of application, on many occasions it takes an hour or even longer. I often find it wastes less time to come and apply one day for a book and to return on the morrow to read it. Consequently, I have explored with some care the reasons for this delay. It is much greater than that in other big libraries that I have used, especially in the United States. There, if a book is not supplied within twenty minutes, you complain to the management.

At the Museum, applications for books are made out with a carbon copy and handed in at a window in the centre of the reading-room. A library assistant classifies the applications according to the area in which the books are stacked, as shown by the press-mark recorded on the application. Since 1905, pneumatic tubes have been available to the seven areas of the library stacks. But, in times of pressure, applications for each area are not despatched until several have accumulated and returned cylinders are available. This may delay up to ten minutes the despatch of the earliest applications by pneumatic tube.

When the cylinder arrives in the office in the middle of the relevant area, the applications are further sorted by a supervisor according to location. There are several library assistants attached to each area who go and search for books. But, on a busy day, it is uneconomical to go and look for a single book. So each library assistant takes a pile of applications, some of which may have waited for a further fifteen or twenty minutes before the search even begins.

The space between the shelves is too narrow and the corners are too sharp for a barrow to be conveniently used; so the books are carried by the assistant in his arms, which limits the number that can be collected on any one round. One copy of the application is left in the space from which the book was taken and the second copy is placed inside the volume. The books are then packed by the assistant into wicker baskets (which takes up more time), the lid is closed and the basket despatched down a steep metal shute. (However tightly the books are packed in, some bindings get rubbed in transit.) Owing to the peculiar construction of this century-old building, the two shutes have to go right down into the basement where the books are automatically transferred to a single conveyor belt that brings them up to the main floor again. To speed up the delivery of books, four more shutes and more conveyor belts might with advantage be installed, as well as two more lifts for returning empty baskets to the upper floors and for transporting the staff.

When the baskets are unpacked on the main reading-room floor, the books are transferred to trolleys after being sorted according to the rooms in which the readers are seated. Those for the main reading-room are further sorted roughly according to the readers' seat numbers. (This takes up more time.) As soon as a trolley is full, it is wheeled into the relevant room, from which other assistants distribute the books by hand to the waiting readers. Hence an hour's wait is comprehensible, even when all the staff are on duty. But there is difficulty nowadays in keeping the establishment of sixty-six assistants up to full strength. The work is as elementary as that of a postman; the physical effort equally tiring; the pay less than that offered in many factories and commercial offices. As the library is open six days a week, and on three of these days for twelve hours, many assistants (who, under Civil Service regulations, work only a five-day week) work overtime one or two evenings a week. What with time off for meals, sickness and annual holidays, there are always some fifteen fewer assistants on duty than the numbers provided for in the establishment. Hence the delay in supplying books occasionally reaches two hours. There seems to be a clear case for an increase in the number of library assistants by fifteen to bring the number *on duty* up to sixty-six.

When a book is supplied to a reader, the assistant initials the second copy of the application and hands it in to one of three windows according to the initial letter of the reader's surname—A to G; H to O; and P to Z. There, the second copies are further classified alphabetically by other assistants. When books are handed in, the reader gets back the copy of his application form as evidence.

Books acquired by readers who come in day after day may, however, be handed in with a slip bearing the reader's name. They are then stored on reserve shelves (and, for lack of space, on the floor!) for three days before being returned to the stacks. When regular readers come in, early each morning, there is much pressure of work in this section, handing out dozens of piles of books.

When books are eventually returned to the stacks by the library assistants at 9 a.m. each day, the first copy of the application is removed and destroyed. Some books are borrowed by members of the staff, mainly for bibliographical purposes: in such cases, a yellow application form is put in the space left on the shelf.

THE BUDGET

The budget of the Museum, as a Government institution, is included in the civil estimates. The first annual parliamentary grant, two centuries ago, was £ 900 (then worth very much more). By 1938–39, it had risen to £ 203,000 (also worth more than today). The budget for the library is not shown separately from that of the Museum as a whole, which, in 1967–68, received £ 2,262,000. In addition, it expects an income of about £ 90,000 from the sale of publications and reproductions. Considerable sums of money spent on the Museum's collections and library are borne on the votes of other Ministries and departments; for example, £ 1,221,000 for furniture, fuel and light (Ministry of Public Buildings and Works), and £ 403,000 for stationery, printing and binding of books (Stationery Office). In addition, municipal rates and the pensions of retired Museum staff are paid for by the Government from other votes. The total cost of the Museum (including the library) is thus about £ 4,059,000 a year. The cost of the Library of Congress is nearly three times as much: but costs in the United States are about twice as high as in Britain, to begin with.

George Bernard Shaw, in his day a grateful user of the Museum library, left it one-third of his residuary estate (or some £ 600,000). By cautious investment, that sum, together with royalties, has now become £ 750,000. But, strange to say, the Museum trustees have still not found a purpose for the Shaw Fund. They do not wish to apply it to anything whose financing has a legitimate claim to Government funds. Hence, the bequest is only used for such minor purposes as special book purchases or for foreign travel by Museum library officials. This is a typical case of the poor little rich boy.

STAFF

In 1939, the library had a staff of 509, which has risen to 741 today. The number of employees in the Library of Congress is 3,500: but staffing in United States institutions is fantastically exaggerated, largely because of hyper-specialization.

Office space for the existing Museum library staff is inadequate. Hence, even if more staff were to be engaged to keep up with the rising tide of printed matter, it would be hard to find place for them in the existing buildings. With specialised departments within the Museum, the redeployment of senior staff to equalise the pressure throughout becomes very difficult.

The allocation of staff in the 1967–68 estimates is as follows:

Bloomsbury and Colindale

Principal Keeper	1	⎫
Keepers	2	⎬ Senior administration
Deputy Keepers	8	⎭

Assistant Keepers	38	Senior academic staff
Research Assistants	33	Junior academic staff (all graduates)
Executive grade staff	36	Office managers; high grade clerical work requiring powers of decision and a good level of education
Clerical grade staff	64	Card-filing, recording acquisitions; normal office duties
Typists	18	
Senior Conservation Officer	1	Liaison with bindery
Library Assistants (all three grades)	93	Handling books in relation to readers' individual requests
Paperkeepers	22	Handling books in bulk; stamping
Messengers	10	Taking round letters, files, etc.; some handling of books; cloakrooms
Catalogue and Labelling Shop staff	67	Physical maintenance of catalogues; labelling of shelf-marks on books

National Reference Library of Science and Inventions
Holborn Division (formerly the Patent Office Library)

Keeper	1
Assistant Keepers	4
Research Assistants	11
Executive grade staff	7
Clerical grade staff	48
Typists	5
Library Assistants	16
Paperkeepers	12
Messengers	16

Bayswater Division (closed to the public; entirely acquisitions, cataloguing and classification work)

Assistant Keepers	16

Research Assistants	27
Executive grade staff	8
Clerical grade staff	49
Typists	11
Library Assistants	7
Paperkeepers	6
Messengers	3
Labellers	4
The grand total is	644

Some of the titles of Museum library posts seem to imply that the books are imprisoned and are trying to escape: at the top there are keepers* and at the bottom there are warders.

Ordinary working-men and women dislike their jobs being described in plain English. Hence, in the Museum library, it is not surprising that men whose sole job is to push trolleys and distribute books should be described as paperkeepers (the title used generically in Whitehall for elderly office messengers).

The ordinary Museum staff are not civil servants but are recruited through the Civil Service Commission. Not only it is difficult for the civil service to compete with industry for good employees, but, within the civil service, it is difficult for the Museum to compete with what are popularly considered to be livelier Government departments or with the universities. Those university graduates who are interested in making a career in the Museum are often more attracted to posts involving independent research than to library work.

Of all the sections of the Museum library that I visited, the oddest was one of those staffed by industrial labour. For example, pasting slips into the catalogue can *only* be done by members of SOGAT (the Society of Graphical and Allied Trades). Vacancies are filled by candidates selected solely by the trade union. But much of the work could easily have been done by intelligent school-girls. Although craft pride is an asset, such a monopoly must make administration of the library very inelastic.

---

* An unimaginative translation from the French *conservateur*.

The normal twelve-month librarianship training courses, primarily for the public and university libraries, are not regarded as particularly suitable for work in the Museum. Essential skills can be more quickly taught on the job.

Some senior Museum library staff are released to go abroad for short periods as advisors to other libraries. But, because of the constant pressure of work, little attempt is apparently made at systematic release in mid-career for further academic study.

Staff relations are important in any institution, and particularly so in one that is as highly departmentalised as the British Museum. There is no house magazine through which the heads of the library can make their ideas known to their subordinates. There used to be an internal monthly bulletin for members of the department of printed books; but it has died for lack of an editor. All that is published today is a dry, periodical list of staff appointments, transfers, promotions and retirements; and a staff magazine, recreational in conception. What is needed is something on the lines of the bulletin that the Library of Congress used to publish, with plenty of officially inspired material.

Public Relations

The Museum library does not do itself justice largely because the public knows so little about its organization and its problems. In the past, the trustees were not much concerned with public relations: they took the Museum for granted and assumed that everyone else did the same. Otherwise, it is hard to understand why no annual report at all was published by the Museum between 1939 and 1966, a matter of twenty-seven years. Now, under the 1963 Act, reports must be published at least once every three years, and the first appeared in 1966. It was nicely produced, but failed to make much impression on the press or the public. There would seem to be a good case for the publication of an annual administrative report, at least on the library. This need not be on glossy paper and full of expensive illustrations of choice exhibits. What many members of the public want is far more information about the development of the library and the organizational problems that beset it. The Museum now has a publications officer; yet it still needs a public relations unit, which is something quite different. But what it *really* needs is a vigorous and continuous publicity campaign to improve its image in Parliament and in other Government department whence the money to solve its difficulties must come.

* * *

The British people tend to approach any new development in a very dilatory manner. The older, larger and more complex the institution, the longer it takes to get anything effective done. By the time the Museum library is in its new buildings and has automated its records, say ten or fifteen years from now, it will inevitably be hit by further technological advances. In several countries, automatic information retrieval of legal or medical precedents at a distance is already in operation. Within ten years, *even using only technical processes already available today*, it will be possible for research workers to stay in their rooms, dial a microfilm library and see, within seconds, on their own home television screen, any page of any book they wish to consult. For many branches of academic study, in particular on history, sociology and literary criticism, consultation of the actual books will still be essential. But, for information in many fields, enquirers will not need to go to the Museum reading-room, or consult its index, or write out an application for a book, or wait to receive it, or read it on the premises. Many books today are already set up in type at a distance by linotype operators punching tape, hence the books themselves can be reproduced on computer memory drums without any further human intervention.

Technological change is becoming more rapid year by year. Forecasts of its impact on library techniques have been made for the immediate future, but not for the distant future. It would be ironical if, after the expenditure of vast quantities of money in the 1960's and 1970's on bringing the British Museum library up to date, wholly new systems of recording and retrieving information would be available by the 1980's that would make the library wholly a museum of fine bindings and illustrations, typography and paper-making and no longer a practical workshop.

The Royal Opera House, Covent Garden

I am grateful to Sir Leon Bagrit, till recently one of the Directors of the Royal Opera House, Covent Garden Ltd. (and one of the Patrons of the Israel Institute of Public Administration), for having introduced me to Mr. John Tooley, then the General Administrator-designate of the Opera House, to whom I am indebted for much information. I am also grateful to members of the Opera House staff, in particular (in the order of my seeing them) Mr. Trevor Jones (an Assistant House Manager); Miss Sheila Porter (Press Officer); Mr. David Jackson (Box Office Manager); Mr. William Bundy (then Stage Director); Mr. Douglas Lund, C.B.E. (Company Secretary and Chief Accountant); Mrs. Joan Ingpen (Controller of Opera Planning); Mr. John Sullivan (then Technical Director); Miss Muriel Kerr (then Personal Assistant to the General Administrator); Miss Stella Chitty (Opera Stage Manager) and Mr. John Field (then an Assistant Director of the Royal Ballet).

Much of the history of the Opera House has been derived from Vol. 35 of the Great London Council's *Survey of London* dealing with the Theatre Royal, Drury Lane, and the Royal Opera House, Covent Garden.

EARLY HISTORY

The history of the Opera House covers over three centuries and dates back to 1662, when King Charles II granted two Letters Patent —one to Thomas Killigrew from which the Drury Lane Theatre developed, the other to William Davenant from which the Opera House developed. Each Letter Patent gave the right to build one theatre in either the City of London or the City of Westminster and

65

to establish a company of actors to perform in it. Thomas Killigrew set up the King's company of actors, William Davenant established the Duke of York's. All other companies then performing in London or Westminster were to be suppressed (this was not strictly enforced). The two monopolies lasted until the passage of the 1943 Act for regulating the theatres; till then, they were valuable properties which were bought, sold, divided, shared and bequeathed.

The ground landlords were originally the Dukes of Bedford; but, in 1918, one of them sold the site to the Covent Garden Estate Company (set up by Sir Thomas Beecham), which, in turn, sold it in 1929 to the Covent Garden Properties Company Ltd., which leased* it in 1949 to the Ministry of Works for operation by the present Royal** Opera House, Covent Garden Ltd., incorporated in 1950.

The Theatre

There have been three theatre buildings on the present site (not all aligned in the same direction), two having been burnt down. The first was the Queen's Theatre, built by John Rich in 1704, with 1,400 seats. In 1731, it passed to Edward Shepherd and was renamed the Covent Garden Theatre. It was in this theatre that Sheridan's *The Rivals* was first performed in 1775. It was destroyed by fire in 1808 and rebuilt by Thomas Harris to the designs of Sir Robert Smirke to seat 2,000. It was again burnt down in 1856 and rebuilt by Frederick Gye to the designs of E. M. Barry, to be re-opened in 1857–8 as the Royal Italian Opera House. In 1899, it was taken over by the Grand Opera Syndicate Ltd., and, in 1933, by the Royal Opera House Company Ltd. It escaped the 'blitz' during World War II, but, as no operas could then be performed, became a popular dance hall. In 1945, it was taken over by Boosey and Hawkes (the public-spirited music publishers), who transferred it to the present company in 1950.

The present building site covers only three-quarters of an acre and

---

* There is some criticism of the expenditure of over £1,000,000 of public money on the maintenance of a building only *leased* to the Government.
** The inclusion of the 'Royal' in the name of the Opera House has no practical effect other than the conferment of a certain status in the eyes of the public.

is now too small for its present purpose. Some of the administrative offices, including the box office, have been moved to leased premises in an adjacent street, while much of the scenery is stored in warehouses in other parts of London and even outside. Some of the rehearsing of operas and ballets to be performed is carried out at the London Opera Centre in the East End and at the Royal Ballet School at Hammersmith. It is hoped that, when the wholesale fruit, vegetable and flower markets adjacent to the Opera House are transferred in 1973 to Nine Elms, south of the River, extension will be possible.

Even so, it is already a very large theatre, with a stage just over 7,000 square feet in area, and almost as large as the auditorium itself. However, by most modern standards it is small, as the following comparisons will show:

West Berlin	19,600 square feet
Munich	26,500 square feet
New York	25,700 square feet

After reconstruction of the gallery in 1964, there is room for an audience of 2,115 (plus 43 standing) compared with 1,903 in West Berlin, 1,798 (plus 323 standing) in Munich, and 3,788 (plus 175 standing) in New York.

It is the policy of the Opera House never to lease the stage for public performances by companies other than those directly engaged by the management. Occasionally, it may be leased on a Sunday to some film company taking pictures of an opera or ballet sequence for which it provides its own performers, or the 'Crush Bar' for a fashion show.

STRUCTURE OF MANAGEMENT

Over a thousand people work at the Opera House, in the following units: *

The Royal Opera Company, with 136 members.

The Royal Ballet Company, with 168 members.

The Orchestra of the Royal Opera House, with a hundred members.

* There is some duplication as a few people work in more than one group.

The Royal Opera Chorus, with some 70 members.

The English Opera Group, with a varying number of members.

Ballet For All.

Most of the rest of the staff are divided between the following major departments:

'Front of the House'	180 employees
Production	153 employees
Stage	125 employees.

The staff also includes the general administration, the box office, the press office and the accounts office, totalling 53 employees.

The chain of command is continually being revised and improved. In the near future it will probably look something like this:

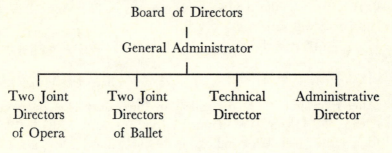

Board of Directors

General Administrator

| Two Joint Directors of Opera | Two Joint Directors of Ballet | Technical Director | Administrative Director |

OPERA

Covent Garden is one of the few opera houses where an attempt is made to give an almost equal number of performances of ballet and of opera. The management structure of opera will eventually look something like this:

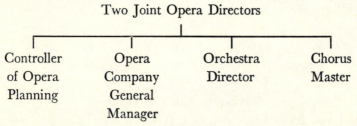

Two Joint Opera Directors

| Controller of Opera Planning | Opera Company General Manager | Orchestra Director | Chorus Master |

The permanent *Royal Opera music staff* consists of:

The musical director, three other conductors and an assistant conductor

The head of the music staff

A senior repetiteur and six other repetiteurs.*

Of the 110 whole-time *opera singers* on the pay-roll, 62 are men and 48 are women. Guest artists are engaged for each production when required.

The Royal Opera Chorus is under the chorus master and assistant chorus master. There are generally an equal number of men and women, and of sopranos, contraltos, tenors and basses.

Associated with the Opera House since 1961 is *The English Opera Group,* an independent company with its own grant from the Arts Council. It works for half the year and presents chamber opera and other works not suitable for a large auditorium. It is under the artistic direction of Sir Benjamin Britten and is managed by the Opera House. In 1968-69, it had on its pay-roll sixteen principal singers, a chorus of nine, a conductor, two producers, a head of music staff and four repetiteurs.

The London Opera Centre

This is a separate organization set up at the old Troxy Cinema in the Commercial Road, East London, to provide further instruction and experience for singers who have graduated from a music college. It receives its own grant from the Arts Council but is administered by the General Administrator of the Opera House, which also contributes to the Centre's running expenses: in return, the Opera House uses part of the Centre's premises for rehearsal and scene-painting.

BALLET

In 1964, when the Opera House was restarted, the Sadler's Wells Ballet Company came over to Covent Garden from the Sadler's Wells Theatre and was eventually re-named the Royal Ballet on the granting of a Royal Charter. In 1957, the Sadler's Wells Theatre Ballet came over and became part of the Royal Ballet, with special respon-

---

* For rehearsing individual singers: they are also stage prompters and undertake other stage duties.

sibilities for touring. Now the two are to be combined, and dancers for tours will be supplied from one central company.

The *Royal Ballet management,* after reorganization, will consist of:

Two joint directors and an associate to the directors

A principal conductor, two other conductors and a guest conductor

Two managers.

There will also be a complement of ballet masters, ballet mistresses, stage managers, teachers and repetiteurs, pianists (for rehearsals) and dance notators.

As far as ballet dancers are concerned, the *company* in 1968-69 consisted of:

35 principals

27 solo artistes

24 'coryphees'

58 artistes.

These were in addition to guest artistes (such as Margot Fonteyn and Rudolf Nureyev) who dance with the company from time to time.

The Royal Opera Ballet (under a ballet master and mistress) with twelve dancers, only for opera performances, is being merged with the Royal Ballet, which will in future supply ballet dancers for opera as needed.

The Royal Ballet Choreographic Group is run by Leslie Edwards, one of the teachers of the Royal Ballet. He arranges for ballet dancers and students to rehearse new works produced by young choreographers who cannot work without dancers to perform for them. The Group is financed, in part, by the Opera House and, in part, by the Friends of Covent Garden (see below).

Ballet For All is an off-shoot of the Royal Ballet, also with its own grant from the Arts Council. It consists of six dancers and two actors who provide explanatory lectures, illustrated by dancing.

The Royal Ballet School is a separate organization with its own grant from the Arts Council. But several members of the board of the Royal Opera House, Covent Garden Ltd., are also members of the board of the School. The two organizations work closely together: most of the young dancers needed for the *corps de ballet* are selected from pupils at the School.

REPERTORY

In choosing productions for both opera and ballet the management tries to provide a well-balanced repertory, including revivals and new productions. The number of new productions depends on the money available for new scenery and costumes, and the stage time available for rehearsals.

The choice of production (and the number of performances) also depends on a balance between what the public wants and those productions, new and revived, that give an adequate representation of operatic repertory generally, including contemporary works.

The selection of any particular production—whether new or a revival—also depends on the availability of the guest artistes proposed for the principal roles. A balance is kept between British and foreign guest artistes. As all are normally booked up to two years ahead, it is necessary to plan productions three or even four years in advance. This is difficult when the Government grant (£ 1,125,000 in 1968–69) is given on a yearly basis. The Arts Council, from which the grant is received, now has a total budget of £ 7,900,000: but it never knows, with the present system of Government budgetting, how much it will get in future years and hence cannot guarantee its grant for more than one year at a time.

When a production is under consideration, the names of possible key participants must be considered—the conductor, the producer or choreographer, the designer and the principal singers or dancers.

Opera Planning

The controller of opera planning (Mrs. Joan Ingpen) is the 'Girl Friday' of the musical director, responsible to him and to the general administrator. She is not a 'line' but a 'staff' official, with no executive control over others. Her job is to go abroad for the musical director and attend opera perfomances in the constant search for new talent. As a former agent for opera singers, conductors and musicians herself, she is experienced in the art of handling temperamental people.

She is a member of the advanced planning group that consists of the general administrator (Mr. John Tooley) and the joint directors of the Royal Opera (Mr. Colin Davis and Mr. Peter Hall). Once the list of operas for a couple of years ahead is agreed on, together with names of proposed conductors, producers, designers and principal singers, it is the controller's function to check their availability. The actual contracts are prepared in the general administrator's office by Miss Muriel Kerr (see below).

For each monthly meeting of the opera sub-committee of the board (see below), the controller prepares a summary of the position for covering approval. She also works out a day-by-day and hour-by-hour schedule of the use of the Opera House for rehearsals and performances of both opera and ballet. The schedule includes the use of the London Opera Centre for many rehearsals because of lack of space and time at Covent Garden.

Music Library

Some of the full scores and orchestral material used by the Opera House is owned by it: the rest is hired from publishers. For some operas and ballets, parts required by individual musicians in the orchestra are copied from the full score by a staff of four music librarians. Copying the notes needed by a single musician for an opera of average length may take a week. On occasion, outside copyists are also engaged. There are two music storage rooms within the Opera House.

Royalties

The Performing Rights Society does not handle royalties for opera or ballet. They are paid by the administrative manager's department to the publishers or, in the case of unpublished works, direct to the composer. Even if the work is commisioned by the Opera House, copyright is retained by its author.

Television and Radio Transmissions

The Opera House and the BBC try to televise one operatic or ballet performance each quarter. To secure spontaneity, this is done when the public is present and not with an empty auditorium. Because of the 'Equity' trade union rules that prevent artistes from performing in front of television cameras before paying audiences, the audience on such occasions is there by invitation of the BBC which then compensates the Opera House for the loss of revenue. Some radio broadcasts of operas are transmitted by the BBC each year from Covent Garden. The gross television and broadcasting receipts are about £ 100,000; but expenses come to some £ 80,000.

PRODUCTION

The eventual structure will look like this:

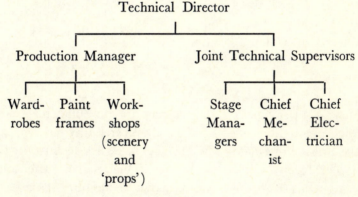

The Workshops

The first stage in the physical production of a new opera or ballet is for the designer and the producer to meet several months before the production is staged. They discuss the scenery, 'props' and costumes needed. The techniques to be employed are decided and the work is given out to the several departments concerned.

Model Room

For the scenery a 1:24 scale model is built on one of the miniature stages in the Model Room. Four people work here.

The Wardrobes

These are divided into two sections:

Production Wardrobes, with 69 people, divided as follows:

Tailoring	23
Dressmaking	32
Jewellery	4
Millinery	4
Stockroom	3
Production Assistants	3

Running Wardrobes, where the costumes actually in use are kept, with 52 people, divided into:

Ladies' Opera	}	
Men's Opera	}	26
English Opera Group	}	
Ladies' Ballet	}	
Men's Ballet	}	14
Ballet For All	}	
Touring Ballet		12

The Armoury

Many of the weapons in the armoury are authentic (for example, duelling pistols). Some, such as pikes, are carried by serving soldiers in the Brigade of Guards who are glad to earn a fee in their spare time. This follows a suggestion by Queen Victoria who, after attending an opera performance, was dismayed at the sorry spectacle presented by the stage army and offered the use of her own.

The armourer is licensed under the Firearms Act, 1968, to handle real arms. He is responsible to the Opera House for their repair and maintenance. A strict check is kept to see that all are returned to the armoury at the end of each opera performance or rehearsal: the armourer is present in the wings.

The armoury is also equipped with machinery to make metal armour for a particular production. More may be hired or bought from theatrical costumiers. Two men work in this section. A prop list is prepared for each production by the producer and the designer.

Scenery-Building Workshops, near King's Cross, employ 19 people.

Scenery Painting is done in two places, one on two vertical frames at the top of the Opera House (five people). The other, employing five more, is the London Opera Centre where the painting is done flat on the floor, as usual abroad. (Metal chamber-pots (for mixing paints) are in great demand.)

Wigs:	8 people
Props:	13 people
Dyeing:	3 people

The workshops have a total of 124 staff, the *minimum* number that can be employed all year round. When more work comes in than they can properly handle, the rest is put out to contract.

THE STAGE

The 119 staff members controlled by the technical director are divided up as follows:

Stage Management

Stage managers for opera	4
Stage managers for ballet	4
Stage managers for the English Opera Group	3
Assistant stage manager for plotting	1
	12

Handling Scenery at the Royal Opera House

Chief mechanist	1
Assistants	6
1st daymen*	13
2nd daymen	43
Motor driver	2
Repair carpenter	1
	66

* This is an old stage name for men employed during the day as well as the evening in contrast to 'show-men' who only work at night while the show is on.

Stage Lighting and Sound Amplification at the Royal Opera House

Chief electrician	1
Assistants (including sound)	5
1st daymen	10
2nd daymen	20
	36

Touring Staff

Stage 1st daymen	2
Electric 1st daymen	2
Electric 2nd daymen	1
	5

Hours of Work for Stage Hands

The stage hands used to be divided up into small and non-interchangeable permanent groups.* They also worked very long hours, including Sundays when technical rehearsals are held. They started at 8 a.m. preparing the stage for the rehearsal at 10.30 a.m. which might last till 1.30 or 2 p.m., possibly involving one or two partial scene shifts meanwhile. They then had to prepare all the scenery for the evening performance involving several scene shifts and remove it all late at night. This situation has been greatly improved by a recent agreement with the trade union introducing the shift system. It gives the men a guaranteed take-home pay, but reduces the hours of work and enables each man to get adequate time off in addition to greater flexibility in the deployment of the stage crew.

Storage of Scenery and Props

No opera house can afford expensive space in the very centre of the city for the storage of all its scenery and props.** In con-

---

* For example, scenery shifters who worked on one side of the stage *never* operated on the other.
** The Opera House must store scenery and props for about 80 different operas and 90 different ballets.

sequence, much is stored in warehouses elsewhere, when not in use.*

The Opera House has little room for storage at the back or at the side of the stage. It has leased some 5,000 square feet of storage space across the adjacent street and 84,000 square feet elsewhere in other buildings.**

The opera scenery, the English Opera Group scenery, the ballet scenery and the props are all stored separately. Two or three large lorry loads of scenery and props must be brought to the Opera House for each performance and taken away again.

STAGE MANAGEMENT

The opera stage manager (Miss Stella Chitty) has three assistants, and there are four more for ballet (two for the resident and two for the touring company). Of the four opera stage managers, one or more are allotted to each production: if the producer is a guest, one stage manager stays with him throughout to make things easier for him.

The stage manager sees that the producer's wishes are carried out, particularly regarding the placing of props, the positioning and operation of lights, the operation of 'flies' (moveable scenery that flies up and down) and the movement of members of the cast.

Before a model of the proposed stage set is handed over to the workshop (see above) it is studied by the stage manager allotted to that production. He or she also studies the score of the opera and discusses with the producer which 'extras' are to be engaged for non-vocal parts.

Stage rehearsals consist of:

musical: where all the singers are rehearsed on stage (in addition to the rehearsal of individual singers separately by the repetiteurs in rooms or studios) in accordance with a music calls sheet;

technical: for scenery and lighting; and

production: for the movement of the cast and props.

Production rehearsals are held initially at the London Opera

---

* The Paris warehouse is larger than the whole Paris Opera House itself.
** One is part of a bus garage: another is out at Maidstone.

Centre (or some other hall) and ultimately at the Opera House itself. If the scenery is not available, its position is marked on the floor.

Rehearsals are arduous, taking act by act, three hours a morning and another three hours in the afternoon, six days a week (and sometimes Sunday night as well), for 3½ to 4 weeks, involving 35 to 40 rehearsals for each production. Members of the cast required for each act are assembled by production rehearsal call sheet. The principal singers are spared as much as possible.

Different 'plots' are recorded by the stage manager as follows:
fly plots, for lifting and lowering any scenery during each act;
prop plots, for placing the props for each act, the props being supplied
   by the workshops under the Technical Director;
setting plots, for positioning the lights, worked out with the Chief
   Electrician; and
lighting plots, for the actual operation of the lights, including their
   colour and intensity. During rehearsal, the exact cues are recorded
   by a girl assistant stage manager sitting at the control board behind
   the Grand Tier (with a view of the stage). During the performance, the control board is operated by two or more electricians.

The stage manager has three interleaved copies of the score. One is the *prompt score,* showing opposite the relevant bar or music the producer's instructions for the movement of artistes and the operation of lighting, curtain and 'flies'. The other two are the *cue scores,* one for each side of the stage, showing the bar when each participant goes on stage and, five minutes earlier, when the participant is called from the dressing-room.

In the wings on each side of the stage are closed circuit television sets showing the orchestra conductor in the pit. Otherwise many of the singers would not be able to see his beat.

Touring Britain

To rationalize the tours of dramatic and lyric companies, DALTA (Dramatic and Lyric Theatres Association) was set up in 1966 under the chairmanship of the present general administrator of the Opera House, Mr. John Tooley, then assistant general administrator. This function is now undertaken by the Arts Council.

Touring Abroad

When the Royal Opera or Ballet performs abroad, a technician is often sent very early on to survey the theatre. He must see what is available locally and what adaptations or additions are needed to existing Opera House scenery and props. On his return to London he must see that they are provided. Then, later, they must be packed and forwarded.* On occasion, containers are held up on the way and have to be traced and their arrival at the destination in time has to be ensured. Returning the containers to Covent Garden is done on a narrow time margin: sometimes the scenery and props for a particular ballet only arrive back a few days before a scheduled performance at the Opera House.

Rehearsals

There is no separate rehearsal stage at Covent Garden as in Berlin or Munich. Rehearsals take place either on the regular stage or in the 'Crush Bar' behind the Grand Tier of Covent Garden, at the London Opera Centre in the East End, or at any other suitable hall. The Royal Ballet has its own rehearsal rooms at Baron's Court, in the west of London. The number of rehearsals depends on the producer's demands and the availability of the conductor and the principal singers or dancers.

Post-mortems

Now matter how careful the planning, how skilled those involved, how well they are directed and rehearsed, things—artistic, constructional or mechanical—sometimes go wrong on the first night. Nor is it always easy to keep costs within the financial allocation authorised for each production. There would consequently be an obvious advantage if, after the first night of each production (and again at the end of the season), all heads of departments concerned could meet under the chairmanship of the general administrator to list what went wrong and to take steps to prevent some of the same mishaps (many are

---

* Recently, some forty-foot containers, weighing 90 tons in all, had to be sent by sea to New York: eleven others had to be taken by road to West Germany.

fortuitous and unforeseeable) from recurring in future productions. The trouble is that nearly every head of department—and the general administrator—is much too busy with current work to do this systematically. In consequence, such post-mortems are only held when specially called for. The stage manager does, however, report daily to the general administrator on anything that goes seriously wrong.

Licensing

Since 1969, the Lord Chamberlain no longer has any authority to censor productions. But the Opera House is still licensed by him and it is his office that prescribes the safety regulations, including the maximum size of the audience and the fire regulations.

ADMINISTRATIVE MANAGEMENT

The structure of the administrative management of the Opera House (under the ultimate supervision of the general administrator) will eventually look like this:

Administrative Manager
and Assistant Administrative Manager

House Manager ('Front of the House')	Box Office Manager	Accountant

Assistant House Manager	Assistant House Manager

Usherette Manageress	Catering Manager	Chief Maintenance Engineer	House Cleaning Supervisor

The Opera House is a large Victorian building in which far more people now work than ever before: the size of the audience is now much bigger, too. Some part of the building is occupied at every hour of the day or night. Only in August is the theatre completely closed (save for the firemen on duty).

To administer the building, 168 people are employed, divided as follows:

House Manager and his assistants	17
Housekeeping staff	32
Staff restaurant (open 12 hours a day)	31
Five buffets (catering for 100-1,200 each)	10
Bar-men and cellarmen	9
Waiters for the Royal Box and other boxes in the Grand Tier	3
Telephone operators	6
Security and stage-door staff	6
Commissionaires	16
Usherettes	26
Cloakroom attendants	6
Firemen	6

Box Office

This is one of the three units controlled by the administrative manager (for 'the Front of the House'). The box office manager, Mr. David Jackson, supervises a staff of 21 who undertake the following functions:

Fixing booking periods

For greater ease of handling ticket applications, the year is divided into six booking periods of seven to eight weeks each. A booking period will provide performances of about four different operas and an assortment of ballets.

Schedule of forthcoming performances

The detailed schedule of all the 40 to 50 performances, including matinees, within the booking period is printed on a single sheet (called a 'throwaway'). It contains programme notes, ticket prices and instructions on dates and methods of application. It is prepared in conjunction with one of the assistant house managers. The programme notes are supplied by the press officer. Although the cast for each production is prepared two or three years ahead, there are often last-minute changes when singers or dancers fall ill.

Mailing list

The throwaway is sent out by post to a mailing list of 35,000. For an annual subscription of 5/– anyone can have his or her name added to the list. The names have all been recorded on a computer tape and the list is constantly updated. About half of the persons on it live within the London postal region; the other half in the Home Counties or further afield.

Applications for tickets

Separate application forms for opera and for ballet are included with each throwaway. About three-fifths of all applications for tickets are sent in by post. The rest are made in person at the Covent Garden box office windows or to London theatre ticket agencies (see below).

Ticket prices

The cheapest matinee seats, very high up, at the side, with only a restricted view of the stage, cost six shillings. Standing matinee tickets in the stalls circle cost ten shillings. For the most expensive special performances, seats in the stalls cost £7.0.0, but for the general run of performances between £2.10.0 and £5.0.0. The pricing of seats for different productions is established by the general administrator in consultation with the manager of the box office. Without a grant of £1,250,000 sterling (in 1968–69) from the Arts Council, ticket prices would be almost twice as high, which would put them out of reach of many music-lovers.* In 1968–69, ticket sales ran from 86 per cent of capacity for ordinary opera performances to 98 per cent for special ballet performances (see below).

Ticket allocation

Performances can be classified into major attractions and ordinary performances. The seats are grouped into the less expensive and those at higher prices. The major attractions are those in which world-famous singers or dancers appear (e.g., Joan Sutherland or Margot Fonteyn and Rudolf Nureyev) and old favourites (e.g., Swan Lake). For such performances there are about three times as many applications for the cheaper seats (42/– and under) than the number of tickets available, and about fifty per cent more for the more expensive seats. Overall, there is about a 50–50 chance of getting a ticket for such major attractions. For the ordinary performances, there is a 2 to 1 chance of getting a less expensive seat and almost a 100 per cent chance of getting a more expensive one.

For the major attractions and for the cheaper seats for ordinary attractions, a ballot is held in the box office by means of random selection of application forms. Tickets for the major attractions are initially sold in response to postal application and not at the box office windows.

Boxes in the Grand Tier used to be taken by the aristocracy and members of the 'Establishment' as a mark of social status. Now, they are bought largely by the commercial firms on subscription (see below). To attract an even wider circle of applicants for seats, an Arts Council working-party is now investigating the possibility of computerized booking from shopping centres along the lines of the system already in use for air-line ticket reservations.

Seats available

The house has 2,115 seats and room for 43 'standees'. Of the seat tickets, 200 are sold to theatre ticket agencies. Forty commercial firms have subscribed to some 50 seats and ten Grand Tier boxes

* At the larger German opera houses, only 30 per cent of the expenditure has to be covered by box office receipts, against 50 per cent at Covent Garden.

each night to entertain some of their more important out-of-town customers. This leaves about 1,800 tickets for distribution by the box office for each performance. Of the 1,000 amphitheatre tickets, 600 are reserved for postal applicants and 400 for window applicants. Of the 800 more expensive tickets, 500 are reserved for postal applicants, 300 for window applicants.

In all, about half a million tickets are sold each year and 50,000 postal applications dealt with. For the more popular productions, 95 per cent of the tickets are sold; but this drops to 65 per cent for the less popular productions. The average sold occupancy is over 90 per cent of capacity.

Special Performances

Eight performances a year are reserved for members of Sir Robert Mayer's 'Youth and Music' organization and for the Friends of Covent Garden.

Box Office Staff

The manager and assistant manager allocate their staff of 21 as follows:

Mailing list	5
Postal applications	6
Window applications	7
Cashiers	2
Typist	1

ACCOUNTS

The head of this department in 1968–1969 was Mr. Douglas Lund, a chartered accountant and one of the original group that helped to revive the Opera House after World War II.* Apart from two principal assistants, 19 people work in his department allocated as follows:

* His work as Secretary to the Company is described below.

Cost accounting	5
Accounts	6
Wages	2
Ticket audit	3
Computers	3

Most salaries and wages are paid weekly. About half the staff are now paid by cheque. Records of hours worked by stage crews, etc., are kept by time-keepers at the stage door.

The budgetary year follows that of the Government and of the Arts Council—from April 1st till March 31st. This is not very convenient, as the theatrical year runs from September 1st.*

The detailed planning of the budget for the year starting in April begins in the preceding summer. The budget is now nearly £3,000,000 a year; the actual amount depends largely on the size of the Arts Council grant. If less is allocated than was anticipated, the draft estimates have to be pruned. The actual expenditure usually comes within half of one per cent of the estimates.

The estimated income from the sale of tickets for any particular production can be calculated within some 5 per cent of the actual receipts.

A cautious policy is adopted in estimating the value of the scenery, costumes and props in store. Although they are heavily written down for the balance sheet, these items are, in fact, insured for some £1,500,000. The insurance value of any item is reduced by ten per cent each year, on the assumption that, at the end of ten years, a new production would be commissioned.

STAFF

Compared with some other venerable institutions that I have studied,** staff morale is very high. This may be due in part to the fact that the curtain *must* go up each night on time. All are on their toes all day. It is this feeling of tension and excitement that may be a major reason why many of the staff accept long hours, cramped quarters and lower salaries than they could get elsewhere.

* With the month of August as a general holiday for everyone.
** For example, the British Museum Library, see Vol. 9 of this Annual.

There is also the fact that working for the Opera House undoubtedly gives considerable prestige. Some of the staff who joined just after World War II to help restart opera in Britain from scratch are still employed today, a quarter of a century later.

Staff negotiations

With such a large number of people of different professions working in and around the Opera House, staff negotiations are complex. Singers and dancers are represented by 'Equity', the musicians by the Musicians' Union, the stage crew and production staff by the National Union of Theatre and Kine Operators. The clerical staff are not members of any union. There is no personnel manager as such. The management has some difficulty in ensuring proper communication with all levels of the staff in such a complex organisation, but steps are being taken to improve it.

Staff training

None of the top administrators or heads of departments has received any management training. The general administrator has considered sending a few to management courses; but it is very difficult, with such a tight schedule all through the year, to spare anyone for such a purpose. The August holiday is too short: few courses are available then, and the month is badly needed for vacation and rest.

Press Office

The press officer and her two assistants undertake several functions:
— Arranging for their own photographers, press photographers and freelance photographers to take pictures of the dress rehearsal of each production.
— Keeping a complete file of the biographies and photographs of the conductors and singers or dancers in each production for supply to the press on demand. Some of the photographs for the file are supplied by artistes' agents; others are taken by the Opera House photographers.
— Preparing material for classified theatre advertisements in dailies and weeklies for distribution through an advertising agency.

— Supplying posters for theatre ticket agencies, travel agencies, public libraries, schools and railway stations.

— Generating feature articles, at least two months ahead, on forthcoming productions.

— Preparing editorial matter for theatre programmes and for the leaflets ('throwaways') notifying forthcoming productions that are sent or given to anyone interested (see above).

— Distributing tickets to music critics. There are separate lists for opera critics and for ballet critics. For new productions, up to fifty tickets are issued according to a list developed over the years. For major revivals thirty critics are invited; for major cast changes about fifteen. The press officer has at her disposal four further tickets for foreign critics who may arrive in London and apply.

— Keeping a volume for each production containing reviews supplied by a press-cutting agency. Most artistes get press reviews of their own performances from their own agents; but, on occasion, they apply to the Opera House for photocopies.

The press officer and her staff attend all first nights with the critics so as to know themselves what is going on.

The Board of Directors

The Royal Opera House, Covent Garden Ltd. is a company limited by guarantee and has no shares: it was incorporated in March, 1950, under the Companies Act, 1948. It is managed by a board of between five and twelve directors: there are at present eleven, of whom Lord Drogheda is the chairman. None of the directors is paid. They each serve for five years; each year two retire, either to be re-elected or replaced. The board meets monthly and has three sub-committees—for opera, ballet and finance respectively. They, too, meet monthly, a week before the main board meeting, at which the minutes of each of the three sub-committees are considered.

The Company Secretary, Mr. Douglas Lund,* is responsible for the legal phraseology of the board's minutes, prepared by the

* Also head of the Accounts Department—see above.

board's own Secretary, Mr. Robert Armstrong. Mr. Lund also submits to the Registrar of Companies the annual return required by law and prepares the balance sheet.

THE GENERAL ADMINISTRATOR'S OFFICE

From 1946, when the Royal Opera was rehabilitated, till the summer of 1970, Sir David Webster was the general administrator. On his retirement, he was succeeded by his former deputy, Mr. John Tooley (who first joined in 1955). The element of continuity at the Opera House is thus very strong and is one of the reasons for its smooth running.

The general administrator is the king-pin of the whole complex organisation and is responsible to the board of directors. He is concerned with forward planning, the budget, relations with the Arts Council, with the Minister of Arts (formerly Miss Jennie Lee and, now, Lord Eccles) at the Ministry of Education and Science, and with the British Council (that helps to finance foreign tours). He is general co-ordinator of the work of all Opera House units and is much involved in smoothing relations with both staff and artistes. He participates in the negotiation of artistes' fees.

Miss Muriel Kerr, another member of the original team that revived the Royal Opera, prepares contracts for the general administrator on special printed forms for guest opera singers, conductors, designers and producers.* She also applies to the Department of Employment and Productivity for permits for foreign participants.

FINANCE

Income

During the 1968–69 season, 543 performances were given, of which almost half were on tour. Of the 273 performances at Covent Garden, 142 were of opera and 131 of ballet. In the four tours by the Royal Ballet, 184 performances were given in the provinces and 86 overseas. Of the 131 ballet performances at Covent Garden, three were given by the Royal Danish Ballet.

---

* The Ballet Company prepare their own—a continuation of the practice when they were still at Sadler's Wells.

Attendances at Covent Garden amounted to 530,270 people and the receipts were £885,500. Income from the tours was £324,000. With £1,250,000 as a grant from the Arts Council, £20,000 net broadcasting and television receipts, £36,000 from profits on the bar, catering, sales of programmes, etc., and some sundry receipts, the total income for that year was £2,630,00.

Expenditure

The major items of expenditure for the year were salaries and wages:

	£	
Artistes (opera and ballet)	832,000	
Orchestra	288,000	
Stage and staff	492,000	
Administration and accounts	70,000	
'Front of House'	80,000	1,762,000
New productions (including salaries and wages)	98,000	
Revivals (including salaries and wages)	147,000	245,000
Rents, rates and insurance of building, etc.	89,000	
Maintenance, replacements and alterations, including wages	47,000	
Stage machinery repairs	6,000	
London Opera Centre (half share of recurrent expenditure)	27,000	
Amortization of leasehold properties	12,000	181,000
Royalties and performing fees	38,000	
Travelling and hotel expenses and subsistence allowances	108,000	
Touring expenses	50,000	
Insurance (including superannuation)	29,000	
Publicity, advertising (including salaries and wages)	48,000	

* Government grants for opera only started in 1930 when Philip Snowden was Chancellor of the Exchequer. The BBC was then authorised to promote opera to the extent of £17,500 a year for five years.

	£	
Donations (including employees on termination)	13,000	
Depreciation	9,000	
Miscellaneous expenses*	173,000	468,000
Grand Total		2,656,000

The cost of the individual new productions and revivals varied from £1,300 for a new ballet ('Intrusion') to £62,000 for a new production of the 'Sleeping Beauty' ballet and £49,000 for a new production of *Die Meistersinger von Nürnberg*. The average for the four operas and eight ballets was £20,000 each. It is not possible to relate the income from each production to the expenditure because of the difficulty in allocating overheads. But the introduction of a system of cost/benefit analysis is now under consideration.

'THE FRIENDS OF COVENT GARDEN'

This Society was founded largely on the initiative of Sir Leon Bagrit, who became its first president. The aim was to raise some money for things which the Opera House could not afford to do with its own funds. The Society also hoped to develop a deeper understanding among its members of operas and ballets to be performed. Talks are given before new productions.** An illustrated magazine entitled *About the House is* distributed to all the members in return for their minimum annual subscription of £5-0-0 (£2-0-0 for Young Friends). Some £10,000 is raised by the Society each year. It was with this money that Mr. Richard Rodney Bennett was commissioned to write a new opera—'Victory'. An album of recordings and the translation of foreign operatic libretti were also underwritten. Finan-

* The miscellaneous expenses include such items as:

	£
Repairs, replacements and cleaning of costumes and shoes	32,000
Repairs, repainting and rigging of scenery	21,000
Manufacture, repairs and replacement of stage props	5,000
Hire of music, repairs to sheets, copying, instrument hire and piano tuning	4,000

** When *Hamlet* was produced as an opera in 1969, a thousand people attended the illustrated lecture in the auditorium.

cial support is given to the Royal Ballet Choreographic Group and scholarships are provided for the Royal Ballet School and the London Opera Centre.

Members of the Society are invited to an annual 'cabaret' provided by the artistes and, on occasion, to attend dress rehearsals. The tight schedule of the Opera House does not allow time for a second dress rehearsal (as in some opera houses abroad) which the public and the critics might attend. Otherwise, headmasters of schools would be invited to send selected children to see dress rehearsals in order to encourage the rising generation to buy tickets when they grow up.

CONCLUSION

The present Opera House is 112 years old: the revived Opera Company has just completed a quarter of a century: the Ballet Company is even older: their repertoire covers nearly 200 years. The thousand people who keep this complex organization running so smoothly for eleven months a year do so under considerable pressure of space, time and money. The gainers are the general public—both British and visitors—who, thanks to a generous Government grant, can buy tickets for superb performances at prices that enough can afford to keep the theatre almost completely full, night after night, for season after season.

Balliol College

This is the fifth of a series of articles that I have written on the administration of venerable institutions. All the previous four have appeared in this journal: the House of Lords (1963), the Catholic Church (1966), the British Museum Library (1967) and the Royal Opera House, Covent Garden (1970).

Balliol College is sufficiently venerable to be done, having celebrated its 700th anniversary in 1964. I am grateful to the Master (Christopher Hill), whose guest I was in College in 1970, for having given me access to all College records. I stayed again in June, 1971, and obtained further oral information from Fellows and College officers. I am particularly indebted to Mr Jacobus de Wet (then Vice-Master); the Rev. Francis Willis-Bund (Chaplain and Dean), Mr. Donald Harris (Estates Bursar), Mr William Weinstein (Tutor for Admissions), Mr Patrick Sandars (former Senior Tutor), Mr. Anthony Kenny (the present Senior Tutor), Mr. Vincent Quinn (Librarian), Brigadier Denis Jackson, CBE (Domestic Bursar), Mrs Bridget Page (College Secretary) and Mr K. W. Jones (a second-year undergraduate, then President of the Junior Common Room).

For those wishing to read more about the College, the following books may be helpful:
— Victoria History of the Counties of England: vol. III, *Oxfordshire,* 1954
— Savage, H.: *Balliofergus,* 1668
— Davies, H.W.C.: *A History of Balliol College,* 1963
— Mallet, C.E.: *A History of the University of Oxford,* 1962
— The annual *Balliol College Record*
— The annual *Oxford University Handbook.*

THE UNIVERSITY OF OXFORD

The University of Oxford has grown out of seeds casually planted in the 13th century by a few scholars who had graduated from the University of Paris. Settling in mediaeval Oxford, they gathered round them small groups of students who paid them direct. The students—and their teachers—lodged at inns in the town: this was neither cheap nor comfortable. Several hostels for them were founded and endowed in the 13th century which are still men's colleges in Oxford today. Other such colleges have been founded during the subsequent centuries, making about thirty in all. To them have been added five women's colleges and five graduate colleges. Each of the forty is a self-governing institution, with its own statutes. Each is a community of Fellows (teachers) and undergraduates or graduates. Each provides accommodation for most of its students, often in ancient buildings forming a quadrangle, with a green lawn inside. Food from college kitchens is provided (separately) for Fellows and for students. Part of the intellectual needs of undergraduates is supplied by the college library and college and university societies; the formal spiritual needs of the community by the college chapel; the undergraduates' need for physical exercise by college sports clubs and playing fields. Each undergraduate is allotted, on arrival, to one or more college tutors who closely supervise his or her studies. Each college has its own income from students' fees and, for many of the older colleges, through rents and dividends from gifts and bequests by alumni. From these funds, college teachers and administrative and domestic staff are paid. All colleges are federated in the University of Oxford, which has its own revenues: these provide for professorships, lectureships, research facilities, and faculty and University libraries. It is the University that arranges intermediate and final examinations* and awards degrees at all levels.

What is true for Balliol is largely typical for most of the other colleges of Oxford and Cambridge.

* Entrance examinations are now arranged by groups of colleges (see below).

94

The College started over seven centuries ago as a hostel for poor students of arts (the humanities) and was built outside the then city walls, near the north gate. The founder was John Balliol,* a powerful baron with lands on both sides of the Scottish border. Involved in a dispute with the Bishop of Durham, he was ordered in 1263, as a penance, to maintain sixteen poor students. After his death in 1269, his widow Devorguilla—a descendant both of the kings of Scotland and of Alfred the Great—continued the payments. Her charter of 1282 is in the possession of the College, which still stands on its ancient site. The charter provided that the students should elect their own principal but that the hostel should be governed by two external masters, one of them a Franciscan. A common table should provide food for the students to a value of eightpence a week (13th century prices!). In 1340, the number of maintained students was raised to twenty-two. They had no chapel of their own but attended the nearby parish church of Mary Magdalene.

The statutes were recast in 1507 to provide for ten Fellows and ten students not over the age of 18. Each Fellow nominated one student who more or less acted as his servant. The College became more completely self-governing, the Fellows electing from among themselves a Master, a Vice-Master, a Senior Fellow, a Senior Dean (for discipline and the library) and a Junior Dean (in charge of the chapel), two Chaplains and two Bursars. It also obtained the privilege of electing its own Visitor (Honorary President).

In 1572, the College began to accept fee-paying commoners as well and, by 1576, there were forty undergraduates. As more gifts were received from alumni (the first in 1294), the College was able to endow lectureships in Greek, rhetoric and logic in 1572, theology in 1591, poetry and mathematics in 1698 and Hebrew in

---

* His name is of French origin—*Bailleul,* derived from the verb *bailler,* from which come the English words bailiff, bailey and bail. According to Murray's *New English Dictionary,* a bailiff, among other things, both tutors and administers. It is thus appropriate that an article on the administration of a tutoring college should be written about Balliol.

1708. By 1641, the number of students had risen to seventy; but, owing to the disruption caused by the Civil War, it fell by 1649 to forty again. In the 1670's, endowments were received from John Snell and others to provide 'exhibitions' for deserving students, in addition to scholarships for scholars.

The intellectual level of the College fell in the eighteenth century; but, with the advent of Richard Jenkyns as Master (1819 to 1859), its fortunes began to rise and, by 1830, the number of students was ninety. In 1856, the College took the step of requiring *all* its undergraduates to take the final honours examination, without the option of sitting for the lesser pass degree. Benjamin Jowett became Master in 1870, by which date the number of students had reached 150: by 1880, there were 200. Today, the College is one of the largest in Oxford with 80 scholars, 50 exhibitioners, 200 undergraduates and 150 graduate students. Not only do its undergraduates attain a higher percentage of first-class honours degree in relation to its size than any other men's college at Oxford, but it also shows considerable athletic prowess, especially in rowing.

THE FELLOWS

The Fellows are the senior members of the College and, together with the Master, form its autonomous governing body. There are by now some sixty Fellows, of whom half are College tutors. There are twelve additional tutors who are not Fellows, making a total of 42 tutors for some 320 undergraduates—a ratio of about one to eight. They are not deeply involved with the 150 graduate students who are largely under University supervision. These have their own Balliol graduate centre, jointly with the St. Anne's women's college.

There are on the establishment, besides the thirty tutoring Fellows, seven senior and four junior research Fellows, four Fellows who are College officers and have little time for tutoring, and fourteen professorial Fellows holding University appointments.* Lastly, there

---

* The University statutes provide for the holders of certain chairs to be Fellows of different Colleges. The holders of other appointments have been individually elected as professiorial Fellows (*ad hominem*) of the several colleges by their governing bodies, including that of Balliol.

96

are numbers of *emeritus* and honorary Fellows who are not members of the governing body.

There is provision of long standing in the College statutes* that no woman may be a member of the College: this applies equally to women Fellows and to women students.

The admission of women students is now under informal discussion between Balliol and other Colleges. But it is generally agreed in the University that no woman should be accepted by any College until it has admitted one or more women Fellows (as has already happened at King's College, Cambridge). That would require a revision of the statute of each College: such revisions would have to receive approval not only from the University but also from the Queen's Privy Council, an expensive and lengthy process.

New Balliol Fellows are co-opted by the existing ones: the seniority of each is determined by the date of his election. Up to World War II, Fellows came in young and spent their whole working lives as tutors. That has now become rarer: Fellows leave to be heads of other Oxford or Cambridge colleges, or professors in other universities in Britain or abroad, or to engage wholetime in research, or to become headmasters or senior civil servants or to join industrial or commercial enterprises. Of the present tutors, over half have held office for less than ten years.

In mediaeval times, when monasticism was more frequent in Britain, Fellows had to be unmarried and live in College. Until a century ago they were obligated not only to take an MA (in Oxford, largely a formal process) but also to proceed within a further four years to ordination in the Church. Today, the great majority of Balliol Fellows are married and live outside the College. Each, however, is provided with a room in College where he gives his tutorials and keeps his professional library. By statute, at least two unmarried Fellows must live in College** to help to maintain good order there.

Up to 1855, Fellows had to be members of the Established (Anglican) Church: then, non-conformist Protestants were admitted. From 1871, Catholics and Jews could be accepted as students but,

* Paragraph VII(6)c of the 1966 revision.
** At present there are five.

as Fellows, not until 1922. Today, there are several Catholic and Jewish Fellows; but most Fellows have no strong religious affiliations.

The aim of the governing body is to achieve a high level of excellence in the College: Fellows are recruited from as wide a field as possible. Being a Balliol man helps; but Balliol men form only about a quarter of the Fellows: another fifth come from other Oxford colleges, and a tenth from Cambridge, making a total of over half from 'Oxbridge'. About a quarter come from other British universities and a fifth from abroad.

Tutors in the different faculty subjects are engaged more or less in proportion to the number of undergraduates admitted to read for their degrees in such subjects. At present, there are the following numbers of tutors in each subject (the numbers in brackets show the distribution of the eleven tutors who are not Fellows: the remaining 32 are Fellows):

Modern history 4	Life sciences and medicine
Languages 2 (+3)	2 (+3)
Philosophy 2 (+1)	Other sciences 5
Economics 2 (+1)	Mathematics 2
Politics 2	Engineering 2
Classics 2	Agriculture and Forestry 2
Jurisprudence 2	Geography (1)
Ancient history 1	Geology (1)
International relations 1	Music (1)
Psychology 1	

When a tutorship falls vacant, the governing body decides whether to refill it or to allocate it to some other subject of increasing popularity for which the present tutors are overworked. The College, on the advice of the Senior Tutor and the Tutorial Board, plans forward in the light of the subjects chosen by freshmen and subsequent applications to transfer from one subject to another, bearing in mind contemporary technological and social developments and the need to introduce tutoring in new subjects.

Where there are too few undergraduates studying any one subject to warrant the appointment of a wholetime Balliol tutor for it, joint arrangements are made with another college with tutoring capacity to spare. Eighty such arrangements were made in 1970–71.

Tutors in the arts undertake twelve hours tutoring a week: those in the sciences (who have to supervise work in the laboratories for some six hours a week) undertake eight. When a tutor becomes a College officer, his tutoring load is lightened but, on principle, never wholly lifted.

Most arts tutors hold University lectureships in addition, for which they are paid a University stipend. The extra work is not very onerous—sixteen lectures over a period of 24 weeks a year (three terms of eight weeks each). On the other hand, most science tutors start as University demonstrators and are elected Fellows, which supplements their income. The combined salary of each Fellow is based on a College scale which starts at about £2,000 a year and reaches a peak of about £5,000 at the age of 45.

About twenty of the Balliol fellowships have been specifically endowed in the past by the payment to the College of a sum (today about £ 50,000 is needed) on which the interest is more or less sufficient to pay the stipend. The balance is made up by the University in respect of the lectureship held by the Fellow and, if necessary, from the College exchequer (known as *Domus*). Some endowments specify the actual subject in which the Fellow is to tutor:* others do not.

The other perquisites of a Fellow include:
— a free room in College for use as a study;
— all meals at the Common Table (to which Fellows now contribute the sum of £ 50 a year (less than 35 new pence a day);
— a standard book allowance of £ 50 a year;
— £ 60 a year to enable tutors to offer coffee or sherry to visitors, including Old Members and present students;
— payment by the College of a premium to BUPA (British United Provident Association) for medical insurance of the Fellow and his family;

* For example, there are three in philosophy, one in philosophy or classics, one each in history, law, economics, mathematics and biology and four in either chemistry, physics or biology.

— a monthly premium paid by the College to the FSSU (Federated Superannuation System for Universities). The monthly premium varies considerably from Fellow to Fellow; but, as a case in point, for a recently retired Fellow, with 31 years service, the College and the University, between them, paid a premium in the last year of £ 419. The Fellow was entitled to either a lump sum of £18,000, or an annuity of about 55 per cent of his terminal salary: he chose the former; and

— paid sabbatical leave at the rate of one year or one term in seven.

Fellows may earn up to 20 per cent above their emoluments from one or more of the following sources (some do not earn anything):

— fees paid by the University for supervision of graduate work;
— University examination fees;
— royalties on books;
— fees for writing articles or book reviews;
— fees from radio or television appearances; or
— occasionally, fees as part-time adult education lecturers or correspondence tutors.

A well-established tutor may have taught up to 500 students. In consequence, he spends much time in friendly correspondence with many of them and in receiving them when they visit Oxford. He is also called on to supply written recommendations for up to twenty former students a year, applying for jobs in other institutions. Recommendations are far franker and less laudatory than those commonly sent by American professors.

Tutors are also involved for about ten days each year in the entrance examinations (see below). *All* papers of *all* candidates are read by *all* the tutors in that subject. *All* candidates are interviewed by those who will teach them, if they are accepted. After the examination, a very full and careful report is written by a tutor to the school of each candidate, with advice on future prospects for those who have been unsuccessful.

Senior and Junior Research Fellows

The senior fellowships are awarded to eminent scholars, coming to Oxford, who have no tutorial appointments. They may also be awarded to Fellows who wish to be relieved of tutoring for a period, or who are too old, or who hold University jobs. The junior fellowships are normally granted for three years, often to graduate students working for their doctorates. Some of both these types of research fellowships are endowed: of these, one or two are in specified subjects. All junior, and some senior vacancies are advertised and selection is made by a committe composed of the tutors concerned plus the Master and Senior Tutor.

Junior research fellows are allowed (but not required) to tutor, if they wish, in return for fees paid by the College.

STUDENTS

Admissions

The minimum University entrance requirements are met nowadays by secondary school 'O' (ordinary) or 'A' (advanced) level examinations. All candidates for entry into any British university register with the UCCA (University Central Council on Admissions). For some departments of some universities there is an excess in demand: for example, thirty candidates for every place at the Bristol University school for drama: or 36 to one for the Sussex University department of social studies. For Oxford and Cambridge, the ratio is about two to one. Candidates may list up to six colleges at either university in order of preference. Each University has a central admissions office. Since 1962, Oxford divides its colleges into three groups, each consisting of larger and smaller, older and newer, and academically highly and less highly-rated colleges. The group examination also serves as an entrance examination to each individual college. The successful candidates, and their marked papers, are then seen at the colleges of their first choice. Those that are not picked are then seen at the colleges of second and subsequent choices. The papers of those good candidates who fail to get into any Oxford college of their choice are then referred to the Cambridge central admissions office, and *vice versa*. By January each year (some nine months before the date of entry), unsuccessful candidates for Oxford and Cambridge are free to apply to any other British university on the basis of their school record (GCE), a three-hour paper and an interview.

Balliol now has a total enrolment of 315 undergraduates, admitting about 105 freshmen each year. Admissions are based on quotas for each faculty subject, related to the number of tutors available in it. The present quotas are as follows:

Politics, philosophy and economics 20*	Physics 10
	Chemistry 10
History 16	Mathematics 7
Classics 10	Medicine and biology 6
English 6	Engineering 5
Law 6	Other subjects 9

Nearly all freshmen are selected on brain alone, but other factors are taken into consideration, such as Balliol family tradition, or prowess in sport at school. But few men get into Balliol for non-academic reasons. The College has always been particularly interested in foreign students and some ten per cent of the total body of undergraduates is of foreign birth, including about ten Rhodes scholars, largely from the United States,** as well as an assortment of princes and, occasionally, of gods. The Tutorial Board (see below) has the right to recommend the admission each year of one or two freshmen of exceptional interest to the College.

A century ago, Oxford and Cambridge undergraduates came almost entirely from the upper classes, having been taught at the better public schools. At Balliol, today, of the ninety per cent of students from Britain only some 36 per cent come from the public schools, nine per cent from the independent grammar schools, while 45 per cent comes from the State school system (which includes a number of maintained grammar schools).

---

* This quota in future will be split up into separate quotas for each of the three subjects taken for a PPE degree.

** Rhodes scholars also come from Canada, Australia, South Africa, New Zealand and West Germany.

Nearly all the British undergraduates are in receipt of State grants. The amount which they can receive is related to their parents' means but, nowadays, can reach £450 a year. It is intended to cover only the three terms of eight weeks each (i.e., half the year). About one third of Balliol undergraduates are in receipt of nominal college scholarships (£60 a year) or exhibitions (£40 a year).* Some 35 such nominal College scholarships and exhibitions are now available each year. Of these, nine are in specific subjects but the other 26 are open. Of the total of 35, 31 were awarded last year.**

Undergraduate Accommodation

All undergraduates reside in College for their first two years; some for all three years. The traditional right of scholars to a third year in College (rather than in 'digs' outside) has been allowed to lapse. The scholars then in residence when the question came up felt that the privilege was both undemocratic and restrictive. The *Camerarius* (one of the junior Fellows) allots rooms in College. One of the Junior Common Room committee members helps third-year men to find accommodation outside. Nearly all students have a bed-sitter; a very few have separate bedrooms, a pair of such under-graduates sharing the same study (mostly in cases where it has been structurally impossible to convert the rooms to bed-sitters). The old days of a separate bed-room and study for each undergraduate are long over. Rooms on each staircase are served by 'scouts' (men-servants) paid by the College, with additional tips from students to whom, by special request, they bring daily morning tea, whose shoes they shine and whose beds they make. But these personal services have largely lapsed as many students from homes without any personal service find such attention embarrassing. They would like only cleaning of rooms to be provided and on a more anonymous basis. 'Scouts' also serve at table in Hall; there is a proposal by students to change over to a cafeteria system.

* From about 1880 to the 1950's, the scholarship was worth about £100 a year. This covered nearly all the scholar's expenses.
** One is held, for a term at a time, by a schoolmaster seconded by his employers. No freshmen were eligible for four of the closed scholarships.

The work of the 'scouts' is supervised by the Head Scout, an experienced College servant. During vacations (except in August, when the College is completely closed), a dozen students, who have nowhere else to go, stay on. Up to a further hundred remain for two or three weeks following the end of term, or arrive a week or ten days before the start of it.

Undergraduate Expenses

Undergraduates pay the following charges each term (the starred items are paid by the State in addition to the annual grant):

General College 'establishment' fee	£ 52*
Tuition in College (see below)	£ 71*
Food in College (see below) (average)	£ 31
Room rent in College (plus bath fee of £ 1) (average)	£ 33
Heating (average)	£ 4
Laundry (students provide their own linen) (average)	£ 3
Junior Common Room membership (see below)	£ 7.50*

This comes to £ 201.50 a term, or slightly over £ 600 a year, towards which a maximum State grant of £ 465 is paid, together with a further £ 391.50 to cover the starred items. An undergraduate's basic expenses for the six months a year that he spends at the University are thus more or less covered. But he still has to pay for his own transportation to and from Oxford; for his books; membership fees for any college or university club or society that he decides to join; his clothing and entertainments; and his examination and other University fees.

College bills are sent to students before the beginning of each term to cover the previous term and the intervening vacation. The bills are called 'battels', a special Oxford University name.* There is a weekly fine for delay in settlement and £ 30 must be deposited by each freshman (called 'caution money') to cover claims, which is returned when he leaves.**

* According to Murray's *New English Dictionary*, the word has an affinity with 'battle', in the sense of settling a score or an account.
** Many Old Members arrange for £ 5 to be retained indefinitely by the

104

Undergraduate Food Charges

The price of food in College is still subsidised; but this is gradually being brought to an end. Students pre-pay £ 16.44 a term, which covers about half the cost. They buy food tickets which they present in Hall to obtain the following alternative meals:

Breakfast: 8 or 12 new pence

Lunch: 11 p (table d'hôte) or 13-23 p (à la carte)

Dinner: 17 p (standard)

Undergraduate Welfare

In order to qualify for benefits under the National Health Service, every freshman, on arrival, must register either with an Oxford doctor of his choice or with the College doctors. The College doctors have a three-man group practice that works for several colleges on retainers. A student who is ill must inform his 'scout', or the Lodge porter, so that he may be seen by the College nurse. If he is confined to his room for more than a day, he must inform his doctor.

A few students suffer nervous breakdowns, usually the result of family pressures to succeed in the face of what appear to the student to be insuperable difficulties. There have been occasional attempts at suicide—usually more as a cry for help. The only recent successful suicide by a Balliol man was due to drug addiction before admission: he took his own life after a period in hospital.

It is the Chaplain (at present also the Dean) who is in charge of student welfare (in addition to student discipline). He is often the first to discern signs of physical or mental trouble and then refers the student for medical advice.

The Junior Common Room

This is the Balliol undergraduate club, occupying five rooms on the ground floor and basement in the inner quadrangle. These are used as lounges (with newspapers and magazines), a coffee bar, a meetings room, a games room, a basement liquor bar, a television

College. This allows them to stay and have meals in College when on a visit and pay the bill later.

room, a second-hand book-shop (where original pictures and prints are available for loan to undergraduates for their rooms). As with most student premises, tidiness and proper maintenance are difficult to secure: many of the members are just not concerned.

Each undergraduate pays a membership fee of £ 7.50 a term, whether he uses the JCR or not (this fee is refunded as part of the student's State grant). The income of the JCR is some £ 2,000 a year which enables it to pay for the services of two secretaries, six pantry staff and a cleaner.

The JCR is managed by a committee of nine undergraduates elected each year and one *ex-officio* graduate member—the president of the alumni association who resides in Oxford. The political party affiliations of the candidates for election are taken into consideration by the voters: the 1970-71 president, a second-year man, says that he is 'on the far Left'.

The work undertaken by the committee is distributed among the members as follows: president; treasurer; second-hand book-shop manager; liaison with the National Union of Students; and Balliol representative on the University Students' Representative Council. Of the three other committee members, one supervises the running of the Lindsay bar;* another is responsible for the coffee bar and is the JCR channel for student representations to the College about the quality, quantity, variety and price of food served in Hall; while the third maintains the JCR premises: he also keeps a file of vacant 'digs' for the third-year students moving out of College.

The president is a member of the University committee of presidents of college JCRs, which meets twice each term. Its importance has, however, been overshadowed by the more recently established Oxford University Students' Representative Council which meets twice a week and on which the Balliol JCR committee is represented, as already stated.

Balliol has the reputation of being a fairly liberal college, as far

---

* The bar got into debt some years ago and is now under the management of a joint consultative committee on facilities. The committee has five members of whom three are junior members and two are senior members of the College.

106

as undergraduate societies, publications, meetings and speeches are involved. The main questions of JCR and undergraduate concern seem (in 1971) to be the demand that the College be thrown open to women Fellows and women undergraduates; and undergraduate representation on the College governing body and its committees and sub-committees. The undergraduates claim, at least, the right to see the agendas of such meetings (as now at the Somerville women's college) and even the minutes.

There is already regular liaison with the Dean, the Academic Committee and the Domestic Committee (see below). Five undergraduates sit on the Disciplinary Committee (see below) and on the Library Committee (see below), apart from their representatives on the joint consultative committee on facilities (see above).

Undergraduate Discipline

For fifty years or more there have always been Left wing activists in Balliol—a healthy sign; but there are a few deliberate disruptionists. Relations between undergraduates and the governing body today are outwardly calm; but eddies below the surface remain. Much has, however, been done to calm the situation, both before and after the publication in 1967 of the Hart Report on University discipline. The theory that the College and the University are *in loco parentis** is largely dead. New and more mature generations of undergraduates have arrived since World War I and, particularly, since World War II. College and University prohibitions have gradually been relaxed. Students may now frequent public houses and are not required to wear academic gowns in the streets in the evening as a means of identification. But, if a young man (or woman)—apparently an undergraduate—is creating a disturbance, a University Proctor**, wearing a white tie and full academic robes, will come up, tip his mortarboard and, in traditional fashion, ask

* This theory is a relic from former centuries when undergraduates were often admitted at fifteen years of age.
** One of the two Fellows who are appointed for an academic year in rotation between Colleges to maintain undergraduate discipline in the University as a whole.

"Are you a member of this University?" And, if the student turns and runs, he will still be pursued by the Proctor's attendants (known as "bull-dogs") and summoned to appear next day before the Dean in his or her own college for disciplining.

The Dean of Balliol is responsible for securing good order in the College. He is a Fellow, elected (and re-elected) for this duty for four years at a time. His assistant Junior Dean is always a bachelor, able to live in College and be on the spot in a crisis.

A copy of the printed College disciplinary rules (together with other information) is given to each freshman on arrival. The rules are subject to reconsideration by the Disciplinary Committee at a series of sessions in February of each year. This committee has nine members, of whom four are Fellows (the Dean, the Junior Dean and two other Fellows nominated by the Nominating Committee (see below) and elected at a meeting of the governing body. The remaining five members (the majority) are undergraduates elected by the JCR. Four 'JCR deans' are also elected by the JCR to help police the College rules. These rules are as follows:

— No interruption of teaching, research or administration.
— No disturbance to the public in—or from—the College (e.g., throwing things from windows of rooms abutting the streets).
— No excessive noise (which covers the third of the three features of a riotous life—wine, women and *song*).
— Compliance with reasonable instructions by a Dean.
— No parties of more than ten persons to be held in the College without three days' notice. Individual (i.e., not casual general) invitations to be given. Uninvited and disorderly guests to be excluded. No resultant damage to property. No unreasonable noise (e.g., no recorded music to be played loudly after 11.30 p.m.). Special permission to be obtained for live music to be played and for the use of any public rooms in College (such as for a dance). The College gates are no longer closed at 10.30 p.m.; but only members of the College and their guests may enter between midnight and eight a.m.
— No women to stay in College overnight. (This prohibition is difficult to enforce and is, in fact, freely disregarded. No-one

has recently been sent down for such a reason. In any case, what happents by day in an undergraduate's rooms cannot be policed without infringing his 'reasonable rights of privacy'—another of the rules written into the code.)

— No absence from College for more than three days without the Dean's permission and leaving an address. (This replaces the old prohibition against going up to London even for a day.)

— No use of drugs in College. This would expose the College to prosecution for aiding a criminal offence. There is probably some experimentation with marijuana; but organised 'pot parties' have not come to light.

— No short cuts across the lawns, except those reserved for primitive forms of croquet and bowls: no other games to be played there. The lawns not to be littered with rubbish or with cutlery and crockery taken out of the buttery. (From my own observation, this is widely disregarded.)

— No firearms to be brought into College.

— No outside aerials to be placed on the roofs.

It is interesting to note that American universities prohibit student possession and use of liquor on the campus, whereas British universities do not. Informal clothing and Shakespearean hair lengths,* however, are customary in both countries.

Tutoring

This is the heart of the Collegiate system. It enables the potentialities of undergraduates to be intensively developed in the comparatively short time customary for obtaining a degree. Over three years there are only 360 working days in College, spread over 72 five-day weeks arranged in nine terms of eight weeks each.

Each tutor has an average of eight undergraduates allotted to him. Some students taking more than one subject at a time (PPE**, for example) will have separate tutors for the two subjects taken simultaneously out of the three. The student normally sees his tutor

* One of the older Balliol Fellows, Russell Meiggs, recently retired, was an early originator of the present fashion.
** Politics, philosophy and economics.

(or tutors) once a week (each) in the tutor's own room in College. Tutorials last an hour. Sometimes the tutor sees a single student (the 'one-to-one relationship'): sometimes, a group of three or four together. The most usual pattern is a pair of students, if possible of more or less equal intellectual ability. Some tutors concentrate their attention on the best (who can hope with special effort by both student and tutor to get a first class honours degree) and on the worst (who may fail to get a degree at all unless specially coached). This allows the average student to develop at his own speed with only ordinary attention.

The essence of the tutorial is the requirement that the student should write a weekly essay on a topic set by the tutor to strengthen his weak spots (science students are usually required to solve a series of problems set by the tutor). The writing of an essay requires a great deal of preliminary planning, reading and thinking by the student on his own, in addition to what he may have picked up from the few university lectures he may have attended. (Attendance is purely voluntary and no records of lecture attendance are kept: science students, however, *must* work in the laboratories.) The student reads his essay aloud to his tutor who points out faulty arrangement, inaccuracies, omissions, lack of precision or poor style. On the other hand, originality of interpretation (if based on the facts) and of the conclusions wins high praise. Thus is the art of clear thinking and good writing (so lacking in American *undergraduates*)* developed under the Oxford (and Cambridge) tutorial system.

The Oxford undergraduate has several sources of books; those he has bought himself (new or second-hand); books lent to the student by the tutor from his own library in his room in College**; from the College library; from the library of the University faculty concerned (see below) or from the great Bodleian reference library (one of the six British libraries of legal deposit).

* American *graduates,* however, can compete with anyone Britain can produce.
** It is for this purpose that tutors who are Fellows get a book allowance of £ 50 a year; they also buy books out of their own pocket, of course, and keep review copies of the specialised new books which publishers send them.

110

Some undergraduates decide to change their subject after admission: this requires permission from the Tutorial Board (see below). A few withdraw from the University (on grounds of ill-health, for example). Occasionally, one will be sent home as a punishment either temporarily ('rusticated') or permanently ('sent down').

Undergraduates are encouraged to compete for one or more of the thirty or so College prizes offered in different subjects and for the more prestigious University prizes.

At the end of every term, each student is seen by the Master (in the presence of his tutor) who discuss freely his progress with him. This is called 'Handshaking' and is a heavy burden on the Master and the tutors.

Many students are so involved in social, athletic or political activity in the College, the University and the town during term time that they try to make up by intensive study during the vacations, in particular the four months of the Long (summer) Vacation. However, 'reading parties' of several students who go together into some secluded spot, possibly with their tutor, to study for several weeks are less frequent nowadays: history and philosophy students sometimes have them.

The Student's Day

There are infinite varieties in the way students spend their day. Some work hard: others do not. There is every degree of participation—or none—in all the different types of activity offered in college, in the University and in the town.

Undergraduates living in College struggle up in the morning: some have breakfast in Hall: others who are too late eat in the Junior Common Room coffee bar: some skip breakfast altogether. The morning is devoted mostly to reading in libraries or the student's own room, to the tutorial or writing the essay for it, to an occasional university lecture and, for science students, work in the university laboratories. Unlike the situation in American universities, no lectures or tutorials are scheduled during the lunch period or the early afternoon. Lunch is usually taken in Hall. Those students interested in sports play until tea-time either in friendly games, inter-college events or, occasionally, in contests with Cambridge. Study continues for most students till supper in Hall. The evenings are spent either in work, attendance at meetings of College or University societies or at public entertainments or in private groups.

Examinations

Undergraduates sit for two public examinations. The first is usually held at the end of the second term of residence.* The second (known as 'Schools') is held at the end of the third year of residence, as the final examination, which fixes the 'class'.

Each final examination paper is set by one examiner, discussed with a second, printed and then approved by the whole board of examiners after checking for correctness and relevance to the syllabus.

Candidates in the arts (humanities) sit for one week of nine or ten three-hour papers. Those in the sciences sit for four to nine papers, together with practical tests in the laboratories.

The 'Schools' are held during June. Papers are marked by two examiners independently. The candidates are not known to the examiners, a few of whom are drawn from other universities.

Some candidates then appear for an oral examination (*viva voce*). In marginal cases, this determines their class: in all other cases it is largely formal. If there are differences of opinion among the examiners over the merit of a particular candidate, the decision is taken by a majority vote. By convention, a tutor withdraws when his own pupil is being discussed. Most of the results are published by the second week in July.

The number of first and second class honours degrees won by undergraduates from each college is jealously watched by all the colleges. The number is graded in relation to the size of the under-graduate body in each college and published as the Norrington Table** each year. Balliol is almost always at the top of the list of

* In Modern History, usually in the first term of residence, as the next best thing to abolishing it altogether.
** Named after the former head of Trinity College, who proposed it.

112

men's colleges. It has been beaten by a women's college: because of the comparatively few women's colleges, the intellectual standard of the entrants is even higher than in the men's colleges.

Graduate Students

The high intellectual level of Balliol also has a special appeal to the *graduate* student, of whom no fewer than 150 are now enrolled at the College (one in three of all students there). A few prefer to live in College: some are accomodated at the joint Balliol—St. Anne's Graduate Centre half a mile to the east, into which Holywell Manor (the former Balliol undergraduate hostel) has now been absorbed. The Graduate Centre is maintained by Balliol, with its own Balliol steward. It is used only by unmarried graduate students; married couples find their own accommodation in the town.

Graduate students are supervised largely by University faculty members and not by the College tutors: graduate fees are paid to the University. Any Balliol tutor who undertakes the supervision of graduate work receives renumeration from the University.

PHYSICAL LAY-OUT

Nearly every Oxford and Cambridge college started in stone buildings set in a quadrangle with college gardens outside. In the centre of most quadrangles there are now beautifully tended lawns. The surrounding buildings usually have two to four storeys with inside staircases at intervals, leading to undergraduate suites on both sides and an occasional Fellow's study. As the colleges grew, a second and sometimes a third quadrangle was added. In each college, including Balliol, other essential buildings have been built: a chapel; a dining-hall used jointly by undergraduates and Fellows; a separate Fellows' dining-room and private gardens; kitchens with a buttery (bar) and stores; a college undergraduate lending library (sometimes incorporating the earlier Fellows' library); senior and junior common-rooms; the college offices and the lodgings of the Master (in some other colleges called President, Rector or Warden).

Balliol has two quadrangles, the first with the porter's lodge controlling access from the street. Next door is the domestic bursar's offices: on the second side, the *old* dining hall (now the College library) : on the third side, the chapel; the rest being occupied by undergraduate suites and Fellows' studies. The inner quadrangle is much bigger, with the Master's lodging (of Victorian amplitude, part now transformed into undergraduate suites), Fellows' studies and College offices; the senior and junior common rooms; the new dining-hall, kitchens, buttery (bar) and stores; the rest being given over to undergraduate suites and Fellows' studies.

There is practically nothing left of the original 13th century College and only a little of the 15th century buildings. Most is of the 18th, 19th and 20th centuries, the latest additions having been built with money raised in the 700th anniversary appeal (see below). They have much more architectural merit than any of the nineteenth century buildings.

Balliol has about 300 rooms in all, in addition to 80 at the Graduate Centre, of which 55 are for Balliol and 25 for St. Anne's. The rooms in College are allocated for use as follows:

Undergraduates	235
Undergraduates' guests	7
Junior Common Room	7
Fellows	43
Fellows' guests	2
Senior Common Room	5
Master's lodgings	6
College offices	11

Lectures open to all members of the University are given in Hall or in the seminar room on staircase 22. College meetings are normally held in the dining-room of the Senior Common Room.

Tutorial Fellows and junior research Felows pay no rent from £29 which they use as studies. Undergraduates pay rent varying from £29 to £39 a term, dependent on situation (inside rooms facing the quadrangle cost more than outside rooms facing the street); size; and type of heating (those with central heating cost more than those with coin-operated gas-fires where each occupant pays for the gas consumed by him).

At the end of each term, the rooms are inspected: the cost of making good any damage to the contents—beyond fair wear and tear—is added to the occupants' battels (bills for the term: see above).

The College also owns about fifty houses or flats in the town: about half are leased to Fellows and the rest of the College staff. No rent is charged for either Fellows' or staff houses or flats.

The Library

When the present College dining-hall was built almost a hundred years ago, the old hall was turned into an undergraduate reference and lending library. In 1927, the Fellows' library—with its manuscripts and early printed books—was combined with the undergraduate library. In 1959-60, the inside of the old hall was reconstructed to provide three library floors, with adjacent rooms used partly for the Fellows' library.

At student insistence, the undergraduate reference library and reading-room are open from 9 a.m. till 1 a.m. the following morning. (This is a sign of the intensity of study at Balliol.)

The College law library is housed elsewhere, while the joint Balliol and Trinity science library is accommodated in the old Balliol basement laboratories, where so much scientific research was done in earlier decades.*

As we have seen, undergraduates have the choice of books from a variety of sources: their own little private library; their tutors' libraries; the College library; the University faculty libraries, in particular those for classics, law, history, English, social studies, theology and science; and, lastly, the Bodleian university library.

The Balliol College has about 151,000 valuable manuscripts and rare printed books, segregated in the Fellows' library behind locked gates, as well as 50,000 more modern books. It acquires about 500 new volumes a year (some fifty being works written by former Balliol men) and it subscribes to many serials.

The oldest College manuscript is a 12th centure copy of Boethius' *De Musica,* bequeathed by Peter de Cossington, who graduated from

* Now done in specially built University laboratories elsewhere.

Oxford even before Balliol was founded and who died in 1276. The College also has the library of 191 volumes (all printed before 1416) bequeathed by Bishop William Gray, a former student at Balliol who died in 1478. Among more modern treasures are the manuscripts of Robert Brownings' later poems.

The library staff consists of the Librarian (now co-opted as a Fellow), a trained full-time assistant and another assistant part-time. The library budget is £ 8,000 a year, which includes provision of £ 2,500 for acquisitions and binding.

DISTRIBUTION OF POWERS

The authority vested in the Master, Fellows, undergraduates and staff is prescribed in the College Statute. All power is ultimately vested in the College Meeting, attended by the Master and all Fellows, excluding only Honorary and Emeritus Fellows. Professorial and junior research Fellows attend and vote (junior research fellows after their first year).

A Meeting has about sixty members and assembles on Friday afternoon or Wednesday morning several times a term. A *Concilium* is held on Wednesday evening: this is an informal discussion and any decisions reached at it require ratification at a formal College Meeting held later.*

In 1967, an enquiry was made by four Fellows, headed by Mr. Donald Harris, (the estates bursar) into the further devolution of authority by the College Meeting on to committees and sub-committees. As a result of the Harris Report, academic affairs are now dealt with, first, by the Tutorial Board and its sub-committees. All other affairs are considered in first instance by the Executive Committee and its subordinate committees. Elaborate provisions have been maintained to keep all Fellows not serving on one or other of these two bodies informed of the decisions arrived at by them; and

---

* *Concilia* used to be held in the Senior Common Room *after* dinner: I suspect that the post-prandial atmosphere was conducive to a more uninhibited exchange of views. But speeches became intolerably long, and the *Concilium* is now held *before* dinner. Growing hunger may serve as a natural 'guillotine'; but the main advantage seems to have evaporated.

116

for referral of controversial matters to the whole governing body at a subsequent meeting.

The Senior Tutor is the executive officer of the Tutorial Board. Its subordinate committees include:

— The Wilson Wilson Committee that distributes the income of a trust fund named after an alumnus who donated the capital.
— The Awards Committee that selects the best among the applicants for the receipt of College scholarships and exhibitions.
— The Library Committee, with a majority of undergraduates.
— The Eleemosynary Committee that deals with undergraduate applications for temporary financial assistance.

The Executive Committee—a particularly Balliol institution—has some 15 members. Care is taken to balance the number of those who hold College posts with those who do not. There are subcommittees for finance, the budget, estates, investments, negotiations with trustees, the gardens and the Master's Field (College sports ground), the Graduate Centre, and portraits. There is, as well, a Nominating Committee and a Chapel Committee that deals also with ecclesiastical patronage.*

The Visitor

The Visitor is the Honorary President of the College and invariably a Balliol man. He visits the College as required, and, among other things, gives the Master leave when he has to be away.

The chief College office-holders are as follows:

The Master

The Master is elected by the Fellows and, by statute, retires at the age of 67. He can be either a Fellow, or a former Balliol man in academic life elsewhere, or an academic from some other Oxford College or other University. The choice is a very serious and difficult matter. It is not easy for any group of men to select one of themselves by majority vote to a post of great authority over the others: many eminent Fellows are inevitably passed over.

---

* Balliol has the right to nominate the parsons of parishes scattered all over England, acquired largely through land ownership by bequest.

The Master not only leads the College in its advance into the future but also exercises considerable personal influence in the University as a whole. He keeps in touch with generations of former Balliol men, many of whom reach powerful positions in the outer world, and can even play the role of political adviser to individual Cabinet Ministers who come to consult them.*

The Master receives a basic salary of £ 5,000 a year, plus a rent-free house in North Oxford. He has a study, bedroom and guest-room in College, together with a dining-room and drawing-room for College entertaining. He is given an entertainment allowance of £ 150 a year as well as all the other perquisites of a Fellow.

Balliol is now one of the biggest colleges in Oxford. The Master is an extremely busy man with endless committee work in the College, and in the University**. He has to keep in close touch with all the Fellows, with the College officials, with the undergraduates collectively and often individually (*and* their parents) and with former Balliol men. The College has no professional fund-raiser: this work devolves largely on the Master. He takes a principal part in the planning of future College academic policies and in the nomination of new Fellows to help to carry them out. On top of all this, he continues to tutor and is relieved of as much administrative detail as possible to enable him to do so.

Vice-Master

Part of this burden is assumed by the Vice-Master, who is always one of the most senior Fellows of the College. Whenever the Master is on a sabbatical, he is wholly replaced by the Vice-Master.

The Chaplain

The Chaplaincy is an ancient post: in fact, in the Middle Ages (as we saw at the outset) Balliol had two chaplains. But few under-

---

* Nearly half of Asquith's Cabinet of 1906 were Balliol men.
** The heads of the colleges used to become Vice-Chancellor of the University in rotation: the last Master of Balliol to do so was Lindsay (1936–38). By the late fifties, all members of the University became eligible for election as Vice-Chancellor.

graduates today consider that formal religious practices have 'relevance'. There is only a handful of devout Anglicans at the College:
about a dozen attend evensong and a score come on Sundays*. The
Chaplain's duties are heavy, with services in Chapel morning, evening
and at night; the preparation for such services, and his own devotions
at home. For the past seventeen years, he has also held the post of
Dean, responsible for both undergraduate discipline and undergraduate welfare.

It is sometimes difficult to draw the line between religious coun-
selling and welfare. Both involve endless and patient listening, usually
late at night, to undergraduates anxious to set out their intellectual
conflicts over belief and conduct and even over their own identity
and purpose. It is often from these talks that students are referred for
professional, medical or psychiatric advice. Those with financial
problems are referred to the Loan Fund.

The Estates Bursar

Different colleges have different management systems. Balliol
employs two bursars—one for its estates and budget planning; the
other as domestic bursar.

All the rural properties bequeathed to Balliol over the centuries
have been sold off and the proceeds reinvested in more profitable
urban buildings leased for use as offices or shops. All the College-
owned urban properties are revalued for insurance purposes every
five years. The last revaluation was at about £ 500,000: this gives
an annual gross income from rents of some £ 20,000 a year. The
value of company shares held by Balliol fluctuates more rapidly with
the state of the stock market; but the total is in the range of
£ 2,000,000. This gives the College a further income from dividends
of some £ 27,000 a year. It is on this annual College income from
property of about £ 47,000 that is based the whole College tutoring
system.

The Estates Bursar is one of the more senior Fellows, elected and

---

* On the other hand, five present Balliol undergraduates intend to apply later
for ordination in the Church.

re-elected annually for as long as he is willing to serve in this onerous post, in addition to his own tutoring*.

Many Oxford and Cambridge college alumni are not yet attuned (as are those of American universities) to being constantly approached for contributions to college development schemes. Nevertheless, 161 have renewed the seven-year Balliol convenants that they have entered into in the past: others have made further donations. Even so, centennial celebrations must be awaited as the occasion for a massive appeal. In 1964, Balliol celebrated the 700th anniversary of its foundation. It planned to raise £ 1,000,000 for its anniversary Fund and, in fact, obtained slightly more. Special trustees administer the Fund. Over £ 500,000 of the money raised has been spent on the reconstruction of part of the inner quadrangle and on building part of the joint Balliol-St. Anne's Graduate Centre. The rest has been invested to endow six existing College fellowships, four new fellowships and four junior research fellowships.

Balliol, together with all other Oxford and Cambridge Colleges, is exempt from payment of income tax and capital gains tax. It is also tax exempt in the United States for purposes of gifts, investments and death duties.

The Budget

The budgetary year (August to July) now wholly includes the academic (October to June).

The total College income for 1970-71 was about £ 250,000, made up as follows:—

Rents and dividends	£47,000
Trust funds	£60,000**
Tuition fees from undergraduates	£60,000
College charges from undergraduates	£58,000
Room rent	£34,000

---

* The former tradition of a life-time Estates Bursar has died out.

** For fellowships—£36,000; for undergraduate scholarships, exhibitions, prizes and travel grants—£12,000; general education purposes—£9,000 and the common table—£3,000.

This £ 250,000 was spent mainly as follows:

Master, Fellows and Tutors	£87,000
Common Table	£ 7,000
Entertainment of students, etc., by tutors	£ 3,000
College officers	£ 3,000
College servants	£66,000
Building maintenance	£54,000
New capital works	£ 7,000
Grants to poorer colleges through the University Chest	£ 8,000

The Domestic Bursar

The present domestic bursar is a distinguished Brigadier (retired), appointed as a College officer and subsequently elected to the governing body as a Fellow. He is responsible for the actual disbursement of much of the budget. This involves the appointment and control of College staff; the payment of salaries to Fellows and College staff; the College feeding arrangements; the maintenance of the fabric, and fire precautions. He is a member of an informal committee of all Oxford college domestic bursars that meets once or twice a term for comparative purposes.

COLLEGE STAFF

There are some eighty College employees engaged as follows:

'Scouts'

In addition to their work in undergraduates' rooms, they also serve in Hall at breakfast, lunch and dinner. One is the Head Scout; 17 are whole-time, while 13 are men and three are women working part-time (equivalent to eight whole-time posts in all) making a total of 26 posts. If service in Hall is replaced by self-service, fewer 'scouts' could be employed. In view of the escalation of wage-scales, this would be a considerable economy for the College. Meanwhile, there is little difficulty in finding men in their forties and fifties (formerly employed at the Cowley Motor Works, for example) who prefer to retire and take on something less regimented.

Senior Common Room

Four and a half posts are allocated, all filled, at the moment, by Spaniards*. Unobtrusive and efficient service at the table is the basis of all good conversation.

Junior Common Room

The staff are employed and paid by the JCR committee from its own budget. The College, however, pays for one man, one boy and one woman part-time to look after the JCR during vacations.

Porter's Lodge

This is one of the main College control and communications centres. Letters, newspapers and messages are received, distributed and despatched: visitors are welcomed and directed or are excluded.

The Lodge, manned 24 hours a day, is staffed by a Head Porter (whose memory for the faces and names of ancient Balliol men is phenomenal), three whole-time and one part-time day porters and one night porter.

Hall

In addition to the staircase 'scouts' who also serve at meals in Hall, there are three men, one woman and one boy who do nothing else but keep the Hall clean, set the tables and wash up.

Catering

Food-buying is undertaken by Head Chef and the catering clerk. The latter collects meal tickets from undergraduates as they enter the Hall.

Kitchens

The Head Chef is assisted by eight chefs, a kitchen porter and three apprentices.

* One was engaged and gradually brought in all the others, mostly relatives. The originator speaks English and serves as interpreter for the rest of the group.

Buttery

Here are sold beer, cider and soft drinks for consumption at the bar. Two men are employed, one of whom is also responsible part-time for cleaning the valuable collection of College silver*. The buttery loses about £ 1,000 a year which would be reduced if the cost of silver cleaning was transferred to another head of expenditure.

Stores

Two part-time men are employed (equivalent to one whole-time post) for the sale of wine in bottles, biscuits, coffee, tobacco, note-paper and such-like. A profit of £ 1,000 a year is made, off-setting the loss on the buttery.

Bursary

Six people work in the domestic bursar's offices: three men—a chief clerk and two assistant clerks, and three women—a secretary, an accounting-machine operator and a wages clerk.

College Office

This is another centre of communication and is housed in part of the Master's lodgings, working closely with him. It has a staff of nine, headed by a woman College Secretary and eight assistants, of whom one undertakes secretarial work for individual Fellows and another is secretary of the Balliol Society—an association of alumni (to whom the *Balliol Record* is sent annually).

The remaining seven posts controlled by the domestic bursar are allocated to a variety of duties, as follows:
— a maintenance man
— a man who looks after the hot-water boilers
— a man who looks after the College bicycles half-time
— a laundress/seamstress who looks after the College linen half time and makes running repairs to undergraduates' jeans and pullovers.

* All the early secular silver was melted down to help the Royalist forces during the Civil War, but some early Chapel silver remains. Each Fellow contributes a piece of silver on retirement and so do some alumni.

— a groundsman who looks after the playing fields

— a head gardener and an assistant gardener.

THE COLLEGE YEAR

Each of the three University terms lasts only eight weeks. The College year starts in mid-October and ends in mid-June, with a ten-day vacation at Christmas and ten days again at Easter—a total of only six months of undergraduate academic work in the year. The Fellows and the College staff are, however, on duty for eleven months. The Christmas vacation is largely taken up with the selection of freshmen for the following October. During the Easter vacation, those freshmen who are candidates for College fellowships or exhibitions are recalled for a second interview. In May, the budget is prepared for the year beginning in August. Students sit for their final examinations in June, which is also the month in which College dances are held. As soon as term ends there is a Gaudy*—a week-end of reunion of alumni from a small group of years. In July and September, the College premises are hired out for conferences. Only in August is the College closed for three weeks for staff vacations: one or two single resident Fellows, however, continue to reside in College, taking their meals by arrangement, in a nearby hotel.

EXTERNAL RELATIONS

Every college is a separate unit, but each is part of a larger organisation—the University. This is not the place to describe the complex series of relationships between Balliol and the outside world in general: they only tangentially affect the administration of the College. But it should be mentioned that the Fellows, staff and students of Balliol have relations with those of other colleges; there are relations between Balliol and the central administrative organs of the University and with individual academics. Balliol also has contacts with the people of the city of Oxford and its administrative municipal machinery, with the County Council and local government officials of Oxfordshire, and with the Central Government in

* From the Latin *gaudeamus*—'let us rejoice'.

London. Lastly, the College must keep in touch with the press and the other mass media, both locally and nationally.

CONCLUSION

The collegiate and tutorial systems of university education at Oxford, Cambridge (and St. Andrews in Scotland) are unique. As a college, Balliol bears some resemblance to an institution with which I am even more familiar—the *kibbutz* in Israel. There, too, is a common table, free accommodation, common rooms and so on. The collegiate system, however, is based on separate societies of Fellows and undergraduates, intermingling at the tutorial and administrative levels: the *kibbutz* has a single society (unless one regards the children's houses, with their own dining-rooms, etc., as a second society). Balliol has a money economy: no one in the *kibbutz* has a private income. The *kibbutz* is rural and agricultural; Balliol is urban and educational. Balliol is venerable: the *kibbutz* not yet. Nevertheless, there is in both the feeling of a closely-knit community and an induced sense of pride in belonging which lasts its fortunate members for all their lives.

Westminster Abbey

This article on the Collegiate Church of Saint Peter is the seventh in a series of studies of the administration of venerable institutions. I am grateful to the Dean and Chapter and others of their colleagues on the staff of the Abbey who gave generously of their time in answering my many questions during the summer and autumn of 1972.

History of the Abbey

The Abbey grew out of a monastery on the left bank of the River Thames. It was founded by the Benedictines, the earliest of the Catholic monastic orders, and followed the rules of Saint Benedict. He had been born near Spoleto in Italy about 480 AD and lived as a hermit east of Rome. His rules were worked out between 535 and 540 for some twelve monasteries, he himself becoming the superior of Monte Cassino near Naples and dying in 547. His Rule was introduced to England in 668 and abbeys[1] of 'Black Monks' were built at Glastonbury, Westminster,[2] Winchester and elsewhere.

The Westminster Monastery was established on a deserted stretch of dry land in the middle of the Thames marshes caused by tributary streams (now underground). The first record of a community

---

[1] An Abbey was originally the jurisdiction or benefice of an Abbot; by extension, the word denoted the religious establishment or corporation itself; and, by further extension, the monastic buildings. The word 'Abbot' is ultimately derived from the Syrian word *Abba* ('Father'), originally applied in the East to all monks; in the West it was eventually restricted to the superior of a monastery.

[2] 'West Minster' was the new Minster west of the (Roman) City of London. The word 'Minster' is another term for a monastery and was eventually restricted to the church of such a monastery.

of Benedictine monks there is apparently a charter given to them by the Saxon king Offa in 785.[3] Gradually, all the buildings needed for a monastery were built:

— an Abbey to pray in;
— a chapter house for all the monks to meet in, daily, with the Abbot;
— a dormitory to sleep in;
— a refectory to eat in, with its attached kitchen and store-room;
— a cloister as 'common room';
— an infirmary for the sick or senile monks; and
— lodgings for the Abbot, and for the day-to-day manager of the monastery—the Prior.[4]

In 960, the monastery was enlarged and remodelled by Saint Dunstan, on the pattern of similar Benedictine monasteries in Flanders.

The First Abbey

Very little is known about the first Abbey, save that it was probably built to the west of the present site and was ravaged during the Danish invasions.

The Second Abbey

The Second Abbey was built in the 11th century by Edward, of the ancient house of Wessex, later to be known as Saint Edward the Confessor.[5] As a result of dynastic quarrels, Edward lived in Normandy between the ages of 13 and 38 (1019–1041). While abroad, he vowed that, if he came back to England safely, he would go on pilgrimage to the grave of Saint Peter in Rome. Becoming king of England in 1042, he could not undertake the journey, and was absolved by the Pope on condition that he founded (or re-founded) a monastery in England dedicated to Saint Peter.[6]

[3] King Offa called it 'a dreadful place'.
[4] The word 'Prior' is derived from the Latin *Prius,* meaning earlier or superior.
[5] A Confessor is one who avows Christianity in the face of danger but does not suffer martyrdom. There are thus two classes of Christian Saints— Martyrs and Confessors.
[6] This is the reason why Westminster Abbey is called the Church of Saint

King Edward chose for this purpose the Benedictine monastery at Westminster, increasing the number of its monks from a dozen to about eighty, drawing them probably from Exeter. He built at Westminster a new Romanesque church in Norman style—the first great cruciform church in England. The King gave a tithe of all his gold, silver and cattle to construct the Abbey and endow it.[7]

The Abbey took many years to build and was only dedicated on December 28th, 1065, when the King was already on his deathbed. He died a week later, on January 5th, 1066, and was buried only nine months later, in a tomb, in front of the High Altar, in October, 1066. Meanwhile, the Norman King—Willam I ('The Conqueror')—anxious to identify himself with the previous Saxon King, had himself crowned in the Abbey on Christmas Day, 1066. Thus began the tradition that the Kings of England should be both crowned and buried in the Abbey.

This second Abbey lasted for two centuries. The only known representation of it—showing the north front—is in the Bayeux Tapestry. With the Abbey's valuable relics—believed to have magical qualities—and its power to issue indulgences, it became a great pilgrimage centre. For the maintenance of the monastery, the King gave it part of the royal estates in what is now Hyde Park, St. James's Park and the greater part of the present districts of Kensington and Belgravia, as well as in fourteen counties all over England.

The Building of the Present Abbey

Henry III, who reigned from 1216 to 1272, was anxious to honour Saint Edward the Confessor more splendidly and began in 1245 to build the third and present Abbey.[8]

In 1296, Edward I removed from Scotland the Stone of Scone and brought it to the Abbey. Twelve years later it was embodied in the

Peter. Peter is frequently chosen as the patron saint of a church, in view of one of the recorded sayings of Jesus 'Thou art Peter, and upon this rock (*Petros* in Greek) I will build my Church' (Mathew XVI, 18).

[7] Among the fifty medieval English monasteries, Westminster became the seventh richest.

[8] It took nearly 370 years to complete.

Chair made for the Coronation of Edward II and Isabelle of France and for all subsequent Kings and Queens of England.[9]

The Reformation

A considerable upheaval occurred in 1539 when all monasteries —including that at Westminster—were dissolved by Henry VIII.

On January 16th, 1540, the Abbot and 24 monks surrendered the Abbey to the King. It was refounded as the Cathedral of the Bishopric of Westminster.

In 1550, the Bishopric of Westminster was suppressed and the Abbey became the second Cathedral of the Bishop of London, still retaining its own Dean and Chapter.

When the Protestant King Edward VI died in 1553 and was succeeded by the Catholic Queen Mary Tudor, obedience to Rome was restored. The Monastery at Westminster was re-established, with thirty monks from the former English Monasteries, and an Abbot was re-appointed.

When, however, the Protestant Queen Elizabeth I succeeded to the throne in 1558 the Monastery was again abolished. The Abbot and his Chapter of monks were replaced by a Dean and twelve Prebendaries.[10] Six Minor Canons, twelve Lay Clerks (adult singers), 16 Choristers and their teacher were also provided for.[11] The Abbey was officially named 'The Collegiate Church of Saint Peter in Westminster', following the collegiate character of two other Royal foundations—Christ Church College at Oxford University and Trinity College at Cambridge.

The Puritan Revolution and Later

The Puritan Revolution under Cromwell a century later caused a further upheaval. In 1643, two companies of troops were quartered in the Abbey. The tapestries were cut up or sold; many of the Abbey statues and much of its stained glass were regarded as idolatrous and, as a consequence, demolished.

[9] Coronations have been held in the Abbey for nine hundred years.
[10] A Prebendary is the holder of a Prebend, or share in the funds of the Church to which the Clergy-House is attached.

Time also caused havoc. The external stone work of the Abbey began to deteriorate as a result of the smoke pouring out of the chimneys of houses that then closely surrounded the Abbey.[11]

THE DEAN AND CHAPTER

Legal Powers

Westminster Abbey has twice been made a Royal Foundation; it was taken over in the 11th century by Edward the Confessor and, five centuries later, by Elizabeth I.

The Abbey is governed by Charters, Statutes, Royal Letters and custom. The Statutes drawn up shortly after the Charter of 1560 were never signed and therefore have no legal effect.[12]

The Dean and Chapter

Westminster Abbey is governed by the Dean[13] and Canons who together constitute the body corporate with a common seal, affixed in the main to Abbey documents involving legal obligations.

They are responsible for maintaining Divine worship in the Abbey and for its fabric, furniture, ornaments and finances.

Rural Properties of the Abbey

The Abbey used to own properties outside the Precincts, not only elsewhere in London but also in the provinces. It thus became the patron of many livings, over which it exercised not only ecclesiastical jurisdiction but also the rights of lord of the manor.

Prior to the surrender of Abbey property to the Ecclesiastical Commissioners[14] between 1868 and 1888, the Dean and Chapter were constantly involved in estate management all over England. This involved contesting the enclosure of commons, canal and

[11] See the section later on maintenance of the Fabric.

[12] It was, however, ruled by the Lord Chancellor in 1911 that the Statutes may be referred to as evidence of ancient custom in cases where the custom is not clear or continuous.

[13] A Dean is the head of a Chapter or body of Canons of a Collegiate or Cathedral Church. The word 'Dean' comes from the ecclesiastical Latin word *Decanus*—the head of ten monks in a monastery.

[14] Now the Church Commissioners.

railway bills, and repairing roads and bridges belonging to Abbey property. The Dean and Chapter were also involved in the filling of benefices, fixing the stipends of the holders and the collection of tithe (originally in kind).

Emoluments of the Dean and Chapter

Up till 1843, the Dean and Chapter shared out the income received from fees paid on leases from the Abbey (called 'fines'). Of the fifteen parts, two went to the Dean, one to the Fabric and the remaining twelve (originally one for each of the twelve Prebendaries) to the Canons. In 1843, this was replaced by a system of fixed stipends from general Abbey funds.

The Dean and Chapter are also provided with rent-free accommodation within the Precincts, entertainment and secretarial allowances,[15] and a share of their telephone bills is refunded. Each receives a pension on retirement.

Pluralism

In earlier centuries, the Dean and Canons often had other benefices as well. For example, at times, the Dean of Westminster was also Bishop of Rochester[16] and Rector of Islip. Some of the Canons resided only during their month of residence. But the Dean and Canons were all required to attend Chapter meetings from time to time. Neither the Dean nor any Canon today may hold another benefice.

Freehold Appointments

In earlier periods, too, many of the appointments to the Abbey were held in freehold tenure; that is, as far as the Abbey was concerned, only on appeal to the Visitor could the holder be dismissed, or even retired for incapacity or old age. Freehold appointments to certain offices were extinguished under a Supplemental Charter in 1951.

[15] The Dean is provided with a private secretary.
[16] Dean Horsley (Dean 1793–1801) on becoming Bishop of Rochester, retained the Deanery at Westminster as a town house.

The Dean

The Dean of Westminster is appointed by the Crown on the re-commendation of the Prime Minister. He must be an ordained priest and a Doctor or Bachelor of Divinity. The Dean is the 'Ordinary'[17] of the Abbey and orders its Divine Services. He takes ecclesiastical precedence at all such Services, even when an Archbishop or Bishop is present.[18] The Dean himself preaches (or appoints a preacher) on the major Church festivals. He decides who may be buried in the Abbey (see later). He appoints the Sub-Dean and also the lay officers of the Abbey. He is *ex-officio* Dean of the Order of the Bath and *ex-officio* chairman of the Governing Body of Westminster School (see later). The present Dean (appointed in 1959, the 35th in line since the first Abbot in 1049–1071) is the Very Reverend Dr Eric S. Abbott, KCVO.

The Canons

The Dean and Chapter originally consisted of the Dean and twelve Prebendaries (see above): this number has gradually been reduced, and at present there are four Canons. Vacancies among the Canons are filled by direct appointment by the Crown. A Canon must be an ordained priest and a Master of Arts. He is usually a man of literary disposition with parochial experience and administrative capacity, and has normally held some responsible office elsewhere.

Each Canon in rotation is in monthly residence at the Abbey, during which time he attends morning and evening services, and preaches at least once each Sunday. The month is sometimes divided between two Canons to allow one to undertake other public duties (e.g., attend a conference outside London). These arrangements allow Canons freedom to preach or lecture elsewhere, even abroad;

---

[17] From the Latin word *Ordinarius,* the official in a medieval religious frater-nity having charge of the Convent.
[18] Archbishops and Bishops cannot even *enter* the Abbey except with the per-mission of the Dean; and a statement to that effect is read out on such occasions.

to teach; do research; write books and articles; serve on ecclesiastical and other committees—all this with complete freedom from Diocesan or even Provincial control.[19] They are expected to use these freedoms by being active outside immediate Abbey affairs. But they must be resident within the Abbey precincts for at least four months and four days of each year.

Between them, the four Canons hold the offices of Sub-Dean, Archdeacon, Treasurer and Steward; to the last three posts they are elected annually by the Dean and Chapter. The duties of these posts are as follows:

Sub-Dean. Acts for the Dean in his absence, when asked to do so.

Archdeacon. Is responsible, with an Assistant, for the pastoral care of all members and servants of the Chapter and their families, and of all other residents within the Precincts. He visits and keeps in touch with all parishes in the patronage of the Dean and Chapter.

Treasurer. Is responsible to the Dean and Chapter for Abbey expenditure and the properties vested in the Dean and Chapter.

Steward. Supervises the maintenance of the grounds within the Precincts, other than the properties of Westminster School or the private gardens attached to Abbey residences. He is also Guest-Master of the Abbey.

In addition to these four posts, there are three other annexed offices. Each is allotted to one of the Canons so that no Canon normally has more than two posts. These offices are:

Chronicler. Keeps a written record of major events in the Abbey. This practice started in the Middle Ages and then lapsed, but it was revived early in the 20th century. The record is still in manuscript and, because the choice of items by the Chronicler may lead to differences of opinion, the record is not now submitted to the Dean and other Chapter members.

Lector Theologiae. Arranges for public lectures to be given in the Abbey during Advent (before Christmas), Lent (before Easter) and Trinity (after Easter).

[19] That is, by a Bishop or Archbishop.

Rector of St Margaret's Church. Under the 1972 Act for the merger of St Margaret's with Westminster Abbey, the Canon with the courtesy title of Rector will in future be appointed from time to time by the Dean and Chapter from among the Canons.[20]

At the moment (summer, 1972) these posts and duties are allocated as follows:

— The Venerable E.F. Carpenter (appointed Canon 1951). Archdeacon and Treasurer;
— The Reverend Canon M.A.C. Warren (from 1963). Sub-Dean and Chronicler;
— The Reverend Canon R.C.D. Jasper (from 1968). Steward and *Lector Theologiae*; and
— The Reverend Canon D.L. Edwards (from 1970). Rector of Saint Margaret's.

Chapter Meetings

The Chapter meets in the Jerusalem Chamber[21] fortnightly (except during August and September). The meeting held around March 25th to receive the accounts and to hear the annual reports of Abbey office-holders is called the Audit Chapter.

The Chapter meeting agenda and minutes are prepared by the Chapter Clerk (see below).

The Chapter Clerk

The present holder of the post of Chapter Clerk is also the Receiver-General and Registrar. The Receiver-General used to receive rents from the Abbey Estates[22] and now administers the Abbey and its finances. The Registrar records baptisms, confirmations,

---

[20] The reasons for the new merger were, first, the moving away from the Parish of Westminster of many former residents, reducing the congregation to under 400 and the consequent loss by Saint Margaret's of much of its income; secondly, Westminster Abbey's need for a smaller additional church for prayer, weddings and religious drama performances.

[21] So called from the wall decorations it had in the 14th century depicting Jerusalem.

[22] Now taken over by the Church Commissioners in return for an annual endowment to the Abbey.

marriages and burials taking place in the Abbey or within its precincts.

The present holder of these three posts in Mr. W.R.J. Pullen, MVO, JP, who has been in the Abbey since 1947 and Receiver-General since 1959. Under the Dean and Chapter he is the mainspring of Abbey administration and looks after everything affecting the 'Abbey Family'. The Abbey's legal work is undertaken by the Legal Secretary, at present Mr John Widdows, MBE, member of a Chichester firm of solicitors.

The Chapter Office

The Receiver-General is assisted by:
— A *Personal Assistant* (Commander W.E. Messinger, OBE, RN (retired).
— An *Executive Officer for Special Duties* (Mr G. Dodson-Wells, MBE).
— *Accounts staff* (see the Section on Finance)

There are also four Chapter Office secretaries; a receptionist/telephonist and a general assistant. Three part-time women cleaners are attached to the Chapter Office, as also the Porter. He lives in the Lodge at the entrance to the Cloisters.

Offices of Honour

These are two ancient posts, now honorific, to which eminent men are appointed by the Dean for as long as the holders are willing to serve. One is the High Steward: the other is the High Bailiff and Searcher of the Sanctuary.

High Steward

Prior to the dissolution of the Monastery in 1539, the stewards of the separate Abbey manors were uncoordinated. When the Abbey was reconstituted in 1560, a High Steward was appointed to supervise the manor stewards. The post today is a sinecure; but the holder still has a stall in the Abbey choir. The post has usually been filled by a powerful nobleman who gives advice—when asked—on public affairs, and intervenes with the State and Parliament on behalf of the Abbey when necessary. (Similar posts of High Steward still exist in the Universities of Oxford and Cambridge.) The present holder (the 20th in succession) is Lord Clitheroe, PC.

The other office of honour is that of *High Bailiff and Searcher of the Sanctuary,* held at present by Lord Redcliff-Maud, GCB, CBE, with functions similar to those of the High Steward.

Other Office-Holders

These consist of:
— Three Minor Canons, who take the appropriate singing parts in the Abbey Services (see that Section)
— The Organist and Master of the Choristers (see the Section later on Music in the Abbey)
— The Surveyor of the Fabric (see the Section later on the Preservation of the Fabric)
— The Clerk of Works (see the Section later on the Preservation of the Fabric)
— The Librarian   } (see the Section later on the
— The Keeper of the Muniments { Library and Muniments)
— The Auditor (see the Section later on Finance).

Committees

The Dean and Chapter are assisted by several Committees (including lay office holders and coopted members) as follows:
— The Investment Advisory Panel (see the Section on Finance)
— The Ornaments Committee (see the Section on the Sacristy)
— The Bookshop Committee (see the Section on the Bookshop)
— The Abbey Exhibitions Committee (see the Section on the Exhibition of Abbey Treasures)
— The Sound Advisory Committee (to deal with the Abbey loudspeakers: see the Section on Abbey Services).

There are also consultants on structural engineering (see the Section on the Preservation of the Fabric), on typography (to standardize the Abbey sign-posting and publications) and on the design of the Abbey Exhibition in the Norman Undercroft.

The Forward Planning of Recurrent Events

Forward planning of recurrent Abbey events is undertaken by an informal committee consisting of the Receiver-General, the Clerk of Works and the Dean's Verger (the work of the last two is described later).

The Forward Planning of Special Services

Forward planning of Special Services and other great events is handled by the Special Services Committee under the chairmanship of the Dean. The other members are the Precentor (the senior Minor Canon), the Sacrist, Receiver-General, Organist/Master of the Choristers, Dean's Verger, the Receiver-General's Personal Assistant and representatives of the sponsoring organizations involved. An agenda is prepared by the Receiver-General after a preliminary meeting with the sponsors. His Secretary keeps the minutes.

Publications

The annual *Memoranda,* compiled in the Chapter office, is an information leaflet of some twenty pages. It lists all the Abbey staff and includes general information. It is for internal distribution only and is re-issued at the beginning of each calendar year.

The Sub-Dean is responsible for the issue of a printed pamphlet entitled *Occasional Paper.* It first appeared in November, 1957, and now comes out half-yearly. In it are reproduced important sermons and addresses delivered in the Abbey, special articles, and domestic news. Some 5–10,000 copies are printed, of which complimentary copies are sent to some 200 persons.[23] The bulk of each issue is placed next to the collecting boxes in the Abbey, with the request for 10p to be placed in the box for each copy taken. (Many copies are, however, taken without payment).

The Chapter Office also publishes a monthly leaflet entitled *Diary*

[23] Including the Queen, the Prime Minister, the Archbishop of Canterbury, the Lord Mayor of the City of Westminster, the Dean and Chapter and former Canons, Minor Canons, the Honorary Stewards, many other members of the 'Abbey Family' and incumbents of all Abbey livings.

of Events. It is compiled by the Receiver-General for distribution to the 'Abbey Family', the Press and subscribers. A mailing list is maintained by the Executive Officer. Names and addresses can be added to the list for an annual postage fee of 25 pence.

The Chapter Office brings the Abbey to the notice of the public by a rather attractive postmark, showing (in addition to 'Postage Paid', 'London SW 1' and the date of posting) the West Front of the Abbey in miniature, with the slogan 'Westminster Abbey Welcomes You'.

Public Relations

The Abbey has no full-time public relations or press officer. Such work is handled in the Chapter Office by the Receiver-General with the help of his Personal Assistant and the Executive Officer.

Staff Relations

A Collegiate dinner is held annually in the Jerusalem Chamber in June on or near St Peter's Day. It is attended by the Dean and Chapter, the officers of the Collegiate Body and their wives. The guests are the Prime Warden of the Worshipful Company of Fishmongers[24] and his wife.

The Abbey is considered by those members of the subordinate staff to whom I mentioned the subject to be a particularly good employer. No need has been felt for a Staff Association.

In 1949, the Abbey introduced a pensions and life assurance scheme for all its permanent staff. This was improved in 1972. The Dean and Chapter also maintain a staff holiday hostel and convalescent home.

In 1965, the Dean and Chapter endorsed a group health insurance scheme (Private Patients' Plan) for the Abbey clergy and members of the supervisory staff and salaried staff. Half the premiums are paid from Abbey funds.

[24] It is on this occasion that a salmon is supplied by the Fishmongers' Guild as token recognition of the Abbey's claim to a tithe of all fish caught in the River.

The Abbey Services consist of:

— Daily Services— some 30 a week—as set out in the Book of Common Prayer; and

— Special Services.

The *Daily Services* are: Holy Communion, Matins and Evensong.

Holy Communion

This is celebrated every day of the week at 8 a.m. in St. Faith's Chapel,[25] except on certain Saints' Days when it is celebrated in Henry VII's Chapel.

There is also a celebration of Holy Communion in St Faith's Chapel on Fridays at 12.30.

In addition, there are Holy Communion Services at the High Altar on Sundays at 11.30 a.m. and on certain Holy Days at 10.30 a.m.

Matins

This service is held every weekday at 9.20 a.m., and at 10.30 a.m. on Sunday. On Tuesdays, Fridays and Sundays it is choral and held in Quire. On Sundays, there is a sermon. On the other four days the Service is said and is held in Saint Faith's Chapel.

Evensong

This Service is sung in Quire on Saturdays and Sundays at 3 p.m., and on all other days at 5 p.m. On Sundays, there is a sermon. On Wednesdays,[26] the service is said.

Other Daily Services

— For *Westminster School*

There is a daily week-day service at 9 a.m. in Quire and Tran-

---

[25] St Faith lived in the 4th century in Aquitaine, and was a Virgin Martyr, burnt during the Diocletian persecution. She was popularized by the Normans and 24 churches in England alone were dedicated to her.

[26] The weekly holiday for the Choir School in place of Sunday.

septs for all boys from the adjacent Westminster School. One day a week, at 9 p.m., Compline[27] is held for the 40 Queen's Scholars in Saint Faith's Chapel.

— *For Visitors*

One minute of Prayer is said from either the Quire or the Nave pulpit on weekdays every hour on the hour between 10 a.m. and 4 p.m. Visiting clergymen, some from the Abbey benefices, take a major share in this. The Abbey Clergy are responsible for the prayer at 1 p.m.

Special Services

There are about a hundred such services a year—an average of two a week. They may be divided into those that are annually recurrent and those that are not.

Recurrent Special Services

These are held on Church Holy Days, Abbey Saints' Days, and other occasions.

All these services are choral and are held in Quire.

Non-Recurrent Special Services

These can be classified as Baptisms, Weddings, Funerals, Memorial Services, religious occasions (such as Coronations and the Consecration of Bishops) and other special occasions such as Centenaries and other anniversaries.

It is not easy to reconcile the role of the Abbey as a place of Christian (more specifically, Anglican) worship with its role as a national shrine. For example, the Abbey must be closed to worshippers for months while it is being adapted for a Coronation. Similarly, the Dean is expected, often at short notice, to receive VIPs and conduct them round the Abbey. The number of requests for special commemorative services is growing, as also for permission to hold concerts in the Abbey.

A special printed Service Paper is produced by the Precentor and a copy placed on each seat in the area of the Abbey to be used.

[27] More properly 'Complin', the last service of the day. The word 'Complin' is probably derived from the Latin *completinus*.

Funerals

Members of the Royal Family are now buried at Windsor, but a Memorial Service may be held at the Abbey.

Burial in the Abbey is considered a unique honour: there is on the average one a year. Permission is granted by the Dean. Sometimes, an offer of burial in the Abbey is made by the Dean to the family of the deceased.[28] Burial is permitted only after cremation.

When a military funeral is organized, senior officers of the Service concerned act as additional Honorary Pall-Bearers. A catafalque, pall and candles are provided by the Abbey. The services of the Abbey Organist, the Choir and Honorary Stewards are also provided by the Abbey. In addition to wreaths sent by relatives, friends and institutions, altar flowers are arranged by the Abbey.

Memorial Services

There is an increasing number of Memorial Services in the Abbey every year. Application for permission to hold one is made to the Dean. Some distinguished person may be invited by the Dean to deliver a memorial address or to read a Lesson.

Weddings

When a Royal Wedding is held in the Abbey, the arrangements are made by the Lord Chamberlain's Office.

When a son or daughter of a member of the Order of the Bath is married, the ceremony may be performed in the Henry VII Chapel—the Chapel of the Order. Weddings arranged for members of families connected with the Abbey or living within the Precincts are often held in Saint Faith's Chapel or Henry VII's Chapel; but, if over 300 guests are expected, the Nave must be used. Now that Saint Margaret's Church is being merged with the Abbey, weddings in that Church will in future also be arranged under the direction of the Dean as the Ordinary.

---

[28] For example, on the death in 1967 of Clement Attlee, Prime Minister from 1945 till 1951.

If one of the couple to be married is resident in the Precincts, banns must be read. For a non-resident, a special marriage licence must be obtained from the Registrar of the Archbishop of Canterbury.[29] After the ceremony, the marriage is registered and a certificate issued by the Abbey Registrar.[30]

Baptisms

Permission for baptism in the Abbey is given by the Dean. The privilege is commonly accorded to members of the 'Abbey Family'. Members of the Order of the Bath are allowed to have their grandchildren baptised in the Chapel of the Order—the Henry VII Chapel.

Consecration of Bishops

A Bishop may be consecrated either in Westminster Abbey or at Saint Paul's, Southwark Cathedral, Lambeth Palace, York Minster or in his own Diocese.

On the average, there is a Westminster Abbey consecration once or twice a year. It is conducted by the Archbishop of Canterbury. The expenses are borne by the Church Commissioners.

* * *

The Minor Canons

The Singing of the Abbey Services is undertaken by the Minor Canons.[31] Originally, in 1540, provision was made for six Petty (i.e., Minor) Canons on the Abbey Establishment: today, there are three.

They must be in Holy Orders, able to read music and to sing. The senior Minor Canon, originally called the Great Chanter, is now called the Precentor (i.e., Pro-Cantor). This post has been held since 1963 by the Rev. Rennie Simpson.

---

[29] He is a partner in a firm of solicitors with offices just outside the Great West Door of the Abbey.

[30] This post is now held by the Chapter Clerk.

[31] Not to be confused with the Canons (dealt with earlier in the Section on the Dean and Chapter).

The second Minor Canon, the Rev. Christopher Hildyard, MVO, has held office since 1932. He is also the Sacrist (see below).

The third is the Rev. William Leah, appointed in 1967.

Minor Canons are appointed by the Dean after a voice-test by the Organist and the Precentor, and enter into a contract with the Dean and Chapter.

The appointments were originally for life ('freehold') but are now for seven years in the first instance, extendable by subsequent periods of five years.

Each of the three Minor Canons takes Matins and Evensong for a month at a time. This is followed by two months off-duty during which he may accept outside work, such as part-time teaching, a hospital chaplaincy or office work.

The Organist submits a weekly list of music proposed for all Abbey choral services (with the exception of the hymns, which are chosen by the Precentor). It is then printed and distributed to all those concerned (see the Section on Music in the Abbey below).

The Precentor is head of the Abbey Choral Foundation and is responsible for the behaviour and welfare of the adult members of the choir—the 'Lay Vicars' (see the Section on Music in the Abbey below).[32]

Since 1951, there has been an Association of Minor Canons throughout Britain— a purely social body. It has some 100 members, of whom forty are active and the rest retired.

The Almsmen

The Almsmen attend on the Dean at Matins and Evensong on Sundays. They date back to the 16th century, when Henry VII built Almshouses for 'twelve poor men decayed in the King's Service'. Their sole duty then was 'to pray for the King's Majesty, for the Church and for the Peace and Safety of the Kingdom.' The Almshouses were situated at the present entrance to Dean's Yard and have long since disappeared. The Almsmen today receive an allowance of £ 3–4 a quarter (a sum much devalued over the last 400

[32] The Organist/Master of the Choristers, however, is responsible for their musical training.

years) in place of the original food and accommodation. There was provision under the draft Statutes of 1560 for ten Queen's Almsmen, of which there are now six. The holders are elderly ex-Servicemen or ex-Abbey servants. Appointments are made for life (i.e., freehold) on the recommendation of the Home Secretary. Warrants of appointments are still signed individually by the Queen.

The Almsmen wear scarlet and blue gowns[33] with a crowned Tudor Rose on the sleeve, and a silver badge. They receive £ 2.60 for each attendance at an Abbey Service.

Medical Arrangements

Whenever large congregations are expected, nurses from the Westminster Hospital are in attendance.

Seating in the Abbey

There is seating only for about 2,000 persons.[34] This is provided by choir stalls and pews (allotted to the Dean and Chapter, office-holders, and other members of the 'Abbey Family'), together with some 1,800 chairs (additional chairs can be added).

The Honorary Stewards

This is a corps of volunteers who assist in seating the congregation on Sundays and at Special Services. There are 38 members, under a Chief Honorary Steward.[35] Names of suitable candidates for appointment to vacancies are usually put forward by existing Stewards. The candidates are interviewed by the Receiver-General and the Dean's Verger. The recommended candidate is then appointed by the Dean, with a year's probation. Each undertakes to attend at least thirteen Sunday services during the year.

The duty roster is prepared by the Personal Assistant to the Receiver-General and is approved by the latter. They appear in morning dress, each with a silver badge of office with the arms of the Abbey and the crossed keys of St. Peter.

---

[33] Redesigned specially for the 900th Anniversary of the Abbey in 1965.
[34] Compared with about 6,500 in Saint Paul's.
[35] At present, a retired Air Marshal.

When the Honorary Stewards are present, it is they who assist in taking up the Collection.

Almsgiving

Collections are taken at all the Sunday Services and at some Special Services. A total of about £ 11,600 was collected in 1970–71, the maximum on any one occasion being £ 450.

About half the Offertories are allotted to causes other than the needs of the Abbey. Over 200 applications for such allocations are made to the Dean and Chapter each year. Of these, some 20–30 are applications from new causes, of which about a dozen are granted.

Of the £ 5,700 allotted to the Abbey in 1970–71, £ 2,400 was transmitted to various Abbey charities: the balance of £ 3,300 was used for the maintenance of the Abbey Services.

In addition, some £ 19,000 was received in 1970–71 from eight collecting boxes placed in the Abbey. All the proceeds go for Abbey maintenance and a notice to that effect is displayed by each box.

The Vergers[36]

The duties of the Vergers include:
— preparing the Abbey for Services (e.g., setting out Service Papers);
— preserving decorum on the part of visitors;
— regulating the movement of visitors at times of Divine Worship;
— answering visitors' questions; and
— showing them round the Abbey.

Besides the Dean's Verger, there are nine Vergers, one of whom is Sub-Sacrist and one the Beadle.

The Dean's Verger (Mr. Algernon Greaves, MBE) is in charge of the other Vergers and is also responsible for the work of the Honorary Stewards at Sunday Services (see above), the Voluntary Abbey Helpers (see below) and the Cleaners. He has an office within the Abbey and, on ceremonial occasions, wears over his black robe a red gown with the Dean's personal coat-of-arms on the sleeve.

---

[36] So called because they carry a gold-headed staff of office—a verge (from the Latin word *Virga*).

146

Vergers work a normal 40-hour week, but are often on duty for longer periods: overtime is paid for the excess. There is an Abbey pension from the age of 65.

There is a Vergers' Room in one of the West Towers of the Abbey. No living accommodation is provided (except, at present, for the Dean's Verger).

Vacant posts of Vergers are advertised in the Press. Some 50 applications may be received for each vacancy. Few of the applicants are members of old 'Abbey families', or were specially devout church-goers. Most applicants seem attracted by the glamour of the Abbey and the television publicity it has received (e.g., during the Coronation). No applicant over the age of 55 is considered. Applicants are interviewed by the Dean's Verger and short-listed: the final selection is made by the Dean.

The Sacristy

There is a small Sacristy in St. Faith's Chapel; but the main one is in an undercroft below the Chapter House.

Before the Dissolution of the Monasteries in 1540, the Abbey had a rich collection of relics and treasures—for example, 330 embroidered copes and 13 gold chalices. Much was lost on the Dissolution and more again was sold or destroyed by the Puritans in the following century. Today, the Abbey has nothing older than 1660, in the reign of Charles II.

Vestments

Sets of vestments have been gradually built up, largely through gifts on special occasions (e.g., Coronations).

Copes are worn by the celebrant at 'plain' Communion Services, and by all priests at choral Communion Service and Special Services.

Plate

All the gold plate has been lost; but silver-gilt Communion plate and silver alms-dishes have gradually been acquired, also largely by gift. There is a Sanctuary Fund built up from gifts for the purchase of new vestments and plate, as decided by the Ornaments Committee.

The Sacristy is under the supervision of the Sacrist (a Minor Canon), assisted by the Sub-Sacrist (a Verger), two other Vergers and an Embroideress.

The Sub-Sacrist is responsible for changing the frontals of the nine Abbey altars in accordance with the colour sequence adopted by the Abbey for particular seasons of the year, major Church Festivals, 'Red Letter' Saints' Days, Abbey Days, Royal occasions and Special Services.[37]

The Sub-Sacrist also looks after the six embroidered silk Banners, borne in Processions. None is over fifty years old. They have been given by various donors and are dedicated to different Saints of the donors' choice, including Saint Peter, Saint George and Saint Edward the Confessor.

For 400 of the chairs in the Abbey, 'kneelers' are provided, embroidered in wool to designs prepared by the Surveyor of the Fabric in 1965 for the 900th Anniversary Year and made by volunteers all over Britain and the world.

The candles and carpets before certain Altars in the Abbey are looked after by the Sub-Sacrist.

MUSIC IN THE ABBEY

Music is an important part of the main Services held in the Abbey, as well as on all special occasions.

The Organ

This, together with the Choir (trained at the Abbey) is the basis of all the Abbey music.

The first written reference is to 'a pair of organs' (i.e., one on each side of the Nave) and is dated 1304. The present Organ was built for the Coronation of George VI in 1937 and is still in excellent condition.[38]

---

[37] For example, for the day commemorating the Battle of Britain, fought in the skies, the colour is appropriately blue.

[38] Some £ 17,000 was spent to reinstate the organ cases before the 1953 Coronation.

The Organist and Master of the Choristers

The post of Abbey Organist is first mentioned in 1553 (over four centuries ago); since then, there has been a long succession of Organists, including Henry Purcell (from 1680 till 1695), whom the present Organist and Master of Choristers (Mr. Douglas Guest) has called "the brightest light in the whole firmament of English music".

The duties of the Abbey Organist are primarily the rehearsal and performance of all music in the Abbey involving the Choir and Organ. In this he is assisted by the Sub-Organist and a Second Assistant Organist, or by guest organists on invitation.

The Organist also submits the music to be performed during all Abbey Services and on other occasions 'as practicable and appropriate'. As already explained, a weekly list is printed and distributed to all concerned. There is a delicate relationship between the Organist (a professional musician, and a layman) who is responsible for the Abbey music, and the Precentor (a Minor Canon who is not a professional musician and is in Holy Orders), who is head of the Choral Foundation. In the event of disagreement, the Dean, as Ordinary, is the final authority.

As Master of the Choristers,[39] the Organist is responsible for the selection, welfare and general discipline of the Choristers and their rehearsal and performance of music in the Abbey. The Headmaster is responsible for the running of the School and the education of the Choristers in non-musical subjects.

All Organ practice is done in the evening, after the Abbey is closed to the public.

The post of Westminster Abbey Organist is today regarded as probably at the top of the profession. When a vacancy occurs, applicants are interviewed by the Dean and Chapter, who seek professional advice. The Dean also appoints the Sub-Organist— usually for a period of five years. The Second Assistant Organist is appointed by the Organist/Master of the Choristers.

[39] The post dates from 1479 when it was entitled 'Master of the Song School'.

The Organist is provided with a salary, free accommodation within the Precincts and a pension on retirement.

Musical Celebrations at Westminster Abbey

There is a number of special organ and choral recitals and orchestral concerts in the Abbey each year. These include:
— Holy Week: the Bach *Saint Matthew's Passion*[40]
— Advent: Handel's *Messiah*.

Organ recitals by invited guest organists from all over the world are given some sixteen times a year.

Other Abbey concerts are given from time to time. The Abbey Organ and Choir have been made full use of; for example, on the following occasions:

1784 Handel Festival on the century of his birth.

1962 The first London performance of Benjamin Britten's *War Requiem*.

1966 The Abbey's own 900th Anniversary was celebrated by a number of musical recitals given by string quartets, chamber and symphony orchestras, with guest singers and conductors. Some of the performances were sponsored by the Arts Council and the BBC.

For a Coronation, in addition to the Organ, there is a big orchestra, the Abbey Choir being reinforced by the choirs of St. Paul's and the Chapel Royal, Windsor, as well as by professional singers.

Each of the three Abbey Organists keeps in the Organ Loft his own personal collection of organ music that he has built up.

The present Abbey Organists are Fellows of the Royal College of Organists which has nearly 4,000 members.[41] Its main function is to act as an examining body for organists and choir trainers.

The Conference of Cathedral Organists now has some 30 to 40 members, including those at Westminster Abbey, St. Paul's, the Temple Church (London), St George's Chapel, Windsor, and the Oxford and Cambridge Colleges.

---

[40] First performed at Westminster Abbey in 1871. Such a performance in an Abbey was then considered to be a daring innovation.
[41] Mr Guest is an Honorary Fellow.

The Abbey Choir

Originally, in 1540, there were ten choir-boys (then called 'singing boys'): now there are 36. In addition, there are twelve 'Lay Vicars'[42] (originally called 'Gentlemen of the Choir'). Originally the Lay Vicars were appointed for life ('freehold'). They are professional singers who normally retire from the Abbey Choir on pension at the age of sixty.

With the opportunities offered by concerts, radio, television and recording, the Lay Vicars have plenty of opportunity for outside singing engagements, and their Abbey contracts provide for this. Candidates are auditioned by the Organist and Precentor and the successful applicant is appointed by the Dean. A legal agreement is then signed between the Abbey and the Lay Vicar, terminable at six months' notice on either side, after a year's probation.

Lay Vicars are salaried, with additional fees for participating in Special Services. They may accept outside engagements if these do not clash with their commitments to the Abbey.[43]

As members of *Equity* (the trade union of professional singers and stage performers), Lay Vicars must be paid high additional fees for recorded programmes. This is not the case with recorded programmes of the King's College choir at Cambridge whose adult singers are undergraduates and not members of *Equity*. Hence, there are comparatively few recordings made by such choirs as the Abbey Choir. Even so, less than half the income of the Lay Vicars comes from the Abbey.

Choir Appearances in the Abbey

The Abbey Choir sings at ten services a week, as follows:
— Matins: three times a week, including Sundays
— Evensong: six days a week, including Sundays

---

[42] Not to be confused with Parish Church Vicars. Compare the similar confusion between Canons and Minor Canons.

[43] If a Lay Vicar is given permission to accept an outside engagement he must select (and personally pay) a replacement from a list of some thirty deputies whose voices have already been auditioned by the Organist/Master of the Choristers.

— Holy Communion: on Sundays twice a month and on major Festivals.

The Organist/Master of the Choristers rehearses the choirboys twice a day (except on Wednesday). The Friday afternoon full rehearsal in term-time is in the Abbey. The whole Choir, including the Lay Vicars, rehearses in the Abbey 'Song School' (in the Cloisters) for twenty minutes before each Service.

The Purcell Club, founded in 1929 as the Westminster Abbey Old Choristers' Musical Society, is a male voice choir. It arranges evening singing tours of the Abbey about eight times a year. The money raised thereby goes to the Restoration Fund.

Choirs from all over the world apply to the Dean and Chapter for the privilege of singing in the Abbey. Some three or four are chosen for an appearance each summer. Others are allowed by the Dean to sing for a few minutes at noon by the Tomb of the Unknown Warrior.

The Choir School

The 36 Abbey choirboys are aged between 8 and 14. They are all boarders at the Abbey Choir School in Dean's Yard near the Abbey. At the same time, they are required by law to receive a proper general education. Originally, they were educated together with the King's/Queen's Scholars at Westminster School. But, in 1868, a separate Abbey preparatory school for the choirboys was established. Since 1914, it is housed in a tall building on the west side of Dean's Yard.

There are about eight vacancies in the Choir School each year and voice trials of candidates (aged 8–8½) are held in February and October. The trials are publicly advertised and some 35–40 candidates apply, mostly sons of middle-class families. The candidates are tested by the Organist/Master of the Choristers on their general musical ability and the quality of their voices. After acceptance and one year's probation, they are given a further examination by the Master of the Choristers to qualify as 'Singing Boys'.

The top 22 choirboys sing at all Abbey Services: the remaining 14 watch or rehearse separately. The top ten are known as 'Choristers on the Foundation'. They are admitted to this position by the Dean at a Sunday Evensong in the Abbey and, thereafter, wear a red girdle on their cassocks and a red tassel to their mortar-boards.

The Choir School Staff consists of a Headmaster (who, in addition to his scholastic qualifications, is chosen for his appreciation of music) and a staff of four teachers, together with a Matron, an Assistant Matron and domestic staff. The second Assistant Organist of the Abbey gives keyboard and theory lessons to the boys, while part-time visiting teachers give lessons on different instruments on demand.

The Abbey Musical Foundation

The Musical Foundation at the Abbey, paid from its corporate revenues, consists of:
— the Precentor;
— up to four Minor Canons (today there are three, including the Precentor);
— the Organist/Master of the Choristers;
— twelve Lay Vicars; and
— ten Choristers (out of the 36 at the Choir School).

The Belfry

The bells of Westminster Abbey used to be hung in a separate Campanile;[44] but it was pulled down in 1775. Today, the Belfry is the North-West Tower. It is in charge of a Superintendent, one of the Minor Canons—the Rev. Rennie Simpson, the Precentor.

There are twelve bells in use. Two of them were originally cast in 1539 (and recast in 1583 and 1593) during the reign of Queen Elizabeth I. They are still in their original frame at the top of the Tower. They have now been fitted with an electric chiming system, operated from the western end of the Nave by one of the Vergers. These two bells are struck alternately on the following occasions:
— for five minutes daily before Matins and Evensong;
— forty times before Services where a sermon is to be preached.

[44] Roughly where the Middlesex Guildhall stands today.

The other ten bells are now lower down in the North-West Tower in view of their great weight and the need to reduce the strain on the masonry. They were all cast at the Whitechapel Bell Foundry.[45]

These ten bells are rung manually by the Abbey bellringers some 30–40 times a year, on the following occasions:

— Whenever the Queen enters or leaves the Abbey
— After most Abbey funeral services (a half-muffled peal)
— On 25 'Ringing Days' throughout the year.

The ringing is done by the Abbey's Company of Ringers. Of its twelve members, one is honorary and another is the secretary. There are also thirteen supernumeraries in reserve. The ringers are all members of the Ancient Society of College Youths—founded in 1637 and almost the oldest Society still in existence. There are many such associations in the United Kingdom, with a total membership of over 40,000 bell-ringers.[46]

There is little opportunity for visiting bell-ringers to be allowed to ring the Abbey Bells, although there are many applications to do so.

Broadcasting from the Abbey

The first studio recording of Abbey anthems was made in 1926. The first broadcast of an Abbey wedding was that of the Duke and Duchess of Kent in 1934. Today, there are half a dozen broadcasts from the Abbey each year, usually of Special Services, often for overseas transmission as well. There are also one or two televised broadcasts from the Abbey each year.

VISITORS TO THE ABBEY

The Abbey is one of London's major attractions for visitors coming from other parts of Britain or from abroad, as well as for re-

[45] The Foundry celebrated its 400th Anniversary in 1970, when a commemoration was attended by the Dean and Chapter of Westminster. To mark the occasion, the Foundry presented to the Abbey a set of ten hand-bells. It was this Foundry that also cast the Liberty Bell for Philadelphia in 1752 and Big Ben' for Parliament a century later.

[46] In the 17th century, bell-ringing for church services was forbidden and it became almost entirely a sport. Today, the objects of bell-ringers' associations

sidents of London itself. That attraction has increased considerably since World War I, through improved means of communication, cheap air fares and the publicity given to the Abbey by the ceremonies held there, all reported in the Press and some shown by television relayed all over the world. Several documentary films of the Abbey have also been made for world-wide distribution.

Visitors spend some £ 500 million a year in Britain—an important factor in the balance of payments.[47] Most of them are on a holiday which includes a visit to London, where the Abbey is one of the most popular tourist attractions.[48] A recent sample test has shown 52 percent of *British* visitors to London expect to visit the Abbey, while no less than 85 per cent of *overseas* visitors also intend to do so.

The number of visitors to the Abbey, in consequence, has increased from two million in 1964 to five million in 1970. It is estimated by the British Tourist Authority to reach eight million by 1975.

A sixth of all visitors to England come on package tours and visit the Abbey in motor coaches as part of a group tour of London. These coaches must set down their passengers and wait for them until they have completed their visit. Such a fourfold increase in the number of visitors in eleven years would therefore impose a heavy burden on the Abbey staff as well as cause serious traffic obstructions in the streets outside.[49]

Congestion in the Abbey

The number of visitors to the Abbey rises from 20,000 a week in the dark, cold and rainy month of February to over 80,000 a week during the six months from April to September. The number of visitors rises in July to a peak of 200,000 a week. But this flood is not spread equally over the week: fewer come on Fridays and Sun-

are to maintain Sunday service ringing, to teach and develop change-ringing, to care for church bells and provide social amenities for their members.
[47] Almost covering what Britons themselves spend in foreign currency when travelling abroad.
[48] It has been called 'The Parish Church of the English-speaking world.
[49] This particular problem is further dealt with later.

days, knowing that there are additional services on those days during which times the Abbey is closed to sightseers: correspondingly more sightseers arrive on Saturdays and Tuesdays.

Three-quarters of the visitors come from five countries: 28 per cent from the United States; 20 per cent from Britain itself; 14 per cent from Germany; seven per cent from Belgium and six per cent from France. The remaining quarter come from almost every other country of the world. This poses additional linguistic problems for the Abbey staff and has resulted, among other things, in the provision by the Abbey of versions of its notices and leaflets in several languages.

Although the Abbey is open from 8 a.m. till 6 p.m. daily[50] (and to 7 p.m. between April 1st and September 30th) a large proportion of weekday visitors crowd in after 10.15 a.m. They then leave in their coaches by 11.15 to see the Changing of the Guard at Buckingham Palace at 11.30 (another immensely popular tourist attraction). Even at 1 p.m., when the rush-hour is over and many people are busy finding somewhere to have lunch, visitors still arrive at the Abbey at the rate of 80 a minute.[51]

At peak periods, there are 3,000 people at a time in the Abbey; this allows only eight square feet of floor space per person, or less than a quarter of the desirable area. The consequences of this congestion are excessive noise, heat and delay, coupled with exhaustion of the Abbey staff.

Conflict of Interests between Worshippers and Sightseers

The Abbey must provide three Services a day and five on Sunday —a total of 23 a week. During the Services, sightseers are encouraged to visit the Exhibition of Abbey Treasures in the Norman Undercroft (see later) which is within the Precincts, yet outside the Church itself; or the Chapter House, which is administered by the

[50] Till 8 p.m. on Wednesdays.

[51] This figure is the result of an actual count during one week in July, 1970. It was made by a firm of management consultants, called in by the Abbey to advise on how to cope with congestion. This count was necessary as no tickets are sold for entrance to a church, unlike entrance by ticket to the Tower of London, the next biggest attraction in London.

(Government) Department of the Environment and not by the Abbey.

The Royal Tombs

These are situated at the eastern end of the Abbey, behind the High Altar. They surround the Shrine of Saint Edward the Confessor and are to be found in the Henry VII Chapel.

Although no charge is made for entry into the Abbey as a whole —a place for Christian worship—charges are made for admission to the Royal Chapel.

The total annual income from this source in 1970–1 was £ 108,000. A further £ 15,000 is received from admission fees to the Exhibition of Abbey Treasures (see later).

The Abbey is not part of any Diocese or Province, nor does it receive any direct Government financial support. Hence this income of £ 123,000 from admission fees to the Chapels and the Exhibition is a valuable contribution towards the £ 260,000 a year that it costs to maintain the Abbey (see the Section below on Finance). Including profits on the Abbey Bookshop (see later), 60 per cent of the Abbey income comes from sightseers.

Only 15 per cent of visitors to the Abbey visit the Royal Chapels; some because they have not read the notices about them at the Abbey doors; others because they do not wish to pay the admission fee. For them, there is free entry between 6 and 8 p.m. on Wednesdays. The Abbey is then staffed by volunteers from a number of organizations, each of which undertakes to provide the supervisory staff required for a month at a time.

To reduce queues at the entrance to the Royal Chapels, conducted tours pay by presentation of vouchers bought beforehand by travel agencies. To speed up the movement of sightseers within the Royal Chapels, no guides are permitted to stop and lecture there to the group that they are conducting.

Entrance to the Royal Chapels, and supervision of the sightseers visiting them, is controlled by a Chief Attendant/Cashier, five Attendants and Relief Cashiers, and two Attendants. They come directly under the Receiver-General.

Voluntary Helpers

These are a group of about thirty—mostly women— who are each able to give one or more mornings or afternoons each week to help visitors to the Abbey: they are unpaid. They wear a badge, but otherwise no kind of uniform as this deters some people from approaching them. Their function is not only to answer questions (many of them speak foreign languages) but to approach the lonely and help to dispel the feeling that the Abbey is impersonal. They serve as public relations staff, imbued with a deep sense of Christian mission.

The Cleaners

With such an immense number of visitors a day, even keeping the Abbey clean is a major undertaking. Cleaning the monuments is the responsibility of the Clerk of Works' staff (see the Section on the maintenance of the Fabric below). But everything at floor level, including the seating, is kept clean by a staff of six men (one a Charge-Hand—i.e., Supervisor) and one woman. They work from 7.30 in the morning until 4.30 in the afternoon from Monday till Friday, and till noon on Saturday. Each undertakes a particular section of the Abbey.

Photography in the Abbey

Photography by sightseers is forbidden inside the Abbey. Professional photographers need a license from the Receiver-General. Filming of special events inside the Abbey has gradually become accepted during the past half century. For example, at the Coronation of King George V in 1911, no filming inside the Abbey was permitted but only of the Regalia Procession in the Cloisters. By 1953, full facilities were given, not only for a colour film of the Coronation itself, but also for television coverage, seen all over the world.

Guides

Unauthorized persons are not allowed to act as guides in the Abbey. Authorized guides are:

— London Tourist Board registered guides, wearing LTB badges;
— tourist agency non-registered guides, carrying one of the numbered permits and numbered badges issued by the Dean and Chapter to the Agency; or
— other guides carrying a numbered personal permit and badge issued by the Dean and Chapter.

All permits are annually renewable: an annual permit fee of £ 2 is charged, including the badge (a new design is issued each year).

Each authorized guide is given a copy of the five-page Abbey code of regulations (the present issue of April, 1971, is the 15th revision). These regulations are enforced by the Dean's Verger.

Vergers' Conducted Tours of the Abbey

Many sightseers visiting the Abbey are not members of conducted tours. For them, the Abbey began in 1972 to offer its own 'Guided Super-Tours' of the Abbey and its Precincts. Each group is limited to twenty persons. The Super-Tours are very popular: between 150 and 250 persons participate each week, dependent on the number of Special Services (when the Super-Tours are suspended). They take place at 10.45 a.m. and 2.30 p.m. on Mondays to Fridays, and on Saturdays at 10.25 a.m. only. There are no Super-Tours on Sundays. The tour lasts about two hours, for which an inclusive fee of £ 1.00 is paid, part of which goes to Abbey funds. Each group is shown round by a Verger: no tipping is allowed.

Public Lectures in the Abbey

There are two series of weekly public lectures given in the Abbey during Lent (preceding Easter in March/April) or Advent (preceding the Feast of the Nativity—Christmas). They are arranged by the *Lector Theologiae* (see above).

There are generally four lectures in each series, mostly on theological subjects. They are delivered from the Choir or Nave pulpits, or in the Jerusalem Chamber. There is no charge for admission; yet in spite of posters, leaflets, mention in the Sunday Service Paper, attendance is disappointing.

Lectures in Lent are given by the Dean and other members of the Chapter, who receive a nominal 75p each from a special trust fund. Lectures in Advent are given by outside lecturers who receive a fee of £ 25 each.

In November, there is the annual Bishop Gore Lecture: the lecturer receives a fee of £ 15 from a special trust fund. Other Memorial Lectures are given from time to time.

In May, when the summer flood of visitors has already begun, there is Wednesday lunch-time music (from 12.30 till 1.00 p.m.) entitled *Come and Sing*. Visiting choirs are invited to participate, for a nominal fee of £ 3–5 for expenses. New hymns are introduced. These musical sessions have been popular, especially with the younger generation.

Plays and readings are also given in the Abbey from time to time.

Communication with Visitors by Poster

Apart from oral communication between visitors, on the one hand, with Vergers, Marshals and Voluntary Helpers, on the other, much information is given by directional signs, notices and posters, both inside and outside the Abbey.

There is a wide variety of lettering and lay-out on Abbey directional signs, notices and posters, as well as on the descriptive notices on individual monuments. A sub-committee appointed by the Dean and Chapter is now considering aesthetic standards and the methods of applying them. As the Abbey has a unique cultural position and influence in Britain, this is important.

Some Abbey notices, and even guide-books, are now provided also in foreign languages.[52]

One pleasing feature is the provision of a table inside the Abbey on which loose pages of a visitors' book are displayed: many per-

[52] This is not really a modern innovation: French and German notices were placed in the Abbey in 1851 for the convenience of visitors to London for the Great Exhibition.

160

sons sign them. This not only gives visitors the feeling that they are personal guests of the Abbey but, by registering their names in such a venerable institution, they will go down to posterity. This reduces the temptation to some thoughtless visitors to write or cut their names on the walls or monuments.

External Traffic Control

Sixteen per cent of all visitors to the Abbey arrive by motor-coach, three-quarters of them before noon. As there is no easy access by road to the North Door, coaches (and taxis) arrive at the Great West Door. Some forty coaches arrive between 10.15 and 11.15 a.m. daily.

The Sanctuary—today a triangular strip of road between the entrances to the West Door and to Dean's Yard—is now too small to allow coaches to wait there: they may only set down visitors. A few taxis may stand there, but coaches must park in Great Smith Street, several hundred yards away.[53] From there, they come round to the east side of the Abbey and draw up opposite the House of Lords and wait for their group who, having visited the Abbey with their guide, come out through the Poets' Corner. There is little chance of better parking-places for coaches being found anywhere near the Abbey.

The same applies to private cars. The entrance to Dean's Yard is now controlled by a lifting barrier, and the use of the Yard for parking is limited to holders of parking permits issued by the Receiver-General. Parking is under the supervision of the Yard Beadle.

The Abbey Bookshop

This is run as a separate department under the Receiver-General. It has four points of sale:

— The Main Bookshop outside the Great West Door

By this door most sightseers enter the Abbey. Participants in guided group-tours, however, have little time to visit the Bookshop

---

[53] Other coaches, to avoid the charge, set down their passengers round the corner. Before the charge was imposed, over a hundred coaches used to

on first arrival. Some return later: others use one of three other points of sale. The Main Bookshop only opens at 9.30 a.m., whereas the Abbey itself opens at 8; but there are few sightseers who enter the Abbey so early. The Main Bookshop closes at 5 p.m., although the Abbey closes at 6 p.m. During the last hour, the Abbey is closed to sightseers for Evensong and there are few Bookshop sales. There would also be staffing difficulties if the Bookshop were to be kept open for more hours a day than at present.

— The Kiosk outside the Poet's Corner Door

The Kiosk is open from 9.30 a.m. till 4.30 p.m. and is much patronized by participants in guided group-tours after leaving the Abbey through this door on their way to their tourist buses.

— A small stall in the Abbey Transept

Only a limited selection of publications can be shown there for lack of space. The stall is shut during all Abbey Services. It opens at 9.30 and closes at 4.30. Although it is open till 8 p.m. on Wednesday nights when the Abbey is open till that hour, the weekly sales are low.

— A small stall in the Exhibition of Abbey Treasures

This is open only from 9.30 a.m. till 4.30 p.m., for the reasons given above.

There are some 350,000 purchases a year from the Bookshop, or 1,100 a day (the Bookshop is naturally closed on Sundays). The average sale works out at 50 pence. Some residents of the Precincts, and Westminster generally, use the Bookshop for ordering books which are not normally kept in stock.

The offices and storerooms are next to the Main Bookshop: there are also storerooms in the cellars under the adjacent Chapter Office. Books are bought in bulk: the stock-in-hand in September, 1971, amounted to £ 17,000. The store-rooms are provided with burglar-alarms.

set down passengers at the Great West Door on some mornings at peak periods of the year.

Bookshop sales in 1970–71 were as follows:

	£
Main Bookshop	121,000
Poets' Corner Kiosk	28,000
Transept Stall	20,000
Abbey Treasures Exhibition Stall	4,000
Total sales (rounded)	174,000

As the original purchase price of the stock sold was £103,000, gross profit was £72,000. From this, £38,000 was deducted for salaries, rent, rates, light, heat, telephones, repairs, printing, stationery, insurance and advertising. This left a net profit of £34,000 in 1970–71 which went in support of Abbey funds. As the Abbey is a religious body and the Bookshop's profits are not subject to Corporation Tax, the ratio of net profit to sales at the Abbey Bookshop is 40 per cent, as compared to the normal 35 per cent for other bookshops of similar size.

The staff of the Bookshop consists of the Manager,[54] two Buyers, an Assistant Buyer, twelve Sales Assistants[55] (some part-time), a Storekeeper and two Cleaners.

Since 1953, the Bookshop is chartered by the Book-Sellers' Association. To be chartered, it has to meet certain requirements, such as minimum floor -and window- space, minimum number of titles stocked (2,000) and the provision of free service to customers ordering, or even only enquiring about, books not in stock. In return, the Abbey Bookshop gets a book-publisher's discount of 35 per cent instead of the ordinary discount of 33⅓ per cent.

Another of the conditions of being chartered is management encouragement to the Sales Assistants to take the Association's diploma in book-selling. This encouragement is now provided; but there is still a difficulty in finding men, or women, willing to be trained for a book-selling career.

[54] A former Regular RAMC Captain and Quartermaster, with experience in stock records.
[55] Not working on a rota system.

Walls and Roofs

The Abbey is a very ancient building; its walls and roofs need constant maintenance and, from time to time, restoration and even reconstruction. Damage to the interior has been caused not only by wear and tear but by vandalism (for example, as a result of the construction in earlier centuries of wooden stands inside the Abbey for Coronations and other special occasions).[56]

Originally, the Abbey had been built with the help of Royal grants; and the State continued to bear part of the restoration costs for several centuries. Nevertheless, the main burden of maintenance and restoration of the fabric is now borne by Abbey funds.

In World War II, the Abbey was, luckily, never hit by a high explosive bomb; but the Crossing, as well as the Precincts, were damaged by incendiaries in the air-raid on May 10th, 1941, when the Deanery, five Canon's houses and Westminster School Hall were burnt out. (All have been since restored).

Cleaning of the inside stonework of the Abbey was finished in 1965, the London Stone Co being employed. The outside stonework, now much begrimed, also needs washing. However, in the process, much decayed stonework would be revealed which would have sooner or later to be replaced.[57] The total cost of hiring and erecting scaffolding is so high that it would be uneconomic to clean the exterior of the Abbey until money is available for simultaneous restoration. That must wait the results of the new appeal for funds.

The Monuments

From the 10th Century, the Abbey was the church of a Benedictine monastery. A few tombs of Abbots remain,[58] but those of indi-

---

[56] Tickets for such ceremonies were sold and the proceeds divided up among the Abbey staff. Hence, every available space was built over for stands and the walls and monuments frequently damaged in the process.

[57] The stone is so friable that some of it is largely held together by the grime. Once the grime is removed, splinters are liable to fall off, endangering the crowds below.

[58] The tombs of only nine of the 30 Abbots have been identified.

164

vidual monks were usually unmarked. The tombs were covered by inscribed flagstones; but most of the inscriptions have been worn down by millions of feet.

Brasses seem first to have appeared in Europe in the early 13th century and in England shortly afterwards. Few remain in the Abbey today.

The Abbey, rebuilt by King Edward the Confessor in the 11th century, was again rebuilt by King Henry III. In October, 1269, the Confessor's body was buried there, in a special Shrine[59] behind the High Altar: Henry III himself is buried nearby. Later kings were usually buried near the Shrine, up to Henry V. Later Monarchs were buried in the Henry VII Chapel, but not after George II.[60]

Other members of the Royal family were similarly buried in the Abbey, to be followed by courtiers, nobles, statesmen, leading sailors, soldiers, theologians, philanthropists, physicians and scientists. Since 1400—when Geoffrey Chaucer was buried in the Abbey—writers, poets, musicians and actors have also been buried there, mostly in 'Poets' Corner' (the Southern Transept). The qualification was originally 'great distinction in the arts of Peace and War'. But, in the 18th century, there was a debasement: Abbey burials were allowed on grounds solely of social rank or mere wealth. Between 1780 and 1800, there were no less than 189 Abbey burials, an average of almost one a month. In 1827, the *Sunday Times* even published the tariff.[61]

Instead of a flagstone, memorials began to be placed on the walls, becoming more and more ornate and often destroying part of the fabric in the process. These memorials were often tasteless—disproportionate in size, incongruous in design, with fulsome inscriptions. Later, free-standing statues were erected to the dead, often blocking the aisles. As Dean Stanley put it a century ago, the Abbey has become 'A Church of Tombs'.[62]

[59] It was despoiled in the 16th century and, today, has only vestiges of its original magnificence.
[60] Since then, they are buried at Windsor.
[61] £54.18.0 for burial in the Abbey, plus 5 guineas for a gravestone: £ 19.6.0 in the Cloisters, plus 4 guineas for a gravestone.
[62] In the 19th century, two Royal Commissions tried, unsuccessfully, to find

During World War II, the Abbey monuments were protected by 60,000 sandbags and hardly damaged at all. But, even in peace-time, many suffer from constant wear and tear—from visitors touching them and even breaking off pieces as souvenirs. In a few cases, the deceased provided in his will for a trust to be set up from which the cost of maintaining his monument could be covered. But the general cost of maintaining and cleaning the monuments is now a charge on Abbey funds. It is undertaken by staff of the Surveyor's Department, which is responsible for the inscribed flagstones and for everything else above floor level.[63] They go round the Abbey systematically and then start again: this takes about three years. Every five years, the monuments and stalls are vacuum-cleaned by a company under contract.[64]

The Surveyor of the Fabric

The first Surveyor, Sir Christopher Wren, having been appointed in 1698, served in this post for 25 years, until he died at the age of 91. The present Surveyor—Mr. S.E. Dykes Bower—is also a distinguished ecclesiastical architect in private practice, with an Abbey office in Little Cloister. He directs the work of his Department and is called on to plan any Abbey alterations or restoration. A Consulting Structural Engineer is retained for specialist advice.

The Clerk of Works

Mr. S. R. Andrews is a fifth generation master-builder from Plymouth.[65] He, too, has an office in Little Cloister and a house in Dean's Yard. He supervises the work of the Maintenance Staff, who undertake the routine care of the buildings and consist of:
— the Foreman of Works

a site for a National Pantheon where some of the worst Abbey monuments (and all future monuments) could be placed.
[63] The cleaning of the floor and the pews is undertaken by the Abbey cleaners, already described.
[64] The intricate carving on the choir stalls presents special problems.
[65] His son is now an apprentice mason on the Abbey Staff—aiming to be the sixth generation.

— the Senior Mason
— two Masons
— two Apprentice Masons
— a Plumber/Tiler
— an Electrician
— a Carpenter
— a Painter
— two Scaffold Riggers
— eight General Workers.

The cost of this staff is some £ 45,000 a year, of which part is debited to the Abbey Restoration Fund.

Members of the Maintenance Staff may join their craft Unions if they wish: but, as the Abbey pays wages above Union rates, there is no strong inducement to do so.

An annual three weeks paid holiday is provided and all posts are pensionable. The Abbey trains its own men; and, long before a skilled worker is due to retire, a 16-year-old apprentice is brought in with the prospect of being appointed to the eventual vacancy. All apprentices are given time off, under the Day Release Scheme, for theoretical training at a technical college.

The Surveyor's Department has premises in Dean's Yard and outside the Henry VII Chapel, The latter is rather an eyesore; but, as stone blocks for the restoration work are sawn there, it must be close to the site.

The Abbey Windows

The Abbey has lost so much of its medieval stained glass that it cannot show anything to rival that at Canterbury or York to say nothing of Chartres. Even the glass in the Henry VII Chapel succumbed to the Reformation and had disappeared by 1643. Sir Christopher Wren reglazed most of the windows of the Nave, Quire and Transepts with plain glass, which makes the interior of the Abbey light and airy. The stained glass in the North Transept Rose-Window dates from the 18th century. The best of the old stained glass was removed and hidden during the *Blitz* in World War II; the rest was blown out. Such glass as could be salvaged has been re-used.

Some modern stained glass windows have been donated to the Abbey, the most famous example being those in the Chapel at the extreme east end of the Abbey, now dedicated to those units of the Royal Air Force that participated in the fateful Battle of Britain in 1940.

One of the mundane difficulties with all the glass windows in the Abbey is the number of panes that are broken by pigeons and that have to be replaced.[66]

Microphones and Loud-Speakers

These were introduced into the Abbey in 1934: they are maintained by the contractors and the Abbey Electrician.

There are eleven microphones in use and 137 loud-speakers; but the echo in the Abbey is such that, in certain parts of it, the sound is very muffled. The microphones at the pulpit are hung round the speaker's neck, thus avoiding the fading that would occur if he moved his mouth away from a standing microphone.

Security

Between 8 a.m. and 6 p.m., when the Abbey is open to the public, the Vergers keep a watch. When VIPs are present for Special Services, admission is by ticket. Between 6 and 10 p.m., there are one-man patrols, inside and outside the Abbey, provided by rota between five men from the Surveyor's Department. After 10 p.m. burglar alarms are turned on. Security arrangements are the responsibility of the Clerk of Works, who has himself had considerable World War II experience in Security matters.

Anything suspicious in or around the Abbey is reported to the Cannon Row Police Station which is responsible for the area in which the Abbey and the Houses of Parliament are situated. If necessary, the Police Station consults the Metropolitan Police headquarters in Victoria Street, nearby. Any such incident is reported later by the Clerk of Works to the Canon in residence.

[66] The pigeons are attracted by the food left by sightseers eating their sandwiches in the Cloisters. A pigeon repellent is used on Abbey ledges and walls but has to be renewed annually.

The Precincts are patrolled by two Abbey constables, with two Constable Reliefs, in addition to two Precinct Night Watchmen under the Clerk of Works.

The Abbey Gardens

All the Gardens are maintained by an Abbey Head Gardener (a woman), an Assistant Gardener, both technically responsible to the Canon Steward; in practice supervised by the Receiver-General.

Abbey Housing

The Surveyor's Department is also responsible for the maintenance and repair of all Abbey Housing.

FINANCE

Abbey Property and Trusts

The Abbey lands and buildings outside its immediate vicinity were made over between 1868 and 1888 to the Ecclesiastical Commissioners[67] against an annual grant of £ 20,000. This was converted into a capital grant of £ 400,000 to be invested by the Abbey on the advice of its Investment Panel. In 1970–71, it produced an income of £ 28,000.

The Abbey still retains property in Dean's Yard and the two houses in the College Garden (mentioned above). All together, they bring in a gross income from rentals of a further £ 46,000 a year.

Abbey Appeals

There is also the income from the Trust Funds set up after each of the two Abbey Appeals previously mentioned. They were:
— *The 1920 Appeal* by Dean Ryle for £ 250,000. It had realised £ 170,000 when it was suspended in view of the even more urgent need to launch an appeal to save St Paul's. The £ 170,000 already raised was invested and produces an income of £ 10,000 a year

---

[67] Now the Church Commissioners.

-- *The 1953 Appeal* for £ 1,000,000, which, in fact, had already raised £ 1,137,000 when it was suspended in favour of an urgent appeal following the inundation of the East Coast of England. The proceeds of the 1953 Appeal were allocated as follows and invested:

— £ 314,000 to the Fabric Fund, producing £ 14,900 a year

— £ 216,000 for the Choir School, producing £ 14,500 a year

— £ 840,000 to the General Reserve Fund producing £ 26,000 a year.

Then there are minor trust funds, to a total of £ 86,000, some of them earmarked (for example, £ 17,000 for the Lead Roof Fund) which bring in £ 6,000 a year.

Finally, interest on deposits and dividends from shares owned by the Abbey bring in a further £ 5,000 a year.

A *New Appeal* is now being planned for some £ 4–5,000,000. At least half will be needed for external restoration of the Abbey fabric. It is proposed to set up a permanent body of eminent Trustees to manage not only the proceeds of this appeal but also to continue the process of fund-raising.

Abbey Income

The total income in 1970–71 was as follows:

	£
Property and investments	147,000
Admission fees to the Royal Chapels and the Exhibition of Abbey Treasures	100,000
Net profit on the Book Shop	30,000
From collecting-boxes in the Abbey	15,000
From Offertories	3,000
Fees for guides' permits	
Fees from coaches setting-down at the Great West Door	2,000
Fees for Abbey weddings	1,000
Fees for brass-rubbing permits	1,000
Total Income (rounded)	£ 300,000

Abbey Current Expenditure

The total expenditure in 1970–71 came to £ 267,000, of which the main heads of expenditure were as follows:

	£
Dean's and Canons' stipends	13,000
Choir expenses (including Minor Canons', Sacrists' Organist's and Lay Vicars' stipends)	31,000[68]
Choir School (less Scholars' fees received)	29,000[68]
Vergers	23,000
Marshals	8,000
Clerk of Works' Department wages, materials, etc.	34,000
Staff pensions	11,000
Printing, stationery, postage and telephones	10,000
Dean's and Canons' secretarial expenses	2,000
Rates, heating, lighting and cleaning	17,000
National insurance contributions for staff	5,000
Maintenance of official housing	20,000
Gardens	3,000
Library and Muniment Room	3,000
Entertaining (by the Chapter, and individual)	4,000
Special Services (e.g., funerals of Abbey staff benefactors)	1,000
Miscellaneous (e.g., preachers, visiting choirs, hymn sheets, leaflets, posters, sound reproduction, belfry, flags, clocks)	22,000

This total current expenditure of £ 267,000 was debited against different revenue accounts.

Control of Expenditure

The control of Abbey expenditure is highly centralised. As there are not many departments, and their heads have offices within the Precincts, all bills within the limits of the budget sanctioned by the Dean and Chapter are sent in to the Receiver-General for payment.

[68] It is interesting to note that the cost of music in the Abbey comes to about a quarter of the whole expenditure.

The present Treasurer of the Abbey is also the Archdeacon. He presents the Abbey's annual financial report to the Dean and Chapter. Financial policy decisions are taken at Chapter meetings throughout the year and are executed by the Receiver-General who also holds the office of Chapter Clerk.

The accounting in the Receiver-General's Department is done by:

The Chief Accountant

An Assistant Book-keeper(for the general accounts)

An Assistant Book-keeper (for the Bookshop accounts)

An Assistant Book-keeper (for the Surveyor's Department, with the trade union experience)

A Salaries and Wages Clerk

A Cashier

Mr I.D.R. Campbell, of Binder, Hamlyn & Co, is the Abbey Auditor.

The Abbey's Financial Year

This still runs from Michaelmas to Michaelmas (September 30th till September 29th), following the old year of the Law Courts and the Universities of Oxford and Cambridge, with Michaelmas, Trinity and Hilary terms. This, in turn, follows the much older agricultural year—from ploughing and sowing to reaping. The usual financial year (from April to March) is comparatively modern and was introduced because the Calendar year, from January to December, put great pressure on accountants over Christmas. So the retention of the old Church calendar would not seem to make things much more complicated. It suits the Choir School.

The Abbey Library and Muniments

The Library is still housed in the northern part of the ancient monastery Dorter (i.e., dormitory). The shell of the structure dates from the late 11th century and has a wooden hammer-beam roof perhaps from the late 15th century.[69] An upper gallery was added in 1932 with the help of a grant from the Pilgrim Trust and is used

[69] The southern part of the Dorter, that became the Westminster School Hall, was destroyed in the *Blitz* in 1941, but has now been rebuilt.

as a reference library and workroom. The main library below consists of leather-bound books still on their early 17th century wooden shelves. Although most of the library of the old Benedictine monastery was scattered at the Dissolution in 1540, the Abbey library consists today of some 12,000 volumes, including sixty *incunabula*.

The Muniments

These are the ancient Abbey archives. 'Muniment' is derived from the Latin word *Munire* 'to fortify'. This implies the fortifying by an institution of its claims to privileges.[70]

The Abbey muniments are still situated in an open gallery provided inside the Abbey when it was rebuilt in the 13th century. This gallery has probably been the Abbey Muniment Room for nearly 600 years. On one wall is a large mural painting of the White Hart badge of Richard II who reigned from 1377 to 1399. The medieval oak cupboards and coffers are still in use.

The gallery has the advantage of possessing a tiled stone (hence, fireproof) floor, stone walls and vaulted ceiling. As it is open on two sides to the Abbey Nave and Southern Transept, the temperature is equable and the air kept well circulated. This has helped to preserve its medieval documents.

The Abbey muniments are of particular importance, as:

they are in their original place;

they are fuller, and more complete and numerous, than those of any other medieval religious house in England;

they are in close proximity to a Royal Palace and hence contain valuable State records as well; and

they have been subject to concentrated research since the 18th century (although there is still no complete picture).

No part of the Muniment Room Library is open to the public; but some of its treasures are displayed in the Exhibition (see below). Conducted tours of the Muniment Room by specially interested persons can, however, be arranged. From Mondays to Fridays, research students are allowed to work in the Muniment Room on

---

[70] Compare another derivation from the same Latin root—'Munitions'.

all but certain classes of documents. Many requests for information about specific subjects are dealt with by the Keeper of the Muniments.

During World War II, 22 boxes of the most precious documents were taken for safety to the Bodleian Library at Oxford and to several houses in the country.

The Administration of the Library and Muniment Room

They are under the Abbey Librarian (the post is at present vacant) assisted by the Keeper of the Muniments (Mr. Nicholas MacMichael), together with a Secretary and an Assistant. Recently there has been formed a special advisory Library Committee,[71] of which the chairman is a Canon, with a secretary provided by the Chapter Office.

The Library and Muniment Room has an annual budget of £ 6,300 for staff, purchase of books, and maintenance of books and documents. Of this, £ 3,700 is covered by endowments and other income, with £ 2,600 as a charge on the Dean and Chapter.

THE EXHIBITION OF ABBEY TREASURES

This is situated in the Norman Undercroft, built between 1060 and 1100. It was probably used originally as the monks' common-room, tailor-shop and shaving-house. In 1908, it was turned into a small Abbey Museum; but, in 1965, (as part of the Abbey's 900th Anniversary celebrations) it was professionally re-designed under the auspices of an Exhibition Committee to serve as an Exhibition of Abbey Treasures, selected by the Keeper of the Muniments and the Committee. The Exhibition illustrates the history of Westminster Abbey from the earliest times until the present day, and shows examples of ancient documents and seals, medieval armour, religious vestments, historical relics, replicas of the Coronation regalia, and a unique collection of the funeral effigies of Kings and Queens and of other prominent persons which have been preserved over the centuries at the Abbey.

[71] The whole administration is at present under review; hence the Committee.

The Exhibition is so popular that it has become permanent and is open from 9.30 a.m. till 5 p.m. every weekday. Its staff is under the Receiver-General: the Bookshop staff is under the Bookshop Manager.

The Abbey and Westminster School

In 1540, after the Dissolution of the Monasteries, a Foundation was set up by Henry VIII called 'The King's Grammar School at Westminster', with provision for two Masters and 40 King's (or Queen's) Scholars. In 1560, Elizabeth I prescribed that Westminster School should be governed by the Dean and Prebendaries of Westminster Abbey. Its Statutes (never actually signed) prescribed that Queen's Scholars should, by preference, be the sons of Abbey tenants.

Westminster School was linked with two other Royal Foundations—Christ Church, Oxford, and Trinity College, Cambridge. For three centuries, the Head Master of Westminster School was nominated by these two Colleges alternately. There are still annual 'elections' of Westminster School boys to scholarships and 'exhibitions' at these two Colleges.

The Master (i.e., Headmaster) and Under-Master (i.e., Master of the Queen's Scholars) still have stalls in the Abbey Choir, while the Queen's Scholars have their own places in the Choir. During a Coronation, the Queen's Scholars walk in the procession of the Regalia and are then seated in the North Triforium over the North Choir Aisle. They are the first to shout *Vivat Rex or Vivat Regina!* when the crown is placed on the Monarch's head.

The average number of boys at Westminster School in the 18th century was about 300. But a typhoid outbreak in 1848 caused the number of boys to fall to under seventy.

A Tercentenary Committee of Old Westminster met in 1860[72] to investigate conditions in the School. A suggestion that it should move out of London to a more salubrious spot was rejected owing to the high cost of transfer.

A Royal Commission on Public Schools recommended that, as

[72] That is, three hundred years from the new Foundation of 1560. The School celebrated its Quatercentenary in 1957.

far as Westminster School was concerned, it should not be wholly dependent on the Abbey Chapter for its income and that more School accommodation should be provided. The Public Schools Act of 1868 largely disentangled the School from the Abbey. New School Statutes were issued in 1869 and 1871, since amended from time to time, the latest occasion being in 1967. The School Governing Body is, however, still partly ecclesiastical. It meets four times a year. As many members are not resident in London, the quorum is only five out of eighteen. Originally, all had to be members of the Established Church; now, non-Conformists and Catholics may serve; but not non-Christians.

The Queen's Scholars are still confined to Christians (Anglican, Non-Conformist or Catholic). Several attempts have been made to remove the ban, but, so far, unsuccessfully.

Scholars pay only half the normal boarding fee, or less if their families cannot afford even that. The 250 or so other boarders, who are all between the ages of 13 and 18, pay a fee of £ 912 a year. Westminster School masters also pay half the fee for their sons.

There are compulsory School prayers at 9 a.m. in the Abbey for all Westminster School boys. Roman Catholics and Jews may be exempted, but few apply for exemption.

This then, in brief, is a description of the administration of Westminster Abbey, its constituent parts and some of its associated bodies. Any errors of fact are solely the author's responsibility.

The Times

This is the seventh in a series of studies that I have made of the administration of venerable institutions.

I must first thank the Editor of The Times—*Mr. William Rees-Mogg—and the Managing Editor—Mr John Grant—for the facilities given for my enquiries. I am also most grateful to their energetic Secretaries[1] for arranging for me some thirty interviews with heads of departments, and other visits. I was thus enabled to visit all parts of the large* Times *building at Printing House Square to see the editorial work and production in full swing at all hours of the day and night. I was allowed to sit in on each of the Editor's different daily and weekly conferences.*

Each part of my analysis has been checked by the person who supplied me originally with the information.[2] The Editor has himself seen the whole study and I have benefited from his comments. I am most grateful for the welcome and help given to me, without exception, by everyone concerned.

My aim in making this study was analytical and not critical. I was not asked by anyone to make any recommendations and have made none: in any case, I am not competent to do so. My object was simply to discover for myself how a venerable London newspaper is organised internally. I wanted to ascertain how it managed to perform the daily miracle of turning out some 150 columns of news

---

[1] Miss Libby Stevens and Miss Mary Kernick: also to Miss Joyce Biggs, head of the Typing Bureau, who co-ordinated much of the drafting, and to Mrs. Era Bennett-Gray, who typed it.

[2] Basic biographical data on each are given as a footnote to the part concerned.

177

and comment every morning, accompanied by a further 100 columns (more or less) of constantly changing advertisements. It is this advertising that enables quality newspapers to cover a large part of their expenses.

Everything on a daily paper is geared to the minute: an enormous amount of careful and continuous planning is therefore involved. During my enquiries, I seemed at times to be present in the medieval kitchens of some baronial hall, with a vast array of men and women hard at work. Here, joints were being roasted; there, vegetables were being cut up and boiled: in odd corners, delicious sauces and syrups were being prepared. Each course had to be ready for serving up, piping hot, whenever the major domo gave the signal.

I took for granted great expertise at *The Times*: what surprised me was the ingenuity displayed in gathering the news, with observers placed at all the most strategic points where information could most advantageously be collected. I was astonished at the speed and accuracy of its transmission to Printing House Square from all over Britain, and the world at large. I was deeply impressed by the seriousness with which every piece of news on arrival is weighed and checked; the skill with which it is rapidly edited to the length required for the page where it will so shortly appear. I found an enormous enthusiasm pervading this venerable institution, which in large measure accounts for the prestige it still commands today.

Some of this enthusiasm is, I assume, due to the policy in recent years of decentralising authority. *The Times* is now produced by a large number of separate departments, the head of each having considerable control over his (or her) own allotted budget, over staff appointments, promotions and assignments. Such decentralisation of authority is essential in any administrative machine geared to work at high speed. At the time when I was making this study (summer, 1973), the financial results for the first part of 1973 showed at last a small profit, after several years of rapidly diminishing deficits. Hence, the spirit of confidence and optimism pervading the upper layers of authority in every *Times* office that I visited.

Journalism is a strange profession. A journalist is like someone who has picked up a germ. It has entered his blood-stream and he can never quite get rid of it. He is continuously possessed by a sort of suppressed excitement, due in part to the spirit of the chase, in part to the spur of competition. Journalists have ringside seats at great events: they are present when history is made. Often they are the first to hear the news and to pass it on. Something of the grandeur of natural upheavals, of major political cataclysms, apparently rubs off on those who handle news of them. Handling it demands energy, knowledge, skill, judgement and taste. Journalists must, therefore, be all-round men or women. The excitement that is involved in journalism is the only explanation that I can find why its addicts are willing to work for long and inconvenient hours in noisy places, day after day, year after year; and to miss it terribly when at last they have to retire.

BIBLIOGRAPHY

Little has been published on *The Times* of today. There is, of course, the history of *The Times* in five massive volumes, published between 1935 and 1952, and covering the century and a half that had passed since its establishment in 1785. I gather that notes for subsequent volumes have been prepared; but they are not yet ready for publication.

A popular history of *The Times* was being written by Oliver Woods, a former Assistant Editor. He, however, died in 1972 and his work has not yet appeared.

Another historical record of the first 150 years was first published as a special supplement to *The Times* in honour of its jubilee in 1935. It was reprinted in book form: ; but still includes nothing that has happened in the past 38 years.

There is a brief mention of *The Times* in a book by Viscount Camrose, entitled 'British Newspapers and Their Controllers',[3] but that is now a quarter of a century out of date.

Some information about *The Times* up to 1966 is, however, given in the (Roskill) Report of the Monopolies Commission (House of

[3] It was published in 1947 by Cassell, London.

Commons, No. 273) on the acquisition of *The Times* by the Thomson Organisation.

Lastly, a small pamphlet on *The Times* was issued in 1972 by its Public Relations Department, primarily for visitors to its offices; but even that is not now wholly up to date.

Hence, my study must begin with a brief account of the development of *The Times* right up to the present day.

OWNERSHIP

The Times is the oldest daily newspaper in the English-speaking world and has been in continuous publication for 188 years. Founded in 1785 as *The Daily Universal Register,* its name was changed to *The Times* three years later.

From 1785 till 1908, it was wholly owned by the Walter family. In 1908, it came under the ownership of Lord Northcliffe: he remained in control until his death in 1922. In that year, Northcliffe's shares in The Times Publishing Company were purchased by Major (later, the 1st Lord) Astor of Hever, who, with John Walter IV, remained joint chief proprietors until 1966. In 1967, 85 per cent of the shares of the Hon. Gavin Astor (later, the 2nd ·Lord Astor of Hever) were acquired by Lord Thomson of Fleet.[4] The management of *The Times* was then merged with that of *The Sunday Times,* of which Lord Thomson had acquired control in 1959.

He is also the owner of many newspapers in Canada and the United States, but their management is in the hands of separate companies with headquarters in Toronto. In 1961, he set up in London the Thomson Organisation for the management of his United Kingdom interests which are now diversified beyond newspapers and include magazines, book publishing, travel and telephone directories. Lord Thomson himself is chairman of the Board of the Thomson Organisation; his son, the Hon Kenneth Thomson, is Deputy Chairman.

The ownership of Times Newspapers Ltd is derived from the Thomson Family Trusts through the following channels:

---

[4] Lord Astor still has the remaining fifteen per cent.

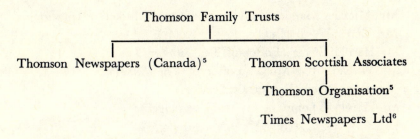

Thomson Family Trusts

Thomson Newspapers (Canada)[5]

Thomson Scottish Associates

Thomson Organisation[5]

Times Newspapers Ltd[6]

Times Newspapers Ltd publishes five separate papers in London:
The Sunday Times (with its colour magazine)
The Times (daily)
The Times Literary Supplement (weekly)
The Times Educational Supplement (weekly)
The Times Higher Education Supplement (weekly).

Lord Astor of Hever is Life President of the Company and the Hon. Kenneth Thomson is Co-Life President. At present, the Company has nine Directors. They are:
Chairman and Editor in Chief: C. D. Hamilton
Lord Robens of Woldingham, PC[7]
Lord Shawcross, PC, QC[7]
Sir Eric Roll, KCMG, CB[7]
Sir Kenneth Keith
Sir George Pope
G. C. Brunton
J. M. Coltart
M. J. Hussey (Managing Director and Chief Executive).

The Executive Directors are:
Mr Denis Hamilton, Chairman and Editor-in-Chief
Mr. Duke Hussey (Managing Director and Chief Executive)
Mr Ian Clubb (Finance Director)

[5] Public minority interest.
[6] Lord Astor retains a 15 per cent interest.
[7] National Directors. At the time of writing, there is a vacancy for a national director, to be nominated by Lord Astor of Hever.

Mr. Michael Mander (Advertisement and Marketing Director)
Mr. Derek Jewell (Publications Director)
Mr Harold Evans (Editor of *The Sunday Times*)
Mr William Rees-Mogg (Editor of *The Times*)
Mr. John Dixey (Production Services)
Mr Harvey Thompson (General Manager).

The main Board of Directors meets quarterly and the Executive Committee meets monthly at Printing House Square.

During week-days, the Gray's Inn Road presses print *The Guardian* (a daily) under contract. On the other hand, the presses in Printing House Square, on which *The Times* is printed each weekday, also print *The Observer* on Sundays, under contract. The three *Times* supplements are printed at Printing House Square. This study is concerned solely with *The Times* and not with its three supplements or with *The Sunday Times*.

THE TIMES MANAGEMENT STRUCTURE

Mr Rees-Mogg, Editor of *The Times,* is responsible to Mr Denis Hamilton, Editor-in-Chief of all five *Times* papers. Mr Duke Hussey, the Managing Director of Times Newspapers Ltd, is responsible for commercial policy.

Mr Hamilton, as Chairman of the Company and Editor-in-Chief, sets the annual budget of *The Times,* as well as for the other papers. Since his appointment in 1967, he has emphasised the importance of business news in *The Times,* on the premise that Britain, after all, is primarily a trading nation. He formally appoints the Editor of *The Times,* but gives him a free hand in running it. That, however, does not properly describe their relationship: they have worked together for years on *The Sunday Times,* and are close personal friends. They know each other's minds almost instinctively and speak to each other directly or by telephone almost daily. Mr Rees-Mogg would not make a major appointment on *The Times* without discussing it with Mr Hamilton beforehand.

Mr Hussey, the Managing Director and Chief Executive, has been in charge of converting the annual deficit of *The Times* for the past three years into a small profit in the first few months of 1973 (see the section later on Finance). This has been achieved by a number of measures:

— By instituting a general awareness of cost effectiveness throughout the whole company, resulting in careful control of all expenditure in all areas (for example, stopping of television promotion at a charge of £ 7,000 for each half minute for advertisements watched by millions of whom only a few are likely to buy *The Times*).

— By reducing staff costs.

— By ensuring strict adherence to editorial quotas (see later).

— By increasing the number of Special Reports in *The Times* to around 200 a year (see later).

— By changing the Business News section of *The Times* from a supplement to an integral part of the paper, thus making its size more flexible and therefore reducing costs (see later).

— Above all, by re-organising the advertisement departments and mounting a sustained drive for more advertising (see later).

Another aim of Mr Hussey has been to enable decisions at Board level to be taken speedily, to match the high speed of newspaper work in general.

The Move to Gray's Inn Road

The Times (and *The Daily Universal Register* before it) have been printed at Printing House Square since 1785.[8] New buildings were constructed for *The Times* between 1870 and 1874 (a century ago) which, in due course, were replaced by the present building, opened in 1962. Since then, however, the circulation of *The Times* has considerably increased; but there is no room on the present site for the installation of additional presses to provide additional copies. On the other hand, *The Sunday Times* presses at Gray's Inn Road are used to full capacity for only one day a week. It has consequently been decided to print *The Times* there on the other six days, together with *The Guardian* (see above). But, as editorial offices for a daily

[8] Even before that date, the King's Printing House had occupied the site from 1667—over three centuries ago.

183

must be adjacent to the presses, a site has been acquired for *The Times* offices adjacent to the Thomson building in Gray's Inn Road. On this site, new *Times* editorial offices are being built; it is hoped that they will be ready for occupation within the next year. Much time is already being spent in allocating between the different *Times* departments the space that will become available there. The printing will be transferred from Printing House Square to *The Sunday Times* presses without interruption. The Printing House Square building and presses have already been sold for £5.5 m. to *The Observer* which has prior rights as tenants of part of the building.

FINANCE

Capital Investment

Times Newspapers Ltd owns *The Sunday Times* (in Gray's Inn Road), *The Times* (in Printing House Square), the three *Times* Supplements and contracts for printing *The Observer* (at Printing House Square) and *The Guardian* (at Gray's Inn Road). The capital employed in the Company's business is approximately £25m.

Income

The main sources of income of *The Times* are as follows:

Advertising	67 per cent
Sales	32 per cent
Other sources (e.g., syndication, sale of waste paper)	1 per cent
Total	100 per cent

Expenditure

The main items of expenditure, in order of size, are as follows:

Production, packing and transportation to rail head	31 per cent
Editorial	22 per cent
Newsprint	16 per cent
Carriage from railhead, and sale	7 per cent

Cost of Advertising Department	6 per cent
Marketing and promotion	4 per cent
Administration, overheads and depreciation	4 per cent

Editorial Expenditure

The Editorial budget for 1973 was just over £ 2.5 million. Rather more than half this sum was accounted for by salaries.

The biggest departments were Home News and Business News, which, together, cost something over 40 per cent of the total. The most expensive department, because of the cost of keeping permanent staff overseas, was Foreign News (20 per cent).

ADVERTISEMENTS

The sale of space for advertisements in 1972 provided 67 per cent of the total income of *The Times,* as compared with 32 per cent from the sale of copies.

The high proportion of income from advertisements is due, in part, to an expanding market; in part to a new policy of 'go out and get it', instead of waiting for the advertiser to approach the paper.

Advertising, which provides 67 per cent of the income, takes up 41 per cent of the space.

Advertising in *The Times* is divided into

	Percentage
Display	20
Financial	14
Classified	53
Special Reports	13

In issues containing Special Reports, there is, on the average, 48 per cent of display advertisements and 52 per cent of classified advertisements.

Classified advertisements occupy an average of six pages in each issue. There are, on the average, four whole-page display advertisements each week.

This side of Times Newspapers Ltd has been handled since 1971 by an Advertisement and Marketing Director, at present Mr

Michael Mander.[9] He is assisted by the Deputy Advertisement and Marketing Director—Mr Donald Barrett.[10] There is also a Group Advertisement Liaison Manager who assists them in administrative and staff matters.

Some of their assistants work both for *The Times* and *The Sunday Times*—for example, the Advertisement Sales Administration Manager. But, under him, are two Controllers, one for each paper as well as a controller of a Central Statistical Office.

There is a special unit for *financial* advertising under a Financial Advertisement Sales Director, both for *The Times* and *The Sunday Times*. He pays special attention to obtaining contracts for large-scale Unit Trust advertising, and for the (paid) publication of company reports that often take up a whole page. He has a total staff of fourteen, of whom some are stationed in Manchester and Birmingham.

Lastly, there is an Advertisement Manager for advertising from the United States, stationed in New York.

I am not concerned here with Advertising Managers who work solely for *The Sunday Times*. For *The Times* alone, there are:

— A *Times* Classified Advertisement Manager with a staff of 47.
— A *Times* Display Advertisement Manager with a staff of 15.
— A *Times* Special Reports Advertisement Manager with a staff of nine.

Classified Advertisements

Classified advertisements are the basis of the solvency of *The Times*. It consequently has offices to accept and solicit classified (as well as display) advertisements also in Manchester, Leeds, Glasgow, Paris and New York (see above).

The intensified *solicitation* of classified advertisements is one of the Thomson 'revolutions'. Lord Thomson brought over an American

---

[9] Born 1935: started in 1957 as an office boy for Associated Newspapers: Marketing Director of the *Evening News* from 1969; *The Times* from 1971.
[10] Born 1928: a Regular Army Officer for five years, then an estate agent and art valuer; joined *The Sunday Times* in 1955 and *The Times* in 1972. As Mr Mander had to go to the United States I continued my study with Mr Barrett's help.

consultant to train advertisement solicitation staff, first for *The Sunday Times,* later for *The Times.* Previously, *Times* representatives (the Field Sales Force) called only on prospective clients. Now, nearly forty girls are installed on the ground floor of *The Times* officers in Printing House Square. Some receive applications from members of the public[11] for the insertion of classified advertisements, others accept insertions by telephone: but the majority spend their whole time ringing up potential advertisers. For this purpose, they monitor all other newspapers and, whenever they read, say, of some property likely to come on the market, they ring up the estate agent and suggest a classified advertisement in *The Times.*

Advertisement Rates

The Times sells about 350,000 copies a day, which would imply that it has about a million readers of one part of it or another. Most live in London or south–east England.

Classified advertisements are printed mostly in narrower columns (nine to the page, instead of eight). The rates vary from £10 to £22 per column inch.[12] There are discounts up to 30 per cent for several consecutive identical insertions.

These advertisements are grouped into many different classes, as follows:

Births, Birthdays, Marriages and Deaths
Charities
Court Circular Page (social engagements)
Postal Bargains (there is often a page of these on Saturdays)
Entertainments
General Appointments Vacant
Legal Appointments Vacant
Public and Parliamentary Notices
Contracts and Tenders
Legal and Financial Notices
Educational
Travel (in *The Saturday Review*)

[11] Tables are provided in the lobby where such applications may be filled up.
[12] According to a new tariff issued in June, 1973.

'Epicure'
'Connoisseur'
Gardening
Property
Furniture and Fine Arts
Restaurants
Art Galleries
Animals and Birds
Announcements[13]
For Sale and Wanted
Forthcoming Events
Holidays and Villas
UK Holidays
Motor Cars
Rentals
Services
Situations Wanted
Women's Appointments
Domestic Situations Vacant
Business Notices
Lectures and Meetings

A Personal Column has appeared ever since the first issue of *The Daily Universal Register* in 1785. It was entitled 'Personal' from 1886 and, later, gradually became known as 'The Agony Column' from the intimate nature of some of its contents, often including cryptic messages. Many people now read it regularly just for amusement at the range of human vagaries. It was traditionally on the front page; but when it was decided in 1966 to reserve that page for news, the 'Agony Column' was removed to Page Two. A year later it found its resting–place on the back page.

Display Advertisements

Display advertising is handled by a Display Advertisement Director. He has four deputies:

[13] Here starts the Personal Column (see below).

188

— A Display Advertisement Manager.

— A Special Reports Advertisement Manager.

— A European Advertisement Manager.

— An International Advertisements Manager.

There are fourteen Advertisement Representatives in London alone. They are in constant contact with the national display advertising agencies and attempt to get for *The Times* the largest possible share of the budgets of large firms for display advertising.

There are sub-offices in Manchester, Birmingham, Leeds, Belfast and Glasgow.[14]

The European Advertisements Manager, stationed in London, has four Representatives.

The display rates (according to a new tariff issued in January, 1973) are based on a charge of £16 per column inch. The price of a whole page is £2,816. The cost of a 'colour' advertisement varies with the page on which it appears. A 'solus' position[15] covering three columns, eleven inches high, facing the leader page, would cost £634 for one insertion.

There are special rates for display advertising in Business News, *The Saturday Review,* or a Special Report. A whole page in a Special Report costs £3,366; in colour it costs £4,600.

There is a fifteen per cent discount for any firm spending more than £10,000 in any one year.

For display advertising simultaneously in all four *Europa* supplements the cost is £7,733 for a full page advertisement.[16]

CIRCULATION

The cover price of *The Times* accounts for nearly a third of its total revenue. Following the Thomson Organisation take–over in 1967, a major circulation sales drive was launched which raised the net sale from 280,000 to 430,000 two years later. This expansion in

---

[14] Some also solicit classified advertisements.

[15] Printed alone, usually at the bottom of the page, to the left or right, and surrounded by editorial matter on two sides.

[16] There is a discount of 15 per cent; but in most of the editions this is counterbalanced by a tax of the same amount.

readership came about through the offer of highly readable and comprehensive editorial matter. This was, in fact, a continuation of the well–known traditions of *The Times* reporting. A more refreshing style had already begun with the introduction of front page news in 1966.

In the last four years, circulation has fallen from its all–time peak to around 350,000, as a result of doubling the cover price within a period of thirteen months. This was essential if the paper was to become less dependent on advertising, which is subject to the economic cycle of boom and slump.

The Circulation Department, as a revenue–gathering department, comes under the authority of Mr M. S. Mander, Advertisement and Marketing Director of Times Newspapers Ltd.

The staff responsible for circulation include:

— Mr F. A. Owen,[17] Circulation Manager in overall charge of all matters connected with sales distribution and administration.

— Mr C. W. Lovesy, Deputy Circulation Manager, whose duties are mainly concerned with promotion, publicity and the three *Times* weekly Supplements.

— Mr M. Paterson–Jones, who covers distribution, office administration and joint Newspaper Publishers Association (NPA) projects.

An Overseas Sales and Subscription Manager responsible directly to Mr Mander looks after overseas sales and subscriptions for *The Times*, *The Sunday Times* and three Supplements.

The information I needed for this section was supplied largely by Mr Clive Lovesy.[18]

DISTRIBUTION

Copies are distributed daily to 680 wholesalers throughout the UK and to over a hundred other countries. UK wholesalers supply

[17] Mr Owen has been with *The Times* for over thirty years, Circulation Manager for the last four.

[18] Mr Lovesy began his service with the Company in 1963 as a circulation representative in the North East and was transferred to Head Office in 1969. A year ago, he was appointed Deputy Circulation Manager.

in turn some 40,000 retailers. Wholesale groups like W.H. Smith & Son and John Menzies also have their own shops and bookstalls, but at the same time supply independent outlets. W. H. Smith have about 550 wholly-owned outlets and John Menzies 260.

Larger towns often have more than one wholesaler. Some wholesalers supply as many as a thousand retailers every morning. Small townships or villages away from the main distribution points sometimes receive copies direct from the publishers.

The Times is despatched by various means of transport:

about 50 per cent by rail;

about 36 per cent by road; and

about 14 per cent by air (10 per cent overseas)

Each night, supplies are sent out from the ten London rail terminals, some on special newspaper trains, others on normal passenger services. Distribution is mainly a joint operation encompassing all the nine national dailies. Bulk supplies are collected from the nearest railhead by wholesalers. If the railhead is some distance away, bulk supplies are transported to local wholesale depots by special NPA road services on a cost–sharing basis.[19]

Night flights are operated to Scotland, Northern Ireland and Eire.

In London, where there are sixteen wholesalers distributing *The Times,* each depot collects its own supplies from the publishing room (despatch department) and collates despatch with other national dailies to over 8,000 retail outlets. This operation is completed within four hours.

Some 32,000 copies are sent overseas: of these, 12,000 are printed on airmail paper to reduce freight costs; these go to countries outside Europe. For Europe, a special lightweight paper is used.

In many cases, overseas distribution is done jointly with the other national dailies to cut down freight costs.

The Subscription Department

There are now only 600 subscribers in Britain (a decline by a third over the last five years) and a further 6,700 abroad. The num-

---

[19] Similar arrangements are made for the Sunday newspapers, with a greater proportion going by road.

ber of subscription copies declines, since the cost to the subscriber includes postage, which is continually rising. Only those readers who live in the heart of the country (and cannot be easily reached by retailers) or libraries, public record offices and certain businesses are willing to go to the expense of subscribing. Subscriber copies are individually wrapped and sent by night postal service.

Unsold Copies

Unsold copies left on newsagents' counters at the end of the day are not normally taken back. Sale or return agreements are made with a limited number of retailers with a high rate of turnover at the discretion of the local *Times* representative, to help the agent cope with fluctuating demand. With the shortage of newsprint becoming critical, *The Times* is now much more restrictive.

Area Managers and their Representatives

The Circulation Department employs 26 Representatives who, in turn, are responsible to three Area Managers. The representative's function is to promote the sale of *The Times* in his area by planned calling on wholesalers and retailers. He is responsible for all matters concerned with the sale of *The Times, The Times Literary Supplement, The Times Educational Supplement,* and *The Times Higher Education Supplement.*

The Times Editions

Three standard editions are printed. Later editions are put out if incoming news warrants it or if the editorial departments wish to alter a page content for some reason.

Airmail supplies are taken from the second edition as it includes the previous day's American stock market prices which, owing to the time difference, arrive in London late at night.

The first edition, scheduled to be off the presses at 9.45 p.m., is sent to Northern Ireland, the North of England, Scotland, Eire and the Continent.

The second edition, off the presses at midnight, is sent to the Midlands and South Wales.

The third edition, off the presses at 1.35 a.m., is for London and the Home Counties.

THE EDITOR

It is the Editor who sets the tone of *The Times*: he has final authority throughout all the editorial departments. During the existence of *The Times*—for nearly two centuries—there have been several Editors who have also exercised considerable influence in British public life.

Over the last 62 years there have been only six Editors, as follows:

Geoffrey Dawson, 1912–19, 1922–44	(28 years)
Henry Wickham–Steed, 1919–22	(3)
Robert Barrington–Ward, 1941–48	(7)
William Frank Casey, 1948–52	(4)
Sir William Haley, 1952–66	(14)
William Rees–Mogg, 1967–	(6 years so far).

The average tenure of office has thus been over ten years for each Editor. This has given considerable stability to the paper and has allowed most of the Editors sufficient time to mould it according to their views.

The policy of *The Times* has traditionally been three–fold:

— To maintain its reputation as a *Journal of Record*. This requires accuracy, comprehensiveness, and a proper judgement on the relative importance of all items of news.

— To provide a *Journal of Opinion,* objective in its own outlook (and, hence, non–party). It is intended for a readership that includes politicians, senior civil servants, leading trade unionists and businessmen.[20]

— To feel free to *criticize the Government,* while recognising that the Government must govern and, as such, must not be belittled.[21]

The present Editor, Mr Rees–Mogg, was born in 1928 and is

---

[20] Many leading businessmen read *The Financial Times*. It is probably the most serious daily competitor to *The Times,* especially in the field of business, finance and the economy generally.

[21] Unlike its counterpart in New York (*The New York Times*) and Paris (*Le Monde*) which are basically in opposition to the Government.

now 45 years old. At Oxford University (Balliol College) he was President of the Union, a sure sign of later eminence. He entered journalism in 1952 through *The Financial Times,* from 1955 as Chief Leader Writer and, from 1957 to 1960, as Assistant Editor. Moving then to *The Sunday Times,* he was, over seven years, successively City Editor, Political and Economic Editor, and Deputy Editor. In 1967, with the acquisition by Lord Thomson of control of *The Times,* Mr Rees–Mogg was transferred to be its Editor. The following year he became a member of the Executive Board of Times Newspapers Ltd.

Originally a Conservative by inclination, he contested a Durham constituency in 1956 and 1959. In keeping with *The Times* tradition he is now non-party, although he remained for a time a member of the Carlton Club. He is also a member of the Garrick Club (being interested in the arts) and it is this which he has normally used.

When Lord Thomson acquired *The Times* in 1967 Mr Denis Hamilton, then Editor of *The Sunday Times,* became Editor–in–Chief of both papers. A limited attempt was then made to unify production and promotion and to share foreign correspondents[22]. But a weekly and a daily have different needs, and Mr Rees–Mogg has been given a free hand.

Under the previous Editor, Sir William Haley, editorial control was highly centralized. The present Editor has gradually decentralized editorial control all the way down. Every departmental editor has his own budget and controls his own staff. This has been accompanied by stricter financial supervision. Departmental heads are required to ensure that their expenditure closely follows that presented in the annual budget. This is one of the reasons why the losses of *The Times* have steadily declined year by year: it is now breaking even once more.

Another innovation has been arrangements to improve relations between *The Times* and the National Union of Journalists. A joint Consultative Committee, comprising the Editorial management team and representatives from the Staff side, meets regularly to discuss

[22] In Israel, the same correspondent serves both *The Times* and *The Sunday Times.*

virtually anything that affects the paper or its staff, though not editorial policy.

The Editor's Day

The Editor starts his day by reading all the London morning papers at home: this takes him over an hour. He reaches his office about 10.45 am and (with time off for lunch) leaves it between 7 and 8 pm. One day a week he comes back at 9.45 pm to keep in touch with the night staff. He then reads at the office the proofs of the following morning's paper. When at home in the evening, he ses the first edition at about 10.15 and remains in touch by telephone with the Night Editor (see later), putting through a call between eleven pm and midnight. It is rare for the Night Editor to consult the Editor after midnight.

Every day, the Editor has editorial conferences with different groups of departmental heads, as follows:

11.45 am	Leading members of the Business News Department (see later).
noon	General editorial meeting of about a dozen, when news items received since midnight are reported in turn, further news items anticipated, and space re–allocated if necessary.
12.15 am	Leader writers' meeting, of about four persons.
4.15 pm	General editorial meeting, to hear reports on news actually in hand.
6.00 pm	Meeting with departmental heads and others concerned with the make–up of the front page: much of the news is by then already in proof.[23]

At the 4.15 pm conference, a cyclostyled Editorial Schedule is distributed to all who attend. It gives the number of pages in the following morning's issue, the total number of editorial columns and

---

[23] There seems to be no time during the day for systematic general or departmental post-mortems on the previous day's issue (with the exception of Business News).

the number allotted to each department (home, foreign, arts, etc).
This is accompanied by detailed lists of the major news items at
home and abroad, and in sport and business news. It ends with the
name of the reporter allotted to each, as well as a list of the pictures.

From 11 to 11.45 am on Tuesday, there is a free–ranging general
discussion of policy with some half–a–dozen senior staff members.
(It is known as the 'Think Tank').

The rest of the Editor's morning and afternoon is kept free for
discussions with senior members of the staff individually (for example, with the Letters Editor at 3.00 pm: see later).

Lunch–time also enables the Editor to meet people. Once a week
he gives a lunch in *The Times* dining–room to someone important
in public affairs or the arts. This lunch is also attended by up to
eight staff members.

On Fridays, the Editor lunches in the office to free him for writing
leaders. On the remaining three days of the working week, he invites
those whom he wishes to see to lunch with him, either at an hotel
or, if they are connected with the arts, at the Garrick Club; or they
invite him to their own clubs. Of these people, about half are political
or international figures: the rest are connected with the business or
legal worlds.

The Editor tries to avoid social engagements in the evening but,
nevertheless, is so involved about twice a week.

He has regular weekly meetings separately with Mr Denis Hamilton (chairman of the Company and Editor–in–Chief) and Mr Duke
Hussey (Managing Director and Chief Executive). Mr Rees–Mogg
sees Lord Thomson, one of the Joint Chairmen of the Thomson
Organisation, about once every two months, and Mr Kenneth Thomson, joint President of *The Times,* at about the same intervals.

He is not in close contact with other London Editors. They all
know each other personally and meet from time to time at BBC
press lunches and elewhere.

He is not much involved with the Press Council, though he has
to deal personally with the more important complaints made against
The Times.

196

Size of Daily Issues

The Times appears every weekday throughout the year, with the exception of Good Friday, Christmas Day[24] and Boxing Day[24]. There are thus 310 or 311 issues a year.

The newspaper is larger in autumn and spring, and smaller over Christmas, Easter and the summer holidays, when Parliament is in recess and the Law Courts on vacation. One whole page for Parliamentary Reports and up to half a page for the Law Report are then saved. Many people are on holiday in the summer and there is less news in general. Broadly speaking, the weekly editorial content of the paper varies between 800 and 850 columns. But additional pages are added on special occasions each year; for example, for.

The Honours List (January and June): three extra pages.

The Budget (spring): three extra pages.

The Conservative, Labour, Liberal and Trades Union Congress conferences (autumn): an extra page a day for each (the organisers arrange the dates so as not to coincide).

The total number of pages available for editorial matter during the year is some 5,430. With eight columns to a page, this makes some 43,400 columns a year for editorial matter.

Editorial and Advertising Space

The daily quota of editorial space varies from about 128 to 151 columns according to the day of the week and the time of year. This provides a reasonably constant basis on which the composing and printing staff can plan the editorial setting. Like other quality newspapers, *The Times* depends for its profitability more on advertising revenue than on sales revenue. The daily space requirements for advertising are therefore added to the editorial quota to determine the size of the paper. This means that the size of the paper can go up or down according to advertising demand without affecting the editorial quota.

[24] One of these may fall on a Sunday, when the paper does not appear anyhow.

Space Allocations for Editorial Matter

Thirty–six hours before each issue (i.e., on Monday afternoon for the Wednesday morning issue), the Managing Editor, Mr John Grant[25], prepares a quarter–size dummy issue on thick paper. Each page is ruled vertically into eight columns. These columns are then allocated among the various departments according to their expected requirements. The dummy shows the exact position of each advertisement and the number of columns for editorial matter for each department. The dummy and the space summary are then duplicated and copies are sent to each department so that the following day (Tuesday for the Wednesday morning issue) each department knows exactly how much space it is likely to get. If, however, there is heavy rain, for example, and no cricket matches are played, the space reserved daily during the summer for cricket reports[26] can be reallocated at the last moment to some other department where the pressure of space is heavy.

The final allocation of space (in numbers of columns) for a typical issue was actually as follows:

Thursday, May 10, 1973

38 page issue = 304 columns.

Of this total, 142 columns were allocated to advertising and 162 columns to editorial, as follows:

Advertising		
	Display	30
	Financial	37
	Classified	75
	Total	142

---

[25] Born 1923: Oxford graduate. In journalism since 1947; with *The Times* for eighteen years; Managing Editor for four years; formerly Defence Correspondent and News Editor.

[26] As cricket reports take up more space than football reports, sixteen columns more are devoted to sport each week in summer than in winter.

Editorial	Front page	7
	Home	20
	Europe	4
	Overseas	12
	Parliament	10
	Women	6
	Arts	5
	Books	10
	Sport	16
	Centre	7
	Leaders/Letters	8
	Court	6
	Law	2
	Business News	43
	Motoring	2
	Broadcasting	2
	Crossword	1
	Weather	1
	Total	162

Running Total

Each week, the Managing Editor enters on a sheet (with a horizontal line for each day) the actual number of editorial columns printed in that week's issues compared with that planned. He thus can calculate the number of pages above or below the estimate since the beginning of the year. As the cost of paper and printing for two pages (the minimum unit to which a newspaper can work) is about £800, and he works on a tight annual budget, he plans to come out even by the end of the year by reducing or increasing the size of subsequent issues.

LEADING ARTICLES

Leaders are always on the right–hand side of the centre–fold under the mast–head clock device. Three columns are provided daily for leaders, compared with only two each for the other 'quality' papers — *The Guardian, The Telegraph* and *The Financial Times.*

The three columns in *The Times* provide space for 2,400 words a day, which allows normally for three medium–sized leaders of varying lengths or, occasionally, a big one and a medium–sized one, or, on a rare occasion of great importance, a single 'block–buster'.

Six out of every ten leaders are devoted to home or economic affairs; the remaining four to foreign affairs.

All leaders are unsigned and represent the collective opinion of *The Times.*

Home Leader Writers

The Editor himself writes about five leaders a month, dealing with major political affairs.

Other home political leaders, as well as some of those on local government and educational matters—some ten a month in all—are written by Mr Owen Hickey.[27] He has recently (1973) replaced Mr Iverach MacDonald as head of the Leaders Department, with the title of an Associate Editor.

There are two other Home staff leader writers: ; one is Mr Geoffrey Smith:[28] the other post was vacant when this study was made.

The Editor, the Associate Editor and the two whole–time home leader writers provide between them about three–quarters of all the home leaders printed. The remainder are commissiond from among *The Times* specialists. Leaders on economic affairs are commisioned from among members of the Business News Department (for example Mr Hugh Stephenson and Mr Peter Jay).

Foreign Leader Writers

There are four whole–time (and one part–time) Foreign leader writers who, between them, divide up the globe, as follows:

The Far East, South-east Asia and India: Mr Richard Harris (himself born in China)

[27] Born in 1924; an Oxford graduate. Joined *The Times Educational Supplement* in 1951. *Times* leader writer from 1955.
[28] He also writes leaders on Scandinavia.

200

Russia, Eastern Europe and East–West relations: Mr Richard Davy (a former *Times* staff correspondent in Germany)

Europe and the Middle East: Mr Edward Mortimer (an expert on France and a former Fellow of All Souls)

The United States, Latin America and EEC: Mr David Spanier (a former *Times* Staff Correspondent in Washington, DC).

The part–time leader writer, Mr Roy Lewis (a former *Times* specialist in Africa and the Commonwealth–i.e., Canada, Australia, etc.) covers those countries.

Planning

When an interesting report is due to be published, a leader on it is planned, some time ahead, for the day of publication. If available, an advance copy of the report is obtained and given to the leader writer or specialist so assigned.

When some important matter is being publicly discussed, it may be decided to prepare a leader on it, and a writer will be designated. No date will be fixed for its publication; it will appear when the writer has done it and space is available.

The remaining leaders on affairs of immediate importance are decided on, the evening of publication, at an Editor's meeting with the Associate Editor and the senior leader writers between 4.30 and 4.50 pm. Any of the other staff leader writers may attend the meeting if they wish. The subject, and the line to be taken, are defined and the writer designated. No specific research staff are available in *The Times* offices, other than members of the Intelligence Department (see later).

At the Tuesday morning 'Think Tank' (see above), current and impending crises are discussed, to crystallise the paper's attitude towards them. Leaders are not directly involved: but this discussion does have an effect on later decisions about leaders.

The Associate Editor

Mr Hickey works a five–day week and is off on Saturday and either Friday or Sunday. In his absence, Mr Richard Harris or Mr Geoffrey Smith acts for him. Mr Hickey arrives at the office at about 11 am and leaves at about 7.30 pm; he writes his own leaders between 5 and 6.30 pm.

All other leaders are sent to him, or to the Editor, for editing; but no major changes are made without consulting the writer.

Printing

Leaders go to the composing room by 7 pm (the absolute deadline is 8 pm).[29] Proofs go back to the Associate Editor for information only, as the leaders will have already been checked before being sent to the Composing Room and the proofs read in the Readers' Department.

Leaders can be replaced during the night, if necessary, in time for the later editions.

Influence of Times Leaders

It is impossible to assess this exactly. But as the leaders are responsibly written, with no axes to grind, they clearly have an impact on the opinions of an elite readership. How often have I heard at lunch at the long table in the House of Lords one Peer say to another: "Did you see that leader in *The Times* this morning?"

LETTERS TO THE EDITOR

For generations "I'll write to *The Times* about it!" has been the standard protest of the indignant gentleman. On the average, some 300 such letters are still received each day. They are treated in *The Times* offices with great seriousness; no fewer than six members of the staff are employed in handling them. The final selection of those letters to be printed is the Editor's decision.

All incoming mail addressed to *The Times* goes first to the Receiving Cashier to be opened; many of these letters are intended for the Advertising Department and contain money. All other letters are sent on to the Letter Editor, Mr Geoffrey Woolley.[30] He

---

[29] In the good old days, leaders could be written after dinner. The dead-line was midnight and there was no frantic rush to get the first edition out in time to catch the night trains.

[30] Aged 58; a Cambridge graduate; has been with *The Times* for 27 years and

is assisted by the Deputy Letter Editor, an Assistant and three women secretaries.

All letters intended for the Business News Department are first hived off,[31] while the rest are carefully listed on typed sheets. Each letter is given a daily serial number, listed with the sender's name and the subject of the letter. The number of letters listed daily varies between 150 and 450. No letter is ever solicited or paid for and all letters must be submitted in writing and not dictated by telephone.[32] No letter addressed in identical terms to several newspapers is considered.

The Letter Editor extracts from the daily list, and puts into a folder, those letters of interest which he thinks the Editor of *The Times* might wish to publish. To these are added the proofs of letters received on previous days, approved for publication and set up in type but held back for lack of space. The Letter Editor puts in a second folder other letters of interest, not recommended for publication, which the Editor of *The Times* might like to read.

At 3 pm daily, the Letter Editor sees the Editor of *The Times* or the Associate Editor and presents those letters recommended for publication in order of importance. *The Times* tries to cover all fields of endeavour and does not neglect the light touch. If there is a heavy mail on some subject—say, a hundred letters—at least one or two will be published in order to reflect that section of public opinion. Special consideration is given to letters from Archbishops, Cabinet Ministers and Ambassadors accredited to the Queen. But letters from Embassy public relations or press officers are not considered, especially if in reply to letters from other Ambassadors who would feel insulted thereby. Argument is encouraged, although replies may be delayed for a day or two to see if other replies are also forthcoming. Important letters not selected for publication are sent by the Letter Editor to *The Times'* own staff specialists for informa-

Letters Editor for the past twenty years.

[31] They have their own Letters to the Editor columns.

[32] Very occasionally, a letter sent from outside London may be accepted on the telephone to ensure publication the next day, if the subject matter will not keep, and the argument is particularly important.

tion. The specialist may urge publication, in which case the letter will be reconsidered by the Editor of *The Times*.

A minimum of four columns (half of the Leader Page—the most influential part of *The Times*) are at the disposal of the Letter Editor each day. Occasionally, an area totalling a further column (below the Leader columns) will also be made available. This allows for the publication of a total of 3,500 to 4,000 words a day, sufficient for twenty letters of an average of 175 to 200 words each.[33] This is more space than any other newspaper provides.

The receipt of all letters not published is acknowledged within four or five days. Standard forms of reply are sent of varying degrees of affability, starting with a printed card on which "The Editor of *The Times* presents his compliments and desires to acknowledge with thanks the communication kindly sent to him." The different forms of reply end with a typed letter addressed to the sender by name by which "The Editor thanks you for the letter you kindly sent recently, which has been read with interest. He regrets, however, it has not been possible to find a place for it in the correspondence columns.'

If a letter received is libellous, no acknowledgement is sent, as the mere acknowledgement is proof of 'publication' of the libel, even if the letter is read only by *Times* staff. *All* letters to be published are read in proof by a *Times* libel lawyer (see later).

If there is any doubt about the authenticity of a letter, the Letter Editor will ring up the sender for confirmation. But there is no system of regular verification, as this would lead to much delay and, in any case, has not been found in practice to be a necessary precaution.

No letter is shortened without the sender's consent. Sometimes a letter is returned to the sender for shortening, or for the exclusion of what might possibly be a libellous remark. Some letters not accepted for publication are sent on in original to the Editor of the Woman's Page, which also occasionally includes a letter of particular importance.

[33] In addition to those Letters to the Editor printed in the Business News Section.

The Letter Columns are made up about 7.15–7.30 pm daily. The Letter Editor or one of his Deputies is personally present to decide on the exact position of each letter on the page. This is not always easy as, unlike other editorial matter, nothing can be eliminated from any letter.

Cuttings are kept of all letters published; they are filed in the Intelligence Department according to subject and, for the last three years, according to sender. Earlier letters are traceable through the printed *Times Index*.

OBITUARIES

The Obituary Columns of *The Times* are almost as famous as the Letters to *The Times*: if you get an Obituary Notice in *The Times,* you are Somebody. That does not mean that you are necessarily aristocratic, rich or powerful, but that you are considered to have been of particular interest to the public in your own walk in life. Most of those mentioned in the Obituary Columns of *The Times* are, of course, British; but there is always room for foreign Kings, Presidents, statesmen, scientists, writers, painters, musicians and so on.

About one and a half to two full columns a day are reserved for Obituary Notices in *The Times,* far more than in any other London daily.[34] When someone of great national importance dies —such as Winston Churchill—his Obituary Notice may cover two whole pages (sixteen columns or 13,000 words, less pictures). In this way, *The Times* publishes some 600 major Notices a year. They very greatly in length, but have an average of 300 words each. In addition, there are brief minor mentions, averaging thirty words each. Subsequent tributes by friends of the deceased may be published. Sometimes, the author is indicated in *The Times* only by his initials, at his (or her) request; but the identity of the correspondent has to be declared to *The Times*.

Some of those whose names get into *The Times* Obituary Columns are decided on long before their deaths. Week in, week out, the Obituary Department keeps up its stock of draft Obituary Notices.

[34] *The Daily Telegraph* comes next.

It was built up largely by F. S. Lowndes (head of the Department from 1920 till 1938) and his successors, H. B. Walton and John Filmer. The stock was substantially overhauled after 1956 by the present Editor of Obituaries and many Notices were discarded. The present stock consists of between 5,000 or 6,000 draft Notices. Of these, some eighty per cent will actually be printed. The more important Notices are kept set up in type and are revised annually. They are further revised the night after the death is announced, for publication the following morning. *Whose* name is included in the files is a closely guarded secret: and, equally, *what* is written in the Notice.

The present Editor of Obituaries is Mr Colin Watson,[35] who has been head of that department for sixteen years. He reads a great many daily papers and periodicals to pick up names of persons whose obituaries might be prepared.[36]

He has an Assistant and a Secretary, and, through the hands of these three Fates, passes the thread of Man's life. They keep a constant watch for severe illnesses among the chosen few so that their Notices may be revised and ready when the moment comes for the thread to be cut.

Suggestions of names for inclusion in 'The Morgue' come from a variety of sources:

— Picked out from the Press by Mr Watson and his Assistants.
— Noted in Home News telex reports continually being received from the Press Association.
— Noted in Foreign News telex reports continually received from Reuters and the Associated Press.
— Reported by *Times* correspondents at home or abroad.
— Noted from daily perusal of the (paid) notices of death in those classified columns of *The Times* devoted to births, marriages and deaths.[37]

---

[35] Born 1919; entered journalism in the Provinces in 1938; joined *The Times* in 1949.
[36] He claims that his chief assets are 'a grasshopper mind' and a range of interests running from birds to railways to the clergy.
[37] 'Hatched, Matched and Dispatched'.

— Received by telephone or letter from relatives or friends of the deceased.[38]

The Notices are commissioned by the Editor of Obituaries who has on his books a wide range of outside contributors as well as members of the staff of *The Times*.

The very strictest anonymity is preserved, before the death occurs, during the time of publication, and for many years afterwards.

Obituary Notices usually have to be trimmed in order to fit the space available. If someone of great importance dies, the Editor of *The Times* will transfer additional space from another department's allocation (see above). When a death is reported late at night, the whole page may be reset for later editions of the next morning's paper.

Occasionally, someone dies whose existence had escaped the attention of the Obituary Department, and for whom no Notice exists nor can be prepared at short notice. In such cases, a tribute from a corespondent is arranged for later publication.

The Times is rarely sued for libel over an Obituary Notice. The dead cannot sue: but an occasional unhappy reference to someone else in a Notice may lead to a demand for an apology under threat of a libel action. Widows or friends of the deceased may sometimes write indignant protests at critical remarks in the Notice or merely at failure to report additional virtues.

A master copy, and three other copies, of each draft Notice are prepared. One is kept in a fireproof safe elsewhere in the *Times* building to prevent the possibility of generations of patient work going up in flames. The remaining copies are kept in cardboard boxes in steel cupboards lining Mr Watson's office. A card index is kept of names both alphabetically and by occupation. A catalogue of typed lists of names in alphabetical order is also maintained, for easier reference.

THE COURT PAGE

The Court Page owes its name to the Court Circular that usually starts in the left hand column of the Court Page, under the Royal

[38] In some cases, these senders are officials of specialised organisations; for example, the Victoria Cross and George Cross Association.

Arms. The Editor of the Court Page (called the Social Editor)[39] is responsible for recording the activities of the Royal Family, the Government, the Diplomatic Corps, the Church, professional, charitable and social organisations, and those distinguished in many walks of life. The Social Editor also compiles the following items:

'Birthdays Today'

'Forthcoming Marriages'

Reports on luncheons, dinners, receptions, dances, marriages, christenings and memorial services.

These items, together with the Court Circular, normally occupy only half the Court Page, the rest being often filled with items supplied by other *Times* departments, as follows:

'The Times 25 years Ago'	Assistant Managing Editor
'Latest Appointments'.	Home News Department
'Wills'	Home News Department
'Today's Engagements'	Home News Department
(and, on Saturdays, Tomorrow's)	
'Obituaries'	Obituary Department (see above).

Some of these items are movable and may appear on other pages. When there is no space anywhere else, the following items may also appear on the Court Page:

'Parliamentary Notices'	Parliamentary Department (see later)
'Sales Room Reports'	Miss Geraldine Norman (Home News Department)
'Science Report'	(see later)
'Law Reports'	Law Reporters (see later)

The Social Editor is Miss Margaret Alexander.[40] She has a Deputy and an Assistant who also does the outside reporting.

---

[39] Her office is called the Social Room, which is sometimes taken by outsiders to mean a Social Club. She consequently gets from time to time invitations for her members to participate in Club Outings.

[40] From a newspaper family. Started as a secretary on another newspaper in 1947; joined *The Times* in 1950 and became Social Editor in 1967.

Court Circular

A *Times* messenger usually calls about 7 pm daily[41] at the Buckingham Palace Press Office for a copy of the Court Circular. Its length is never known beforehand: when there is a State Visit to Britain or some other major ceremony, several additional *Times* columns are kept free in anticipation.

Birthdays Today

This item was introduced in 1963 by the previous Editor, Sir William Haley. Originally it was intended to accommodate up to twelve names daily of people distinguished in any walk of life: but it often contains more names if many well-known people were born on a particular day. A watch is kept on press reports, the names of men and women of interest noted, and their birthdays ascertained. These names are available to complete the daily roster when a 'vacancy' occurs. It may happen that, on some days of the year, very few distinguished persons (of interest to *Times* readers) were born, and, on such occasions, the list of names is shorter.

University and Church News

This is compiled by the Court Page Sub–editor who is also responsible for marking the type-face to be used in the headings of all other copy.

FOREIGN NEWS

The net space allowed in *The Times* for foreign news varies on different days of the week, as follows:
Saturday: ten columns, plus four on the Front Page = 14
Monday: twelve columns, plus four on the Front Page = 16

On these two days (before and after Sunday), there is less advertising: advertisers believe that readers are not susceptible to advertisements around the week–end, and newspapers are generally smaller.

---

[41] A telephone message is received from the Palace saying exactly when copies of the Court Circular will be ready for collection.

$$\left.\begin{array}{l} \textit{Tuesday} \\ \textit{Wednesday} \\ \textit{Thursday} \\ \textit{Friday} \end{array}\right\} \text{16 columns, plus about a half of the Front Page} = 20$$

When something happens overseas of great interest in Britain (e.g., the 'Watergate Affair' in Washington, DC) up to six additional columns for foreign news may be allowed daily for this particular matter.

Of the columns not on the Front Page, one quarter is devoted to Western Europe and the rest to Overseas. (The make–up of the pages would become too complicated if a special section were devoted to American matters.)

Considerable space is regularly devoted to Common Market affairs. The Editor of *The Times* considers that the space formerly devoted to British imperial news has now to be replaced by additional West European news. In fact, the European Parliament at Strasbourg is regarded almost as a third House of the British Parliament.[42]

Foreign News Staff

The Foreign Editor of *The Times* is Mr Louis Heren,[43] who also acts for the Editor of *The Times* in his absence.

The staff at his disposal consists of:
— A Foreign News Editor (Mr Jerome Caminada)
— A Deputy Foreign News Editor
— Two secretaries
— Three assistants[44] to the Foreign News Editor

[42] Reports on the proceedings at Strasbourg are sent to *The Times* House of Commons Gallery Reporters' office for sub-editing and not to the Foreign News Department Sub-editors in *The Times* building.

[43] Mr Heren is now 54, the son and grandson of East End printers. He joined *The Times* as a boy messenger in 1933 and has worked his way up largely overseas, eventually becoming Chief Correspondent in Germany (1955–60) and in the United States (1960–70). He returned to London in 1970 as Deputy Editor (Foreign). In 1973, he became Deputy Editor as well as Foreign Editor.

[44] One or more are always in the Foreign News Room from 10 am till 2.30 am the following morning.

— Five staff leader and feature writers on foreign affairs, under the Deputy Foreign Editor
— Sixteen foreign correspondents[45]
— Forty 'stringers' overseas (on retainer or linage, or both)
— Four staff technicians and secretaries overseas.[46]

Recruitment of staff

About a dozen applications for employment are received by the Foreign Editor each month, largely from experienced journalists on other newspapers, Reuter's men, etc. The policy of recruiting University graduates without journalistic experience and then training them on *The Times* was dropped some years ago. Vacancies for Foreign Correspondents are not frequent, and they are usually filled from within *The Times,* since the capacities of staff men are already known. Selection from within *The Times* for such promotion is good for staff morale.

Sources of Foreign News

Two–thirds of the foreign news printed in *The Times* comes from its own correspondents abroad, the rest from press agencies—such as Reuters, the Associated Press (AP), the United Press International (UPI: American) and the *Agence France Presse.* As far as news from the United States is concerned, there is a joint financial arrangement with the *New York Times.* In addition, *Times* news is syndicated to other newspapers (see later): this reduces the direct cost to *The Times* of foreign correspondents.

Transmission of News to The Times from Abroad

The Times first rented a Reuters channel in the late 1960s to connect the Washington and New York offices to London. This was, and remains, a channel rented exclusively by *The Times* for 24 hours a day. The two American offices are equipped with teleprinters and can send and receive messages at the rate of 66 words a minute.

[45] There are, in addition, Business News foreign correspondents—in Washington, DC, and Frankfurt—who also work for the Foreign pages.
[46] There are others locally paid.

Because of the success of this arrangement—and the under-used capacity of Reuter's world-wide communications network—*The Times* in 1971 extended the service to many more of its other foreign posts.

These do not have exclusive use of lines, but send messages over those used by the local Reuters office.

News messages handed over to the local Reuters office are pre-fixed 'Proprint'. When the message reaches Reuters Fleet Street office it is automatically identified as *Times* property and is diverted directly to Printing House Square for exclusive *Times* use. News from countries with no Reuter's office, or where the local *Times* correspondent so prefers,, *Times* messages may be transmitted by other systems.[47]

Transmission may be by cable or via Telstar. Sometimes, news messages from overseas are telephoned to *The Times* Communications Centre (see later) where they are automatically recorded. At the same time, they are taken down direct by high–speed typists (wearing earphones) onto typewritten sheets of special paper. Some twenty copies of each message are then immediately run off and distributed within *The Times* offices to the Foreign News Room, the Foreign Editor, the Foreign Sub-editor, the Foreign News Specialists concerned, the Syndication Department, etc.

The Foreign News Sub–editors' desks are staffed in shifts from 3 pm till 4.30 am the following morning, with maximum concentration on the period between 4.30 pm and midnight.

About one–third of all news received from overseas is not printed: some is cut out by sub–editors as redundant; some is considered relatively unimportant or unreliable. Some cannot be used for lack of space.

Post Mortems

From 6.45 am, while still at home, the Foreign Editor scans the front page and foreign news columns of all other British morning

[47] Messages for New Delhi, for example, are transmitted over an extra AP circuit.

papers to see where *The Times* has secured a scoop or has *been* scooped. Later in the morning, the Foreign News Editor congratulates or criticizes *The Times* overseas correspondents concerned.

HOME NEWS

The Home News Department was put in charge of a new Home Editor (Mr Charles Douglas–Home[48]) in the spring of 1973. He has at his disposal an average of sixteen columns (or nearly two pages) of the newspaper daily, plus a share of the Front Page and the Court Page. He also has overall responsibility for the two daily Sports Pages, a further 15–16 columns a day.

There is a staff of 51 (in addition to the Home Editor), as follows:
— 22 Reporters (see later)
— 17 Home Specialists (see later)
— Four at the Day News Desk
— Five Provincial Staff Correspondents[49]

There are also approximately 1,000 local 'stringers'[50]

The twenty–two Reporters are deployed in any one of the following ways:
— The Home News Editor keeps a diary of forthcoming events, such as press conferences or important Court cases, and allots reporters accordingly to cover them.
— Reporters are encouraged themselves to suggest matters for investigation and follow–up. If the Home News Editor approves the suggestion, the Reporter then carries it out.
— Tip–offs and suggestions from other members of the staff and from outsiders.
— When news breaks spontaneously (for example, an aircrash or a bomb explosion) Reporters already engaged on other enquiries as described above are re-assigned as needed.

---

[48] Born in 1937: educated at Eton; entered journalism in Glasgow in 1960. Joined *The Times* in 1964 as Defence Correspondent; Features Editor, 1970; Home Editor, 1973.

[49] Manchester and Birmingham (England), Cardiff (Wales), Edinburgh (Scotland), and Belfast (Northern Ireland).

[50] Paid by the linage used: a few are on retainer.

— Some of the Reporters have responsibility for special subjects (Arts, Motoring, Medicine) but are available for re-assignment when news breaks spontaneously, and also for the general roster for Sunday duty.

The following Home News Specialists are employed by *The Times:*
— Four political
— Three for labour affairs
— One for home affairs generally

A Parliamentary Correspondent (in addition to the Political Editor's staff and the Gallery Reporters (for both, see later)

Others for:
— The Social Services
— Education
— Local Government
— Agriculture
— Science
— Medicine
— Aviation
— Shipping and Transport
— Motoring
— Law (apart from Law Reporters: see later)
— Property
— Sale–rooms
— Defence.

Specialists (like Reporters) are expected to keep the paper abreast of all developments in their field, in consultation with the Home News Editor.

The proportions of Home News received in *The Times* from various sources are as follows:

Staff Correspondents and Specialists	68 per cent
News Agencies	22 per cent
'Stringers'	10 per cent

As already said, 'stringers' are not exclusive *Times* correspondents but are normally paid by the linage used.

The chain of command under the Home Editor is now as follows:

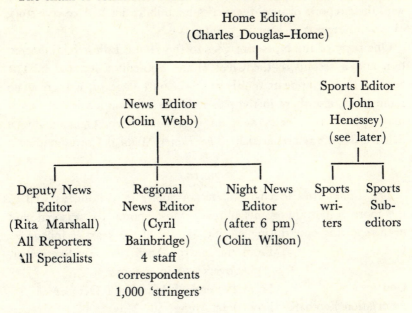

Home Editor
(Charles Douglas–Home)

News Editor
(Colin Webb)

Sports Editor
(John
Henessey)
(see later)

Deputy News
Editor
(Rita Marshall)
All Reporters
All Specialists

Regional
News Editor
(Cyril
Bainbridge)
4 staff
correspondents
1,000 'stringers'

Night News
Editor
(after 6 pm)
(Colin Wilson)

Sports
wri-
ters

Sports
Sub-
editors

Defence Correspondent

Till 1970, *The Times* Defence Correspondent used to be responsible jointly to the Foreign Editor and the Home Editor. In 1970, when Mr Louis Heren became Foreign Editor, the Defence Correspondent became a member of the Foreign News Staff. When Mr Douglas–Home (a former *Times* Defence Correspondent himself) became Home Editor, the Defence Correspondent was transferred to the Home Department.[51] Even so, he covers NATO meetings abroad as well as wars in any part of the world (including Northern Ireland). Events in Eire are covered by a Home News Staff Correspondent in Dublin, reporting to the Home News Department, yet living the life of a Foreign Correspondent.

Science Report

This is handled by the Home News Department. Since 1967, a daily Science Report is supplied to *The Times* by the scientific

[51] This transfer may symbolise the loss of the British Empire and Britain's increasing concern with Home Defence.

journal *Nature* (to which scientists in many disciplines habitually send their reports of new discoveries for publication). A reserve stock of several reports is kept in hand.

One copy of the typescript goes to the Home Editor for information and a second to the Chief Home Sub-editor for action. The Science Report appears mostly on the Court Page or, if there is no room there, elsewhere in the paper. If the information is startling it may appear as a news item on the Front Page. Occasionally, a Science Report is prepared by *The Times* Medical Correspondent.

SPORTS

The Times tries to cover all major sports in Britain, as well as the more important events abroad. Most sports are seasonal and need reporting only during specific months of the year, as follows:

Cricket:	From the end of April till early September, plus overseas winter tours
Golf:	From the end of March till October
Association Football:	From late August till May
Rugby Football:	From early September till the end of April, plus overseas summer tours
Athletics:	The summer months, though winter indoor events are increasing
Boxing:	The winter months
Racing: Tennis:	} All the year round.

The total amount of space in *The Times* allotted to sport consequently varies according to the season, and even according to the day of the week, as follows:

Winter: An average of one and a half pages a day (twelve columns). This may rise to sixteen columns on a busy Wednesday (a popular day for mid-week sport), while falling to ten or eleven columns on other days.

Summer: Two full pages a day—that is, sixteen columns (less an occasional advertisement).

The distribution of columns between different sports works out somewhat as follows:

Winter		
(twelve columns)	Racing	Four
	Association Football	Two
	Rugby Football	Two
	Other events	Four
Summer		
(sixteen columns)	Racing	Five
	Cricket	Five
	Golf	Two
	Tennis	One
	Athletics, Rowing, Yachting and Equestrian events	Three

The Sports Editor is Mr John Henessy;[52] he is assisted by Mr Tom Freeman as Deputy Sports Editor. The Sports Editor is responsible to the Home Editor (Mr Charles Douglas-Home), and attends Mr Rees-Mogg's 4.15 pm daily Editorial Conference.

Sports news reaches *The Times* from several sources:

— Its own full-time salaried staff
— Part-time correspondents receiving fixed annual retainers
— Freelance writers, paid by linage
— The news agencies.

Reports are handled in *The Times* office by nine sports sub-editors, under Mr Freeman.

The full-time staff consists of:

A Cricket Correspondent—John Woodcock (assisted by two or three others). When the English season is over, he goes on tour overseas with the English cricket team. At other times, he might report golf or football.

A Golf Correspondent—Peter Ryde, who occasionally also reports tennis.

[52] Born 1918, a mile from Printing House Square. Went to work in a City business in 1934. With the *Sunday Times* from 1945 and then *The Observer*. With *The Times* Sports Department from 1948: Sports Editor from 1954 (19 years).

The Association Football Correspondent—Geoffrey Green. When the English season is over, he, too, goes on tour abroad. During the Wimbledon Tennis Championship, he does a daily piece. During the summer, he broadcasts for the BBC.

A Tennis Correspondent—Rex Bellamy. During the winter, he covers indoor tennis, racquets, squash and occasional tennis tournaments in America.

An Athletic Correspondent—Neil Allen, who sometimes also covers swimming during the summer. He becomes the Boxing Correspondent during the winter, though sometimes there is an overlap.

Two Racing Correspondents all round the year—Michael Phillips and Jim Snow.

The part-time correspondents working mainly from April till September, cover:

Rowing—Jim Railton
Yachting—John Nicholls
Polo—Andrew Porter[53]

The freelance writers cover:

Summer:

Cricket: Alan Gibson (BBC commentator); Peter Marson (covers Rugby Football in the winter).

Equestrian events: Pamela Macgregor-Morris (from March till November).

Winter:

Motor racing: John Blunsden (from April till October); Association Football: Brian Moore (TV commentator); Gerald Sinstadt (TV commentator); Gerald Harrison (TV commentator); Brian James (*Sunday Times*).

Hockey: Brian Lewis.

Racquets and Real Tennis: Roy McKelvie.

Rugby Football: Peter Marson (see above).

[53] Sir Andrew Horsbrugh-Porter.

Several *Times* Sports Sub-editors[54] report on sports events over the week-ends (Tom Freeman and Norman Fox on Association Football, Gordon Allan and Richard Streeton on Rugby Football, Sydney Friskin on Hockey). Such reporting helps Sub-editors to keep their hands in.

The news agencies supplying sports news to *The Times* under contract are:

Home: Press Association; Exchange Telegraph.

Overseas: Associated Press; United Press; Reuter's; *Agence France Presse.*

The total number of whole-time sports staff employed by *The Times* is eighteen. Overseas events covered include:

Golf and Tennis: tournaments in the United States and Europe.

Athletics: major events all over Europe.

Boxing: world championships (mostly in the Western Hemisphere) and European championships.

Cricket: accompanying the English cricket team (1973 to India: 1974 to the West Indies).

Association Football: many European competitions.

Rugby Football: Peter West may[55] go as commentator to Argentina in September, 1973.

Racing: *The Times* gives more space to week-end racing in France than any other London paper. Michael Phillips (one of *The Times* Racing Correspondents) is given practically *carte blanche* to go over whenever necessary.[56]

The Sports Editor himself (Mr John Henessy) was due to go to Varna (Bulgaria) in September, 1973, to cover the International Olympic Committee meeting, where world sports policies are determined. He covers Winter Sports (skiing and skating), as well as filling in for his own staff specialists on Association Football, Golf, Tennis and Cricket when they are indisposed or several events occur simultaneously.

[54] Michael Hardy, the *Times* Night Editor, also reports on Rugby football.
[55] At the time of writing (July, 1973).
[56] Racing in France is also covered for *The Times* by a French racing correspondent.

The Times makes a special feature of important sporting events that occur periodically, such as World Cup Football and the Olympic Games. It claims to offer better coverage of the Olympic Games than any other British newspaper. It had six correspondents in Munich for the Games last year, together with Mr Hennessy himself, who was reporting the International Olympic Committee meeting.

POLITICAL EDITOR

It is rare for *The Times* to use home political news supplied by news agencies (apart from speeches outside London). Most home political news is gathered—directly or indirectly—from Government departments, politicians, Party organisations and so on. It must have a proper address and be correctly evaluated. This is the function of Mr David Wood,[57] the Political Editor, and his three assistants:

Mr George Clarke (deputy)
Mr John Groser[58]
Mr Michael Hatfield.[58]

They have their own tables and typewriters in *The Times* room behind the Press Gallery in the House of Commons, where *The Times* Parliamentary Reporters (see later) also sit. This is more convenient for covering Whitehall and Parliament than is Printing House Square.

Mr Wood starts his day at home skimming the national dailies and making appointments by phone. At the office, he sees the overseas press and looks at the advance copies he receives of Government reports, White Papers, Ministerial statements and, sometimes, their speeches. He may arrange to have a talk with the author of a report, or with a Minister, either at the Minister's departmental offices or in his room at the Palace of Westminster. Mr Wood sees the Prime

[57] Born in 1914. At the age of sixteen entered provincial journalism; joined *The Times* in 1948; Political Correspondent, 1957. Political Editor, 1968.
[58] Mr Groser is specially interested in business matters, Mr Hatfield in labour affairs (for example, he covers the Labour Party national executive committee's meetings). But both are all-rounders and, very late at night or at week-ends when they are on their own, have to deal with anything that comes up.

Minister at irregular intervals—sometimes as often as once a week and then only after a long interval. Three or four times a week he is called to other Ministries.

He will lunch with someone in the Press Gallery restaurant, or at a club or a hotel. He may have a drink with a visiting journalist or with an academic interested in the British parliamentary system and its conceptions of liberty. When Parliament meets in the afternoon, Mr Wood goes into the Commons Gallery at Question Time to get 'the feel of the House', and invariably when the Prime Minister or the Chancellor of the Exchequer is replying. Mr Wood always spends several hours listening to the Budget debate and other important debates. Occasionally he will visit the House of Lords, when there is an important speech. On the average, he spends an hour a day in the Press Galleries.

After the House of Commons rises, he will stay on for discussions with some of the MPs who happen to be around, with a particular end in view. Someone may try out a new idea on him: he thus learns much that is off the record. Occasionally, someone riding a particular hobby-horse may try to buttonhole him, but he knows from whom to disengage himself.

Sometimes he writes reflective pieces, on which he may work for days or weeks: mostly he deals with the everyday flow of news which is pumped over, hot, as it happens.

There are usually two columns a day written by Mr Wood with more pieces by his three colleagues, either over their own names or without by-lines, sometimes including some of his own ideas.

Some of the political stories are typed out and copies distributed in the office and to the Syndication Department (see later). Some stories are telephoned to the Communications Centre (see later); some are passed direct to the Sub-editors when there is a running story involving considerable changes. When necessary, Mr Wood will discuss by phone with the Editor (Mr Rees-Mogg) the implications of what he has discovered. On Tuesdays, he attends the Editor's 'Think Tank' (see above). When Westminster business permits, he also covers the monthly meetings of the European Parliament at Strasbourg.

It was in 1771 that daily newspapers in Britain began to report speeches made at Westminster. During the 19th century, the regular reporting of parliamentary debates gradually developed. The name generally used to describe the official reports is *Hansard,* due to the fact that T.C. Hansard was first the printer and then the publisher of the official reports of parliamentary debates (covering both the House of Lords and the House of Commons) inaugurated by William Cobbett in 1803. The present system of an official verbatim report was adopted in 1909, although it was not until 1943 that the word *Hansard* was added to the title —"Parliamentary Debates, Official Report."

Since its inception, *The Times* has been supreme in its coverage of parliamentary debates. It was at the centre of the 19th century controversies surrounding the reporting of Parliament, still technically a breach of privilege. Members of the staff have always been prominent in the affairs of the Parliamentary Press Gallery: the 1973 chairman of the Press Gallery is one of the Parliamentary Reporters of *The Times*—Mr John Winder.

In common with a number of other newspapers, *The Times* has its own room at Westminster, opposite that occupied by the staff of *Hansard,* with whom there has for very many years been a close and cordial relationship.

In *The Times* room there are the following staff:
— Mr Alan Wood,[59] Head of the Parliamentary Staff, who edits *The Times* Parliamentary Report
— Mr Robert Morgan, Deputy Head
— Eleven parliamentary reporters.

There are also a compositor (who has his own room, elsewhere, for transmitting reports), and four messengers.

The Times room also provides accommodation for Mr Hugh Noyes, *The Times* Parliamentary Correspondent, who writes sketches and impressions of the debates, taking in the main points. This is

[59] Born in 1927; entered journalism in 1943; joined *The Times* as a Parliamentary Reporter in 1956; Head of the Gallery Staff from 1968.

supplemented by the Parliamentary Report, which gives a much fuller account of what was said.

There is also accommodation in *The Times* room for the Political Editor (Mr David Wood) and his three assistants (see above).

The Times staff has four seats in the Press Gallery of the House of Commons and two in that of the House of Lords. Two of the Commons seats are for the Parliamentary Reporters, a third is for Mr Noyes and the fourth for Mr David Wood, or for one of his colleagues, whenever they wish to listen to the proceedings.

The Parliamentary Reporters

The Times is now the only national British newspaper publishing a full, self-contained, formal report of the proceedings in both houses of Parliament. Members of *The Times* staff do not depend on Press Association or other reports of Parliament: *The Times* does all its own reporting. Since January, 1973, consequent upon Britain's entry into the European Economic Community, the reporting has been broadened to include the European Parliament.

The Reporters, who cover the debates in turn, select for reporting what they consider to be the main points of interest to readers. Their reports from both Houses provide more than enough material to fill approximately one full page (eight columns) of *The Times* after every day on which Parliament sits. On Fridays, the parliamentary day is shorter and a briefer report appears.

Although the Head of the Gallery Staff and his deputy report frequently to the Home News Desk in Printing House Square, they and the rest of the Gallery Staff come administratively under the Managing Editor (Mr John Grant). The object of this administrative arrangement is to ensure that *The Times* Parliamentary Report can be produced as an entity in its own right, giving the Head of the Gallery Staff the freedom he requires to edit it as a whole.

Parliamentary Reporters are recruited nowadays mainly from provincial newspapers. *The Times* Parliamentary Reporters must have had at least three years of journalistic experience and possess a minimum shorthand speed of 140 words a minute (rising to 200) and a typing speed of 50–60 words a minute. The work is highly skilled: it takes at least a year for a newcomer to the staff to become fully acquainted with what is required of him. After a further year, having experienced the procedures of Westminster for at least two sessions, he becomes a fully competent Parliamentary Reporter.

Gallery reporters work a basic 35-hour week, four days from 2.30 till 10 pm and five hours on a Friday (from 11 am to about 4 pm). It is not customary for Parliament to sit on Saturdays or Sundays, although this has happened at times of crisis. Each night, two Reporters (known as 'Victims') stay on throughout the night along with the Gallery Head or his deputy. If Parliament remains in continuous session, one Reporter stays on after the last edition of *The Times* is sent for printing until the sitting is ended or he is relieved the next morning.

Reporters also cover morning and afternoon meetings of Parliamentary committees on major Bills or of important Select Committees. During the recesses, the Reporters work in other departments at Printing House Square, mainly in the Home News department or on Home or Foreign sub-editing. One man goes to the Sports Department.

Selection of Material

The Head of the Gallery Staff (Mr Alan Wood), knowing the agenda of forthcoming business, estimates each week the amount of space in *The Times* required for Parliamentary Debates. The number of columns of *Hansard* each day in both Houses runs into hundreds: *The Times* generally has eight columns (with about a thousand words in each, depending on the size of the headlines). Hence, *The Times* reports are highly selective. Space requirements can be adjusted each day as last minute additions are made to business, mainly statements on matters of current importance.

The Gallery Chief devotes the space at his disposal to the most interesting exchanges at Question Time, and the best points made by back-benchers. *The Times* prides itself on devoting more space nowadays to back-bench views than any other newspaper. The Head of the Gallery Staff is in the House of Commons Press Gallery during

Question Time to indicate which questions need to be reported, and also for Government statements. Throughout the debates, however, Reporters are on their own; for very important matters a colleague has also to be present to take a check note. This arrangement is also followed during Question Time and Government Statements.

Of the eleven Reporters at Mr Wood's disposal, two are usually in the House of Lords and the remainder in the Commons. When there is an important debate in the House of Lords, as many as five reporters may be sent there for the day, leaving the remainder to report on the Commons. At Question Time, or during the main speeches by Ministers and Opposition leaders, each Reporter does a ten minute stint: high-speed stenography is tiring. They work according to a roster, each Reporter returning to *The Times* Room to type his report, and to have a break before returning to the Press Gallery for his next turn of duty. At other times, they report for up to twenty or even thirty minutes.

Sub-editing

All other newspapers edit Parliamentary Reports at their own head offices. *The Times* report on Parliament is sub-edited in *The Times* Room at the House by Mr Alan Wood and Mr Morgan, assisted at times by other colleagues. The advantage of this system is that those who sub-edit the report are very closely acquainted with what has been happening in the Chamber: it is easier to convey 'the sense of the House'. The choice of which questions or speeches must be omitted because of pressure on space is made in *The Times* Room at Westminster.

Transmission

The edited reports of Debates or Questions are sent by messenger to another *Times* room on an upper floor where *The Times* compositor transmits the reports by punched tape to *The Times* computer in the Composing Room at Printing House Square. Continuous tape is fed into the computer which automatically divides up the messages into lines of equal length (to fit *The Times* columns) and inserts hyphens where words are split. Copy is then set into type on line casters which equalise the spaces between all the words in the same line ('justification'). A page of *The Times* is produced each day from Parliamentary proceedings.

The resultant type is sent to 'the stone' (see later) to be inserted into its correct place on the page. This has been laid out and designed by Mr Alan Wood at *The Times* room at Westminster. Meanwhile, a copy of each transmitted report is sent back to Westminster by tape machine for checking. These 'monitors' are used to cut reports which are too long for the space available.

Lay-out of Page

As just stated, this is done in *The Times* room at the Palace of Westminster in the same way as other pages are designed and put together at Printing House Square. Mr Alan Wood has miniature dummy pages; on these he will set out where he wishes each report to appear. For greater ease, the vertical columns are divided into 32 segments which allows of easy division into a half (16 segments), a quarter (eight) and so on. To the top of the page that leads is allotted the most important subject discussed in either House, whether it be by answer to a partliamentary question, by Government statement, or debate.

In this task, the Gallery Chief uses his own judgment, uninfluenced by outside sources, save the knowledge of the topics in which *The Times* is currently most interested. Each night, a member of the reporting staff goes by Underground railway to Printing House Square to supervise the make-up of the page on 'the stone'.

The European Parliament

The European Parliament meets at Strasbourg or Luxembourg every month (except August), for about a week at a time. Its proceedings are covered by *Times* Westminster Gallery Staff. Depending on the importance of the business in the European Parliament, extra space is allotted in *The Times* to enable the *three* Houses of Parliament to be covered at once. The reports are sent from Europe by telex to Printing House Square and transmitted to the *Times* Room at Westminster where there is a special receiver. This enables the European report to be sub-edited in exactly the same way as, say, that on the House of Lords. Such an arrangement enables the European Parliamentary Report to be sensibly related to the proceedings at Westminster.

The Law Report

The Times daily Law Report is produced by barristers and may therefore be cited in Court as authoritative. It aims at providing summaries of legal decisions that:

— make new law;

— develop legal principles;

— throw light on social questions (e.g., immigration, gambling, divorce or the custody of children); or

— are of special importance to particular groups of readers (e.g., 'who is a Jew?').

Hence the Law Report is not concerned with cases heard in the lower Courts or in Scotland (where a different body of law prevails).[60] Nor is it generally concerned with *facts* of interest disclosed even in cases in the superior Courts. These are reported in *The Times* news columns.

The Law Report confines its attention to the following Courts:

	Number of Judges[61]	Number of Courts sitting[62]
In the Strand		
Court of Appeal (Civil and Criminal Divisions)	14	3 / 4
High Court: Queen's Bench Division	44	12
Chancery Division	10	18
Family Division	16	10
In Chancery Lane		
National Industrial Relations Court[63]		3

[60] Some Scottish appeals that come to the House of Lords are reported in the ordinary way.

Also reported are appeals heard by the House of Lords and the Judicial Committee of the Privy Council.[64]

These figures show that the Law Report has to cover legal decisions in over forty different Courts.

The Times can call on the services of about 25 reporters, all of whom must be barristers, though they are never all available on the same day. Even so, the reporters must cover more than one court; this happens almost exclusively in the courts of first instance—in the Chancery, Queen's Bench and Family Divisions. The House of Lords and the several divisions of the Court of Appeal, both civil and criminal, are seldom left uncovered. They hear cases with issues that are often both difficult and important. Two reporters are allocated to each division of the Court of Appeal (the Civil Division, for instance), and they work one week on and one week off.

The selection of cases for publication is made in discussions between the reporters and the editor of the Law Report, Mr. W. J. H. Evans, himself by profession both a journalist and a barrister.[65] The reporters run briefly with him through cases which they believe are worth printing in *The Times*. Some days, Mr. Evans may have brought to his notice up to seven or eight cases of interest that are going on in the courts. Of these, some may not finish that day, or judgment may be reserved; he consequently asks the reporters to write up two or three of the others. Factors influencing his decision are how much space has been allocated to the Law Report that day and how long a report is likely to be.

---

[61] Some sit together: some are detached to sit in other Courts or to undertake other duties (e.g., chairmen of Commissions).

[62] For example, on June 21st, 1973, the day preceding my visit to the Editor of the Law Report of *The Times*.

[63] As a rule, a professional judge presides, with two members.

[64] The number of cases from Commonwealth countries that reach the Privy Council is now very small. All cases heard in the House of Lords are heard by Lords of Appeal in Ordinary.

[65] Born in Wales, 1917. Called to the Bar in 1956 and then moved from provincial journalism to Fleet Street. Joined *The Times* in 1961 as a Home News Sub-editor. Editor of the Law Report from 1967.

Mr. Evans has a desk in the room of the Council of Law Reporting at the Law Courts, and another desk in the Library at *The Times* office. He works at the Law Courts from about 12.30 noon till 5 or 6 p.m. He then moves to *The Times* where he gets his final allocation of space, draws up his lay-out and reads proofs. He sees the Report 'to bed' by 8 or 9 p.m. and may stay even later if there is much cutting and rewriting to do.

Some four to five hundred reports are published each year in *The Times*. Theoretically, cases summarized in *The Times* should be published the day after judgement is given in Court. But the flow of reports is never even: on some days there are half a dozen worth publishing, on others only one; hence one or two may be held over till later.

On the average, two and a half columns[66] are set aside each day for the Law Report. When there are several particularly interesting but lengthy reports worth publishing on the same day, the Editor of *The Times* may transfer additional space for this purpose from some other department. On the average, two cases are reported in each issue, in addition to those that appear as news items.

The Law Report does not always appear on the same page in each issue, as with certain other material (such as Leaders, Letters to the Editor, and the Court Page). The Law Report never appears on the front page or on the centre-spread; but it can be printed almost anywhere else in the paper, and thus is traceable only through the daily list of contents on the front page.

During the long court summer vacation (August and September) there are now several Vacation Courts. The National Industrial Relations Court now sits for most of September. Mr. Evans is thus free to take his own holidays only during part of the Long Vacation. If he is ill, he is replaced by *The Times* Legal Correspondent or by one of *The Times* libel lawyers (see later).

[66] As they are set in smaller type, there are 1,200 words to the column instead of the normal 800. This allows for the publication of 3,000 words of Law Report each day.

The Feature Page

Miss Margaret Allen,[67] the Features Editor, is one of the several women in senior editorial posts on *The Times*. Her Department is also responsible for the Woman's Page, for fitting in the daily Diary and the Crossword (see later), and for commissioning the Saturday religious article on the Court Page.

The Features Page is invariably on the left side of the centre-spread, and provides eight columns a day (less any space taken for an advertisement). This allows four Features to be printed daily (or three if there is advertising), a total of some twenty Features a week. Each Feature is an article of between 800 and 1,000 words—occasionally up to 2,000—providing an analysis in depth of some matter of interest.

Times Features are obtained from three sources:
— Salaried *Times* staff writers (about half the articles) at home or abroad.
— Freelance writers on retainers, some of whom suggest subjects for Feature articles.
— Other writers.

Some articles are sent in 'on spec', but only about one in twenty is accepted.

The general schedule of the Features Page is planned a week in advance, although certain anniversaries (for which special Feature articles will be commissioned) are entered in a diary a long time ahead. The deadline is 4 p.m. on the day previous to publication.

Part of the make-up of the Features Page on certain days is fixed in advance. For example, at present, Bernard Levin's commentary appears on Tuesday and Thursday, together with two or three other articles, one of which, on Thursday, is by Ronald Butt. Victor Zorza's column on Soviet and Eastern European affairs appears on Tuesday: Richard Crossman's political commentary appears on Wednesday. On Monday and Friday, the Feature articles are more ge-

---

[67] Miss Allen, now aged 40, holds an economics degree from the LSE. She entered journalism sixteen years ago, joined *The Times* ten years ago and became Features Editor this year.

neral.[68] Some of those on Monday may be connected with the news received during the previous week-end. On Saturday, when there is rarely advertising on the Feature Page and no Diary, and readers are more relaxed over the week-end, the full eight columns are usually taken up by Feature articles on subjects not of major importance, such as a sports analysis or a historical feature. On Monday there is a political column on the leader page by David Wood (see above). Once a month, there is a feature on Property in Britain and another on Property in Europe, printed in the back part of the paper. These are not Special Reports, but editorial articles surrounded by advertising matter. Similarly, Feature articles on Women at Work are supplied for the Woman's Page.

Staff for the Feature Page and Woman's Page

In writing, Miss Allen is assisted by:

The Deputy Features Editor (Mr. Sheridan Morely)

The Assistant Features Editor (Miss Crawford Poole, who is responsible for the Woman's Page)

The Fashion Editor (Miss Prudence Glynn)[69]

Three free-lance writers, on retainer:

— Miss Sheila Black, whose articles on Shopping appear three days a week (she has an office in *The Times* building);

— Miss Katie Stewart, on Cooking; and

— Dr. Hugh Jolly, the pediatrician.

Home News Specialists who contribute both to the left centre page and the Woman's Page.

The Woman's Page

The Times management does not believe that there are many women subscribers to the newspaper. Most women readers are married and read *The Times* because their husbands subscribe. Nevertheless, there are believed to be about 80,000 women *readers* between the ages of eighteen and twenty-four, and also older women.

[68] Though Lord Chalfont, former Disarmament Minister, now writes a defence feature article on alternate Fridays.

[69] Who is Lady Windlesham.

The number of columns and the contents of the Woman's Page vary on different days of the week, as follows:

Monday: 4–6 columns, devoted to 'Viewpoint', intended both for career women and general readers. It contains three articles:
— a signed Leader;
— an interview with an interesting woman (or sometimes a man);
— a general article.

Tuesday: 6 columns, devoted to 'Fashion Page'—sometimes a single article, with peripheral pictures, on what women are wearing (clothes and accessories), hairdressing and new ideas for clothing design. Direct merchandising is rarely included in the articles.

Wednesday: 4–5 columns, devoted to 'Children and the Family', with one article every three weeks devoted to Children's Health, and another to Children's Books. The third week, there are three articles, one on the general activities of children and families (especially during school holidays), family problems, and social welfare.

Thursday: 5 columns, entitled 'Home Page', with three illustrated articles of consumer interest (e.g., cutlery, design or cooking).

Friday: 5–7 columns on merchandising, entitled 'Shopping Around', by Sheila Black.

Environmental and welfare matters are often dealt with on the Home News Pages and not always on the Woman's Page or the left centre page. But Letters to the Editor on matters of special interest to women sometimes appear on that page rather than in the columns of Letters to the Editor.

The Woman's Page publishes separate pamphlets half-a-dozen times a year, on such subjects as:
— Where to live after retirement.
— Holiday activities available for children.

Most of the pamphlets are distributed free of charge on request.

Sometimes the Woman's Page offers goods to readers at reduced prices (e.g., an asparagus steamer) by arrangement with the manufacturers and linked with articles published in the same issue (e.g., on how to cook asparagus) (See also later).

The Crossword

This daily problem was introduced in January, 1930, and, to date, over 13,500 problems have been set, at the rate of about 300 a year. The diagram (normally 15 squares by 15),[70] together with a miniature diagram showing the correct answers to the previous day's problem, takes up two-thirds of a column. The material is handled in Miss Allen's office: it always appears on the back page for ease in handling by those travelling to or from work by trains or bus.

The problems are set by one or other of a team of six contributors under the direction of Mr. Edmund Akenhead, a retired solicitor living in the country. The contributor who has provided problems for the longest period is Mr. Adrian Bell, who first started in 1930 with ten problems a month, and still supplies four monthly. About one month's supply (25 problems) is kept in stock.

They are enormously popular, even among readers abroad. They are frequently done by commuters to help pass the time. Quite a lively correspondence about the legitimacy of individual clues goes on between solvers and Mr. Akenhead.

The Diary

The Times Diary first appeared in 1966 on the Leader Page under the heading 'As It Happens'. In 1967, after the Thomson take-over, it was moved to the bottom of the Feature Page on the other side of the centre-spread. The Diary is intended as part gossip column, part light relief. It occupies the equivalent of two columns, of which a little is taken up by the daily 'Marc' cartoon.[71] This leaves some 1,200–1,500 words a day for the Diary.

The Diary is now edited by Mr. Michael Leapman,[72] assisted by:

---

[70] In the holiday season, Jumbo Crosswords, 27 squares by 27, are set. Answers can be posted to *The Times* and the senders of the first three correct solutions receive small prizes.

[71] By Mr. Mark Boxer of *The Sunday Times*: he submits between one and three cartoons daily, for selection of the one that appeals most to the Editor of the Diary.

[72] Born 1938: entered journalism in 1958; with *The Sun* from 1964; a *Times* New York staff correspondent from 1969; Editor of The Diary from 1972.

Mr. Robin Young (for music, opera, theatre and much general reporting).

Miss Mirabelle Cecil (for the other arts and light humour—for example, a 1973 series on the quality of teas served by different London hotels).

A Secretary.

Nearly all the material for the Diary is generated from within *The Times* office, quite a lot being written by Mr. Leapman himself.

The Diary appears over the initials 'PHS', which simply means 'Printing House Square', the present address of *The Times* office.[73]

The 1,200–1,500 words a day are sufficient for some six items, separated by headlines. From time to time, the Dairy is wholly devoted to one subject, usually written by Mr. Leapman. Although the successive paragraphs are still separated by crossheads, it is, in effect, The Leapman Column, even though it is laid out more horizontally than vertically.

Some of the material for the Diary is planned in advance: most of it, however, is written the day before. About half of the material has to be gone after outside the office.[74] If there is a shortage of material, left-overs from previous days may be drawn on. (When they get out of date they are scrapped.)

The lead stories are briefly announced by Mr. Leapman at the Editor's noon conference. Technically, the Diary is a Feature, and most proofs are shown to the Features Editor, Miss Margaret Allen (see above) at 6 p.m. each day.

It is hard to assess public reaction to the Diary. About forty readers' letters about it are received weekly. Some of these letters form the basis of an item in a future Diary. Occasionally, such a letter will be included in the Letters to the Editor columns.

About a fifth of Mr. Leapman's budget is spent on outside contributions: the rest goes for staff salaries.

[73] It is shortly moving to Gray's Inn Road.
[74] Mr. Leapman intends to devoted more space to first-hand reporting and, for that purpose (when I saw him last summer) was about to go abroad in search of material.

The Arts Page covers the following subjects, both at home and abroad,[75] more or less in the order of importance indicated:

Music

The Theatre

Art

The Cinema

The Ballet

Television

'Pop' Music

The Arts (Assistant) Editor is Mr. John Higgins[76] who is also the Editor of The Saturday Review (see later). He is assisted by the following *Times* staff and 21 outside critics (some abroad):

The Assistant Arts Editor (Mr. Ion Trewin, who is also Literary Editor)

The Staff Music Critic (Mr. William Mann), with 25 years service in this position

Two Staff Assistant Music Editors

Ten outside music critics

A Staff Art Critic

A Staff Dramatic Critic

One regular outside dramatic critic

A Staff Film Critic

An outside Ballet Critic

A Sub-editor

A Secretary.

The Art Page tries to give an authoritative assessment of current events through 'notices' (reviews), interviews and feature articles.

The space available varies from day to day, according to the area on the Arts Page taken up by advertisements.

---

[75] During the season for European festivals (July and August), a third or more of the material published may come from abroad.

[76] Now aged 39, an Oxford graduate. In 1963, he became Arts Editor of *The Financial Times* (which recruited several members of its staff direct from 'Oxbridge'): in 1970, moved to *The Times*.

There are generally several 'first night' notices daily. When there are seven columns available for editorial material, there are often features or interviews in addition.

Mr. Higgins is in telephonic contact with his chief critics each day, and himself contributes regularly to the page, concentrating on music. The music coverage is planned six weeks in advance; theatre coverage one week ahead. A weekly sheet showing all the performances to be covered each day[77] from Friday to the following Thursday is cyclostyled and distributed inside the office. It shows the name of the critic responsible for covering each performance, and the hall where it will take place. A 'T' in the margin indicates that the review will be telephoned in. Most television and radio programmes are reviewed by the critics from their own homes and the reviews also telephoned in.

A critic receives two free tickets for the first night (abroad, only one free ticket is customary). The tickets are always for gangway seats, to enable the critic to get out of the theatre or hall quickly as soon as the performance ends. If it ends at 9.45 p.m., he will be back in *The Times* office by 10 p.m. The deadline for reviews is 11.40 p.m.; but, to prevent congestion, the earliest come in by 10.45 p.m.: this imposes rather a tight schedule. First night reviews are not ready in time to be included in the earlier editions intended for the provinces and abroad: in those editions they come out a day later. But they do appear in the last edition the morning after the first night, which enables Londoners to form an early opinion.

The precise space likely to be available for the issue prepared in the evening is not known until the morning of the same day, when the Advertising Department informs the Arts Editor how much space is needed for advertisements.

If a review is very unfavourable, the Night Editor will consult the Arts Editor at his home by telephone. This happens perhaps once a year, as critics follow the tradition of never attacking severely a young artiste or actor whose career might be severely impeded thereby.

---

[77] Sometimes up to seven in a day.

Musical and dramatic reviews are rarely submitted to one of the Libel Lawyers[78] for scrutiny: it is some time since a threat of legal action has followed an unfavourable review. Few artistes or actors adversely criticised write indignant letters to the critic or the Arts Editor unless they happen to know them personally. But friends of the artistes or actors—and members of the general public—often write to *The Times* about its reviews. About fifty such letters are received a week, in perhaps half of which the writer differs from the critic's assessment. Occasionally such a communication will be published in the Letters to the Editor columns: there is no space on the Arts Page.

No paid 'puffs' are ever published by *The Times*. Nor is there any link between the appearance of a review and the insertion in the same issue of a paid advertisement by the promotors of the performance or exhibition. Any attempt by an advertiser to influence the critic or the Arts Editor would be sternly repelled.

THE BOOK PAGE

The space available for book reviews varies with the publishing season. In January, when fewer new books come out, reviews occupy a single page (gross) or less: in spring and autumn this will be expanded to $1\frac{1}{2}$–2 pages (gross). About one quarter of each page (two columns out of eight) is taken up with advertisements, leaving six for editorial matter. Hence, in the peak seasons, up to twelve columns will be available for reviews each week, the bulk of which appears on Thursdays.

Mr. Ion Trewin is Literary Editor, and he has an assistant. Also on the staff is the Chief Book Reviewer, Mr. Michael Ratcliffe (formerly Literary Editor) and a Secretary. The Book Page has a pool of some forty freelance reviewers.

The Times automatically receives from British publishers a copy of nearly every new book for review, with the exception of textbooks and highly specialised works on economics, etc. Some 500 volumes (including children's books and paperbacks) are received

[78] See later.

each month, and are divided up in the Book Review Department into categories such as:

Fiction (sub-divided into new novels, crime and science fiction)
Non-fiction: political books
              biographies
              travel
              art
              music, theatre, films
              paperbacks
              children's books
              poetry.

Novels are sent to the outside fiction reviewers, sometimes with a note from the Literary Editor asking the reviewer not to overlook a particular book. A fiction reviewer may be sent a dozen books to consider for review, but, after reading them all, he may review only five or six.

Children's books are reviewed every three weeks on the Woman's Page, with additional coverage on the Book Page three or four times a year (Spring, Summer (twice) and at Christmas).

The Literary Editor himself picks reviewers and is always looking out for new talent.

Books sent to *The Times* which are not, however, selected for review are offered to *Times* staff news specialists for information.

The Saturday Review

The Arts Editor is also responsible for The Saturday Review. A typical issue consists of six pages, including advertising.

It includes:

A film feature article
Theatre, film, music and other programmes
Dramatic, concert and film reviews
Articles on broadcasting and records
Gardening notes
Travel feature articles and notes
Bridge and chess notes
Food notes.

The Business News[79] pages used to be a special separate section: hence it had to have an even number of pages. This made the daily adjustment of its size to the amount of material available somewhat inflexible. Since 1971, it has been incorporated in the body of *The Times:* but this still results in virtually two front pages. The Front Page of *The Times* is for the most important general news (including major business items): a second page in the back of the paper is devoted to other important business items, followed by other Business News pages with comment, features and news of lesser importance.

The Business News section occupies about six to eight pages daily, or up to a third of the whole paper. It covers British business, European and American business, and economic affairs anywhere likely to be of interest to British businessmen. It covers:

Commerce
Industry
Economics generally
Technology
Business education.

It includes daily a complete page of stock market prices[80] and, once a week, stock market capitalization figures, together with all the other material. It is more comprehensive than that of any other daily paper, save the specialist *Financial Times*.

Space in a seven-page Business News section (gross, less advertising) is allocated more or less as follows (not in the order shown):

A Front Page
A Centre-spread: two pages, of which the right-hand side would include City comment by the Financial Editor, business or economic features and a business diary. The left-hand side would contain Letters to the Editor on business matters, and some news items

[79] The first Editor, in 1967, was Anthony Vice, now a Director of Rothschild's.
[80] Containing investment data, price/earnings ratios, dividend yields, all set by computer.

Two pages of company and financial news

A page of market reports, equities, commodity prices and unit trust figures

A page of stock exchange prices.

The Editor of Business News is Mr. Hugh Stephenson.[81] He is assisted by about sixty journalists and seventeen clerical employees. The staff is allocated as follows:

Managing Editor (and Deputy to Mr. Stephenson), Mr. Dennis Topping

Economic Editor, Mr. Peter Jay

Two Assistants

Financial Editor, Mr. Andrew Goodrick-Clarke

Nine Assistants (producing the sort of material that used to be included in the City Pages)

Industrial Editor, Mr. Maurice Corina

Eleven Assistants.

Of the Industrial Assistants, three are permanently stationed outside London, at Manchester, Birmingham and Leeds (working also for the Home News Department).[82]

In addition, Business News has its own permanent Staff Correspondent at:

Frankfurt

Washington, D.C.

The Business News London-based staff includes four senior journalists, dealing respectively with:

Features

Personal investment (for the Saturday issue): Miss Margaret Stone

Business Diary

Business News Office Staff matters.

---

[81] Born 1938: Oxford graduate: Harkness Fellow, USA, 1962–4: Diplomatic Service, 1964–68: joined *The Times* in 1968: Editor *Times* Business News from 1971.

[82] In return, the Home News Staff Correspondent at Glasgow also works for Business News.

There are also:

Seventeen Sub-editors

Six Company reports Sub-editors

Eight Clerical officers (dealing with the stock market pages)[83]

Two Librarians

Seven Secretaries.

The senior staff of Business News keep in close contact with senior members of the Treasury, the Bank of England and the City in general. Mr. Stephenson's own mornings (as well as lunch-time) are devoted largely to this end. Each week, *The Times* Business News invites some leading figure to lunch at *The Times*. Senior Business News staff are frequently invited to attend formal City functions.

At 11.40 a.m. daily (before the noon Conference), *The Times* Editor (Mr. Rees-Mogg) has a meeting with Mr. Stephenson and the senior staff of Business News (the three Editors, the News Editors and those responsible for the Business Diary, and Letters to the Editor on business matters).

Between 5 and 5.15 p.m. daily, Mr. Stephenson has a meeting with his own senior staff.

The morning after each issue, he conducts a brief post mortem on its contents.

Mr. Stephenson visits the Continent personally about three times a year and the United State usually once a year.

Special Reports

Each Special Report consists of several pages devoted to a single topic, covered in depth; for example:

a single town or county in Britain (e.g., Glasgow or Cornwall);

a single foreign city or country (e.g., Barcelona or Afghanistan);

a financial, economic or technical activity (e.g., Portfolio Management, Building Societies or Telecommunications);

a cultural activity (e.g., Italian Ceramics or Food and Drink in Europe);

sport (e.g., Cricket).

---

[83] Before computerization, eighteen were employed.

These reports were first started in 1909 as Special Supplements. But they are now called Special Reports as some are embodied in the paper and are not strictly supplements. Their aim is, first, to interest and inform readers; and, secondly, through advertising, to make a profit for *The Times*. No subsidy is ever solicited or accepted by *The Times* from Governments, organizations or persons interested in the publicity given.

Special Reports come within the maximum of 48 pages that can be produced for any issue of the newspaper. They may run from two to 24 pages, with an average size of six pages. It is easier to have multiples of four pages—a spread of two sheets printed on both sides. Such a Special Report of four pages can be pulled out and read on its own. If it consists of eight pages or more, it is usually folded separately and placed at the back ('backset').

The size of a Special Report depends on the advertising obtained for it by the Advertising Department. The proportion of advertising aimed at is one half. If a Special Report of eight pages is planned, but only three pages of advertising is obtained, then the Report may be reduced to six pages.[84]

Because colour printing reduces the size of the paper that can be produced, Special Reports are not published on 'colour days' unless they are relatively small.

In spite of such considerations, Special Reports appear almost every other day. The frequency and size are increasing, as the following figures show:

Year	Number of Reports	Total number of pages
1971	115	642
1972	170	870
1973 (Jan.–June)	88	517

[84] The gross annual value of the advertising obtained for *The Times* Special Reports is around £1,200,000. From this must be deducted 10–15 per cent commission to salesmen, and other discounts.

Some subjects for treatment in a Special Report are decided up to six months ahead: detailed planning and commissioning normally start three months in advance. Seventy per cent of ideas for subjects originate within *The Times:* the rest are derived from suggestions in readers' letters, from trade associations or from foreign countries (for example, in connection with a national day, a new five-year plan or the inauguration of, say, a new hydro-electric scheme). Of the ideas originating within *The Times,* two-thirds are produced by the Special Reports Department and one third from other departments.

The Department commissions some two million words a year for publication in Special Reports. It consults orally *The Times* news specialists concerned with each subject before deciding from whom to invite contributions.

Of the illustrations used in Special Reports, half are supplied free of charge, twenty per cent come from *Times* sources, while the remaining thirty per cent are bought.

To prevent overlapping, the Special Reports Editor notifies his plans to the News Editors, the Woman's Page Editor, the Features Editor and other departmental heads. Copies of the Special Reports Department's programme, week by week for two months ahead, are distributed. These programmes show for each Report the proposed date (a few are without dates yet), the subject, and the minimum and maximum number of pages involved. A second and more detailed schedule for a whole year ahead is compiled for use within the Department. It shows various other factors (e.g., Bank Holidays, important exhibitions, conferences and sports events) to which certain Special Reports are tied. Also, where a subject is part of a series, the serial number is shown. Changes in the schedule are marked by an asterisk. The schedule also gives the initials of the planner in charge of the editorial matter for each issue, whether colour is to be used, the initials of the Advertising Department staff member concerned, and the number of columns of advertising (a) aimed at, and (b) sold.

There is a Commercial Manager for Special Reports in the Advertising Department, who coordinates the selling of space.

Each Special Report is printed as part of the issue of *The Times* for that day and the number of copies of any Special Report printed is thus fixed. But up to 30,000 extra copies have been ordered for sale separately later to persons interested. Most distributors, especially in foreign countries, are unwilling to order extra copies of Special Reports until they have seen the original issue.

Many Letters to the Editor concern Special Reports just published. The letters are sent over by the Letters Editor to the Special Reports Editor to see as specimens of public reaction. Cuttings of those letters on Special Reports which *The Times* prints are pasted into an album by the Special Reports Department.

The Special Reports Department is of considerable size: it has twenty-six whole-time, and two part-time members. These consist of:

The Special Reports Editor, Mr. John Greig[85]

An Assistant Editor (Planning)

A Business Editor

A Production Editor

Seven Planner-Writers (of whom two are whole-time reporters)

A Chief Sub-editor

A Deputy Chief Sub-editor

Five Sub-editors

An Art Editor

An Art Sub-editor

A Staff Photographer

Four Secretaries

A Clerk.

The two part-time members are a Special Writer and a Photographer.

About twice a year, the Department publishes a series of Special Reports: for example, on *The Towns of Britain* or *The Financial Centres of the World*. They are subsequently republished with a semi-stiff cover. A typical print order could be for 5,000 copies.

Between February, 1972, and June, 1973, *The Times* published Joint Special Reports in co-operation with *Le Monde* (Paris), *Die*

[85] Now 39 years old; a Cambridge graduate; in journalism for 18 years; with *The Times* for 15 years and Special Reports Editor for six years.

Welt (Hamburg) and *La Stampa* (Turin). These Joint Special Reports appeared approximately every two months. Each newspaper in turn assumed editorial control for one issue. The Joint Special Reports came out simultaneously in English, French, German and Italian. *The Times* edition was backset; the other three were integral parts of the issue for that day.

Arising from this co-operation, *The Times* and the three other newspapers are bringing out from October, 1973, a regular monthly newspaper to be called *Europa* to deal with economic, financial and industrial matters. This will also be in the four languages and printed as an integral part of *The Times,* although its format will be tabloid size. It will not be sold separately: if it is in demand, *The Times* circulation should increase.

Sub-Editing

After news has been collected and transmitted to *The Times* it must be evaluated and edited: hence it is passed to the Sub-editors. Their work starts in the afternoon and, with a shift system, continues until the early hours of the following morning until the final edition of the paper goes to press.

The first edition of *The Times* is scheduled to clear the Composing Room at 9.15 p.m.: the second edition at 11.35 p.m. (copy for the inside pages must reach the Printer not later than 10.45: the front page by 11 p.m.). The third edition must be away by 1.05 a.m. copy for inside pages by 12.15 p.m.; front page by 12.30).

The Sub-editors are divided into three sections, with the following number of staff in each section:

Home	20
Foreign	16
Sport	10

At each section, copy comes first to a Copy Taster in the form of typescript or printed telex messages. The Copy Taster rejects some items and passes the rest of the Chief Sub-editor of the Section. The 'Chief Sub' selects items to appear in the next morning's issue and passes each to one of the several Sub-editors of the section, together with instructions for length, handling and the headline. The item, when edited, then goes to a 'Revise Sub' for checking and back to the 'Chief Sub' for final approval, and despatch to the Composing Room for setting.

The Sub-editor has in front of him dummies of the pages at his disposal and indicates on them the space to be occupied by each item, with pride of place given to the lead stories.

This process goes on to a background of consultation with the 'Back Bench' (the Executive Editor (Night) and the Night Editor who supervise the contents of the paper). They are supplied with duplicates of all material, and they select the pictures for the news pages.

Material suitable for the Front Page is normally held for discussion at the 6 p.m. Editorial conference, when the Editor decides which story shall lead the paper.

The Executive Editor (Night) is Mr. Michael Hamlyn;[86] the Night Editor is Mr. Michael Hardy:[87] they work in close co-operation.

The Executive Editor (Night) has budgetary and operational responsibility for:

The Night Editor's staff

The Home News Sub-editors

The Foreign News Sub-editors

The Executive Production Editor and staff (see later)

The Photographic Department (see later)

The Design Department (see later).

Mr. Hamlyn works from 3 p.m. till 2 a.m. on a nine-day fortnight. Mr. Hardy also works a nine-day fortnight, starting at 4 p.m. One member of the Night Editorial Staff stays on all night until the final edition has gone to press.

---

[86] Born in 1936; an Oxford graduate; entered journalism in 1959 with *The Journal*, Newcastle-upon-Tyne, a Thomson paper. Brought to London in 1961 as a reporter on *The Sunday Times*. Became News Editor 1965, and an Assistant Editor 1968. Transferred to *The Times* in 1970.

[87] Born in 1916; a Leeds graduate; entered provincial journalism in 1937; moved to London (*Daily Telegraph*) in 1950 and to *The Times* in 1951 as a Foreign Sub-editor. Night Editor from 1970.

Material sent to the Composing Room from the editorial areas is cut into suitable length 'takes' for the linotype operators.[88]

In the Composing Room, type is made up in pages on 'the stone' (strong metal benches) in formes (heavy metal frames) in accordance with the dummies prepared by the editorial staff. The News pages are supervised by the 'Stone Subs' on the Night Editor's staff. Sub-editors from the specialized departments (such as Sports and Business News) handle their own sections.

THE LIBEL LAWYERS

English laws of libel are paticularly strict. An incautiously phrased remark in *The Times*, even on a wholly unrelated subject, could land the writer and the Editor in court. If the libel is proved, heavy penalties or damages may be imposed.

Most newspapers protect themselves by submitting to expert legal opinion proofs of what is to be published. Sometimes the checking (and rewording if necessary) is done by solicitors. At *The Times,* it is done by barristers.

The checking is done by a team of five barristers, working in rotation. Each evening, one is in *The Times* office from about 5 p.m. till 11 or 11.30 p.m.: he is then on call at home by telephone up to about 3 a.m. Once every fifth week-end, each barrister is on duty at *The Sunday Times* on Friday evening and Saturday for the same purpose. Of the five barristers now on *The Times* roster, three are in Libel Chambers.[89]

In *The Times,* the one on duty uses a table in a room adjacent to the Editor's. The work can be divided into two parts.

---

[88] By tradition, the copy is folded so that its nature is not visible to the operator when he lifts his 'take'. This is a legacy of the piece-work system, when one particular piece of setting might be more rewarding than another. While there is now a comprehensive pay agreement, the habit of folding still persists.

[89] One is Douglas Hogg, son of the present Lord Chancellor. The Libel Lawyer whom I interviewed was Mr. Alexander Bradshaw (Lincoln's Inn, called in 1965), who specializes in the day-time in civil law (in particular, employers' liability) with some criminal cases as well. He has worked as a Libel Lawyer for *The Times* since 1968.

The first is checking the proofs of the entire paper to appear the next morning, including all the advertising, but excluding the supplements for which other arrangements are made. The Parliamentary Report and the Law Report are privileged and cannot be challenged in Court: hence, proofs for these columns are not checked. As *The Times* leader-writers and the Editor of Obituaries are men of long experience, little checking is needed here either.

The Libel Lawyer draws the Sub-editor's attention to anything that involves the risk of an action, and will suggest appropriate alterations or deletions. In cases where the Libel Lawyer's decision is challenged, the matter will be referred to the Editor, or, in his absence, to his deputy, for a final decision.

The main part of the Libel Lawyers' duties is to serve as consultants to *The Times* staff, in particular to the Sub-editors (on their initiative) before copy is sent to the Composing Room. Such consultations may take place two or three times an evening.

The other part of the Libel Lawyers' duties is to check the proofs, as they come in, for legal problems. This may involve the Libel Lawyer on duty in quite a lot of running about, although a query on the proofs is comparatively rare.

The Libel Lawyers come under Mr. James Evans, the Legal Adviser to *The Times,* and his deputy. Their offices are in the Thomson Building in Gray's Inn Road. It is they whom the Libel Lawyers consult on particular legal points when in doubt. Mr. Bernard Levin, the hard-hitting and controversial *Times* feature-writer, usually consults them direct.

The Intelligence Department

In 1898, *The Times* acquired the *Encyclopaedia Britannica,* and preparations were made to publish a reprint of the ninth edition. For that purpose, an Intelligence Department was set up in *The Times* office to collect the necessary information. A library of some 20,000 books was therefore established. When *The Times* interest in the *Encyclopaedia* ceased, about half of the books were disposed of and the rest became the present *Times* editorial reference library, still retaining till today the name of the Intelligence Department.

About a third of the time of the staff is spent in supplying Editorial staff with information to ensure accuracy and completeness of the published news. The remaining time is spent in preparing, classifying and filing cuttings from *The Times* and other papers; in dealing with a continuous flow of Government publications, brochures, pamphlets and so on; in ordering and cataloguing books, and in work for the public. The Department is often called upon for help also by the commercial and managerial sides of the paper.

Much work is involved in dealing with letters addressed to *The Times* but not concerning any specific department (e.g., asking for information; commenting on the accuracy of statements made in the Letters to the Editor column; requesting up-to-date information for the preparation of lectures, projects, theses, etc.).

The Library

About 2,000 volumes are dictionaries, encyclopaedias and year books. To keep them up to date there are standing orders for the purchase of new annual volumes to the total value of some £600 a year.

The remaining 10,000 volumes are standard works, primarily on history, biography and English literature. A further £600 a year is spent on acquiring new Government publications and £250 for other books. Only a few of the new books sent to *The Times* for review end up in the Library.

An author/subject card catalogue is maintained.

The Business News Department has a small library of its own.

Cuttings Library

Cuttings are made in the Intelligence Department (I.D.) of all editorial matter printed in all editions of *The Times*. The Sports Department provides its own cuttings: the Business News Department cuts out economic, financial and industrial items, but all *biographical* cuttings are made and filed in the I.D.

Cuttings are also made in the I.D. from other newspapers if the item was treated there more fully than in *The Times* or had been omitted altogether.

Items to be cut are marked by senior I.D. staff: the cutting and pasting on slips (showing the date of publication) is done by junior I.D. staff. The results are returned to senior staff for classification and filing. Cuttings on specific subjects are filed in drawers by subject, in alphabetical sequence. The classification is highly detailed (for example, one drawer contains cuttings on all subjects from Muffins to Mummy Wheat). Biographical cuttings are filed in alphabetical order in boxes within a *Compactus* storage unit. There are approximately two million cuttings filed on home and foreign affairs and another million on persons, living or dead.

A duplicate set of *Times* cuttings is pasted daily in albums, divided into two series—a blue series for subjects and a red series for countries. This is done because the original cutting may get mislaid; or because a Sub-editor may find it quicker to use the book for a running story, rather than use the classified system in the drawers. The album categories are wider than those of the subject drawer classification. (For example, the album will show Aviation, where, in the trays, B.E.A., B.O.A.C., etc., will be shown separately.) Editorial staff may use these books without having first to consult the Library Assistants, as they do with the cuttings files in the drawers.

The head of I.D. is Mr. Jack Lonsdale,[90] assisted by a staff of [91] sixteen, with the following duties:

— The Deputy Head of I.D.
— Eleven senior staff (of whom one is a chartered librarian). Eight work in two shifts of four. One week, the shift will work from 10 a.m. till 6 p.m.; the next week they will work the following hours: one member from 10 a.m. till 6 p.m.; a second from 3 p.m. till 10 p.m.; a third from 4 p.m. till 11 p.m.; and a fourth from 6 p.m. till 1 a.m. I.D. is thus adequately staffed with two staff on duty for 15 hours every day (except on Saturday when, working with a skeleton staff of two, the Department

---

[90] Born in 1914; a chartered librarian in Leeds; *Times Book Club* 1948–1958 (then owned by *The Times*); with *The Times* newspaper from 1958; head of I.D. from 1959.

[91] There is also a Librarian and an Assistant Librarian in the Business News Department Library.

closes at 1 p.m.). The remaining four senior staff work permament day duties from Monday to Friday. They have the particular responsibility of answering telephone calls and letters from the public.

— Three junior staff (under 21 years of age) for cutting, pasting and routine work, not involving much responsibility.

All I.D. staff are members of the NATSOPA trade union (National Society of Operative Printers, Graphical and Media Personnel).

PICTURES DEPARTMENT

In 1973, Mr. Norman Hall,[92] Pictures Editor, had a staff of 31, as follows:

— Four Staff Photographers (plus two more on retainer)
— A News Pictures Editor (who is also the Deputy Pictures Editor)
— Four on the Pictures Desk, working day and night shifts
— A Secretary
— A Dark-room Manager
— Nine developing and printing staff
— A Manager of the Photo Library and Photo Sales
— A Deputy Head of the Photo Library
— Six Photo Library Assistants
— A Photo Library Clerk.

Photographic Assignments

The Pictures Editor keeps a Pictures Diary, covering fixed forthcoming events throughout the year. From this, and from information supplied by the Home Newsroom, a Pictures Day Sheet is compiled, 24 hours ahead. It lists the assignments (totalling some 3,500 a year), the Photographer assigned, and the dead-line for delivery of the pictures. A folder is prepared for each day, containing relevant information about all the assignments for that day (programmes of events, catalogues of exhibitions and sales, tickets of admission, names of contacts, etc.).

[92] Born in Australia, 1912; in journalism in Britain from 1949; on *The Times* since 1962; Pictures Editor from 1962.

Photographers

Staff photographers are journalists and, hence, liable to be sent on any assignment; but, in practice, they specialize. Lists are kept of free-lance photographers in London and, separately, in the provinces. If all Staff Photographers are busy and an urgent assignment must be made, a free-lance in the area is engaged by telephone. Provincial free-lance photographers sometimes telephone to the Pictures Department offering photographs.

Photographic Equipment

The Pictures Department supplies each Staff Photographer with two miniature cameras and a selection of lenses. Each Staff Photographer has his own locker in the Pictures Department. There is a Photographic Strongroom for specialized and reserve equipment, as well as a Film Store. Each Staff or freelance photographer signs for the rolls of film he takes. Some 75,000 exposures are made annually, which, at 36 frames to a roll, involves over 2,000 rolls of film a year. The number of exposures made on an assignment varies from half-a-dozen for, say, a bridge opening, to 20–30 for a portrait. As film today is cheap, the amount used is not a factor. The aim of the Photographer is to give the Sub-editor a wide range from which to select the most suitable shot.

Developing and Printing Photographs

Each photographer, on the conclusion of an assignment, is expected to develop his film or films in *The Times* darkroom. When the film has been developed, fixed, washed and dried, it is left for the darkroom staff to make contact proofs while the photographer writes his captions. For ease of handling, each film of 36 exposures is cut in half and both 18-exposure lengths are printed side by side on strips of sensitized paper. The contacts are then examined by members of the Picture Desk staff: certain frames are chosen and indicated on the contacts for enlargement. The required prints are made in the darkroom and returned to the Picture Desk for subsequent submission to the Night Editor.

Three additional contact proofs are made from each film: these go to the Picture Library for filing and syndication.

In addition to the 75,000 pictures supplied by Staff Photographers and free-lance photographers, a further 4,500 pictures a year on the average are supplied to the Library by outside agencies. About 20,000 prints a year are provided by AP and UP under contract.

The Picture Library

The Manager of the Picture Library is Mr. Ernest Mynn[93] (part of the Night Editor's Department). He is responsible for:
— The syndication or sale of all *Times* pictures (see below); and
— The indexing and storage of all pictorial matter prepared by *The Times* (pictures, charts, maps and cartoons).

Pictures

Of the four 'contacts' supplied with each negative of up to 36 frames, one goes to the *Times* Sub-editor for selection; a second is cut up for enlargement of the pictures selected; a third is kept unpunched and whole in the Picture Library for future reference, while the fourth is used for syndication.

Syndication of Pictures

At the same time that the first copy of the 'contact' is sent to *The Times* Sub-editor concerned, the fourth copy is sent by messenger to the Central Press Agency (off Fleet Street). This Agency handles syndication in Britain; it is privately owned and one of the biggest. There the frames that appear marketable are marked and dozens of enlarged prints are made which Agency runners then offer to different publications in London. The Agency makes over to *The Times* sixty per cent of all payments received for pictures published. Here *The Times* is in competition with other newspapers, with other agencies and with free-lance photographers.

[93] One of the members of *The Times* staff with longest service. Born in 1912; joined *The Times* in 1927 as a 15-year old boy messenger in the Art Department (then in charge of pictures). From 1945, Manager (then called Librarian) of the Picture Library.

The 'contact' is meanwhile returned by messenger to *The Times* Picture Library. A packet of 'contacts' is sent by hand next day to the London Express News and Features Services, together with a marked copy of *The Times,* indicating which pictures in the 'contacts' have been used by *The Times.* This Agency, also off Fleet Street, is owned by Beaverbrook Newspapers, and handles *overseas* syndication. Hence, *The Times* is in competition, not only with other British newspapers, agencies and free-lance photographers, but with their overseas counterparts. Payment is made monthly.

The Picture Library negotiates direct the sale of *Times* pictures for television, advertising and private purchase, as well as pictures taken for special occasions (e.g., Princess Anne's engagement). The captions stuck on the back of the prints are cut out from the issue of *The Times* newspaper concerned.

Picture Indexing and Storage

One or more 'bags' of 'contacts' are placed in an envelope marked with a serial index number. Where pictures have been actually printed in *The Times* (some 9,000 a year), the index number is entered in a card catalogue arranged by subject. Enlargements of pictures of personalities are filed in their personal folders (alphabetically arranged in a *Compactus*). The rolls of developed film are kept in shallow steel drawers. There are in these drawers 1,150,000 frames, some going back to before World War I.

All Picture Library Assistants are trained to undertake any cutting, pasting, indexing or filing to be done in the Picture Library.

DESIGN

The Design Department was set up in 1971. Miss Jeannette Collins[94] is the Design Editor, responsible to Mr. Michael Hamlyn, Executive Editor (Night). She has an Assistant and a Secretary.

Miss Collins is responsible for the lay-out of *The Times,* in particular of:

[94] Born 1939, a graduate of the Central School of Art and Design, London; Magazine designer; joined *The Times,* 1967, as Art Editor of the new Woman's Page: appointed Design Editor of *The Times* 1970.

— the Feature Page (daily)
— the Woman's Page (daily)
— the Saturday Review (since 1968).

In 1969, she redesigned *The Times Educational Supplement,*
produced in another building, and designed *The Times Higher Educational Supplement* when it was started in 1970.

The Times layout was redesigned also in 1970, when the present
modular system was introduced and a Style Bible was issued. This
specifies headline types and setting styles for the whole paper.

The Special Supplements have their own designer (Miss Valerie
Sargent) and an Assistant. They work on their own within the general style of the paper as a whole.

The Map Room

Since 1971, the Map Room has been administratively under Miss
Collins, the Design Editior, but operates largely on its own. It has
existed for over half a century, and now produces whatever maps,
graphs and drawings are required by *The Times* and the three
Supplements,[95] particularly *The Times Educational Supplement.*

The Map Room produces about 24 maps and twelve graphs a
month, plus two weather maps a day, with an occasional drawing.
Many of the graphs are for the Business News Section.

The Map Room has always had three cartographers;[96] they work
in shifts from 11 a.m. till 8 p.m. When a war breaks out (e.g., in
Bangladesh in 1971), and a new map of the area of operation is
needed almost daily, some of the staff stay on late to prepare a revised map for the later editions as the news comes in.

It normally takes about four hours to get a new map drawn. The
latest news on the situation is received from the Foreign News Department with a request for a map. One of the cartographers on
duty looks up the area in atlases[97] and makes a list of the limited

[95] *The Sunday Times* has its own Map Room.
[96] Two of them are members of the Society of Lithographic Artists, Designers,
and Process Workers, and one is a member of the National Union of Journalists.
[97] There is an adequate selection of atlases in the Map Room, including of
course, *The Times'* own five-volume atlas, and its subsequent productions.

number of place-names to be shown in the *Times* map. This list is sent at once to the Composing Room, indicating the type-face[98] to be used. Meanwhile, the map is being drawn. When the list of printed names is received from the press, it is cut up: each name is pasted on the drawn map. Cross-hatching is pasted on, to indicate occupied areas, etc. All this saves time on the drawing table. The resultant map must reach the Picture Process Department (see above) by 7.45 p.m. for a block to be made, if the map is to appear in the first edition. This means that maps must be ordered before 3.45 p.m. If an order for a map is received after that time, an old *Times* map may be brought out and adapted.

In the Map Room there is a stock of drawings for old *Times* maps, filed by country or region.

After printing has been done, the map is removed from the heavy supporting block in the Pictures Process Department, where the plate is kept for six weeks, in case it is needed again. Some *Times* maps are syndicated (see below).

Occasionally, a Letter to the Editor is received from a foreign Ambassador in London, or some other patriot, protesting against a *Times* map that has accredited to a rival country territory in dispute.

THE COMMUNICATIONS CENTRE

In all newspaper offices, it is essential for incoming news to be received with the greatest possible speed, accuracy and economy. Competition between newspapers is intense; the slowest goes to the wall.

Much of the news is received from the news agencies by tele-graphy; but *The Times* prides itself on the high proportion of its contents that comes from its own correspondents and specialists.

The Times has its own private lines from *The Times* room near the House of Commons Press Gallery, and type-sets direct. It also uses the surplus capacity of lines to the United States and the Far East belonging to Reuters and the Associated Press.

[98] Italics for seas and rivers.

On reception in *The Times* Communications Centre, all stories are duplicated and copies sent direct to all the editorial departments. Most stories from within Britain are telephoned in to a staff of highly skilled copy-takers who stand by in a special room in the Communications Centre to receive messages through earphones and transcribe them directly onto typewriters at a rate of eighty words a minute.

About a hundred thousand words a day are transmitted to *The Times* from all sources.

Pictures are also transmitted by wire. They normally take ten minutes each to come through. If they are urgently needed, the time can be halved, but the result is not so clear. Some seventy are received each day by wire, in addition to pictures received from the Picture Department (see above). Pictures are also received from a mobile *Times* transmitter that can be plugged in at the scene of an event.

The Communications Centre also serves *The Times* advertising and promotion departments. Some eighteen foreign newspapers with head offices for their London correspondents within *The Times* Building receive news through the Communications Centre and transmit some of it back to their own countries.

Within *The Times* offices there are several alternative methods of inter-commuication:

— internal telephones;
— pneumatic tubes (directionally controlled by dialling);
— overhead belts for taking copy along to the Composing Room;
— a lift to and from the Business News Department, situated on an upper floor; and
— messengers.

THE TIMES ARCHIVES

The Times Archives date back to 1785 and are valuable historical records. The early issues of *The Times*[99] have been bound and are kept in a fire-proof vault in the basement of *The Times* offices.

[99] The only known copy of the very first issue of the *Daily Universal Register* is in the British Museum Library.

The present Archivist is Mr. Gordon Phillips. His functions are:
— to look after the Archives;
— to collect important current correspondence at the end of each
  year and to file it; and
— to answer enquiries from research students, and others, all over
  the world.

Production

I am not going to describe in detail the organization in existence
for printing *The Times:* newspaper printing is a fairly standard
system and much has been written about it. I would, however,
like to describe the work of *The Times* Executive Production Editor,
Mr. Ernest Russell,[100] and of the Night Production Editor, Mr.
Anthony Norbury, who form the Editorial Production Unit.

The Production Unit was created in 1966 to organize the production of *The Times* and to coordinate this with the production of the
three Supplements—the Educational, the Literary and, eventually,
the Higher Education—as well as the growing series of Special
Numbers. It became necessary to have a senior man as a trouble-
shooter, authorized to give quick decisions.

It is essential for production to be carefully planned, because the
same plant is used to print *The Times,* its Supplements, and, on
Saturdays, *The Observer*. This requires the Composing Room to be
at work for nearly twenty-four hours a day,[101] with day and night
shifts.

The Times has three main editions, scheduled to be completed in
the Composing Room by the following hours:
— The First Edition   9.15 p.m.
— The Second Edition   11.35 p.m.
— The Third Edition   1.05 a.m.

Subsequent editions, with 'stop-press' news, are printed if ne-

---

[100] Born in 1917: the son of a *Times* night editor: joined *The Times* in 1936
  as a Reporter; 15 years on the Parliamentary staff, eventually becoming
  Chief Home News Sub-editor and Deputy Night Editor. Production Editor
  from 1967.
[101] From 8 a.m. till 4 a.m. the following day.

...y. Normally, the print order has been fulfilled by 4.30 a.m. Beyond that hour, not only does overtime have to be paid, but difficulties arise with distribution (see later).

Advance Production Planning

Mr. Russell has a blackboard on the wall of his office on which details can be entered in chalk. It is ruled vertically into columns for every day of two months, with blanks for Sundays and three other non-publishing days.[102] Horizontal lines are ruled, providing for entries for each day showing:

— The planned size of the paper for that day (total number of pages).

— The total numer of advertisement columns.

— The total number of editorial columns.

— The number of pages in Special Numbers.

— Whether any pages are being printed in colour.

For each week, the total number of pages is also given for each of the following periodicals printed on the same presses:

— *The Times Literary Supplement;*

— *The Times Educational Supplement;*

— *The Times Higher Education Supplement.*

The sizes of the paper are forecast a week ahead, based on editorial requirements and the anticipated volume of advertising. The size of a particular issue becomes firm the day before publication and is notified to the Machine Room. The size governs the number of "units" (a unit is 8 pages) to be brought into use on the presses. Thus, 32 pages require four units; 34 to 40 pages require five and between 42 to 48 (the maximum size that can be handled) require six units. A size increase, say, from 30 pages to 32 pages, is a simple matter, as it does not involve any unit increase; but an increase from 32 to 34 pages involving an additional unit needs an extra 'crew' in the Machine Room. Only in exceptional circumstances would a size change involving an extra unit be decided upon on the night of publication.

[102] Good Friday, Christmas Day and Boxing Day.

At 3 p.m. daily, a Target and Performance Schedule is pre̶
for inclusion in the Editorial Schedule. This is the basis for discussio̶
of the day's news at the 4.15 p.m. Editor's Conference. The Target
Schedule sets the latest time for the receipt of copy for each of the
pages of the following day's issue.

Pages are scheduled to meet the ability of the Foundry to cast two
pages every five mnutes.

The earliest deadline is at 4.30 p.m., for part of the Arts Page,
followed by 5.30 for the Law Report. The latest deadlines are 8 p.m.
for the Business News main page and 8.15 p.m. for the Title (i.e.,
Front) Page. Some thirty columns of 'stock' are prepared in advance, including some Feature Articles, Book Reviews, Letters to
the Editor, the Woman's Page and part of the Art Page.

Estimates of copy received in the Composing Room Desk at the
end of every half hour are recorded, showing separately:

City (i.e., Business News)
Court (i.e., Court Page)
Foreign
Home
Arts
Leaders
Law (i.e., the Law Report)
Obituary (i.e., Obituary Page)
Debate (i.e., reports of the Westminster and European Parlia-
    ments)

The volume of classified and display advertisemets handled is also
recorded.

The total number of columns of copy (and parts of columns)
received each half hour is calculated, and a running total is kept,
showing, at the end of each half hour, how much has been received
and, hence, how much has still to come.

A detailed typed report by the Night Production Manager, sup-
ported by statistics, is submitted the following morning to *The Times*
Editor-in-Chief (Mr. Hamilton) and the Managing Director (Mr.
Hussey). The report covers Composing, Reading, Picture Processing,
Machine Room, Colour Printing and Distribution to Wholesalers.

The statistics show the times of copy flow (see above), the target, and actual times 'off stone' of each page of *The Times,* the total number of copies printed for each edition on various qualities of paper, and the distribution of copies at home and abroad.

Journalist Staff

The total journalist staff of *The Times* is about 285, including Foreign Correspondents and Special Numbers staff. There are a further ninety clerical editorial staff—Library Assistants, Prices Clerks, Secretaries and so on.

Among the 18 women journalists employed, ten are in executive positions.

Staff Supervision

Staff supervision is now highly decentralised, the prime responsibility resting with heads of departments. To them, the Managing Editor issues memoranda on matters affecting more than one department. Copies are filed in his office by subject: they are not numbered circulars.

There is no formal daily post mortem on the last edition of the paper. Heads of departments discuss the more obvious errors with the staff concerned. The Editor may discuss errors or omissions at the morning Editorial Conference of heads of departments.

Appointments

About five per cent of the posts fall vacant each year. *The Times* seldom advertises vacancies but keeps a waiting list of applicants. Occasionally, someone leaving is asked to suggest a possible successor from outside, if there is no obvious candidate already on the staff.

In accordance with a national agreement with the National Union of Journalists, applicants for journalists' posts on *The Times* are normally required to have had at least three years journalistic experience. Some applicants have started on provincial newspapers and then came to another London paper: others apply direct to *The Times* from the provinces. From July, 1973, the minimum salary for a journalist on *The Times* (as on other national newspapers) was £ 2,900 a year.

All applications are referred to Mr. John Grant, the Managing Editor. He weeds out the obviously unsuitable applicants and interviews the remainder. Those whose skills and personality are acceptable are recorded in a register for consideration when vacancies arise. There are several hundred names on the register; but most applicants have probably already found work elsewhere. The number of suitable candidates on the register and still available at any one time varies between thirty and fifty, which makes possible a short list of up to half-a-dozen for a particular vacancy.

When a vacancy occurs, the papers of the short-listed candidates on the register are sent to the head of the department concerned for one to be chosen.

The higher posts—such as those of leader writers—are normally filled by promotion from among more junior *Times* staff: and it is the lower post that then becomes vacant.

Occasionally, some useful member of the staff who begins to get stale in his present work is offered a cross-posting to work of equal importance elsewhere on *The Times*.

Special consideration is given to 'high-flyers' for whom experience in a number of different departments is specially arranged to fit them eventually for senior posts while still young.

Staff Leave

Journalists are entitled to five weeks paid holiday a year. Clerical staff get four weeks a year for their first five years of service, and then five weeks.

Termination of Appointments

No-one can be dismissed without the explicit authority of the Editor or of the Managing Editor.

When the number of staff was reduced after the Thomson take-over, no-one was actually dismissed. The number employed was run down by wastage, leaving vacancies due to normal resignation or retirement unfilled.

Pensions

Times staff become eligible for pensions at the age of 65 (women at 60). There are two pension schemes:

— *Scheme A* (for mechanical staff). The Pension Fund has 1,250 members, of whom 840 are still working, 240 are pensioners and 170 are widows of members.

— *Scheme B* (for editorial staff, etc). The Pension Fund has 877 members, of whom 610 are still working, 190 are pensioners and 77 are widows.

Neither Pension Fund is tied to the cost of living. Both Funds are now closed and new members join the Thomson Organization pension scheme.

Labour Relations

Labour relations with the *Times* Chapel of the National Union of Journalists are handled by the Managing Editor (Mr. Grant). There is also an Editorial Consultative Committee, on which the staff side provide twelve representatives. It meets about once a month, and enables editorial matters to be discussed between editorial management and journalists and allows the staff to be consulted about new developments. Each side puts out its own version of the proceedings.

Other Unions involved in the production of *The Times* include:

N.G.A. (National Graphical Association)

    Compositors

    Readers

    Machine managers

    Stereotype workers

    Press telegraphists

N.A.T.S.O.P.A.

    Clerks

    Machine assistants

    General assistants

    Copy readers

    Revisers

S.O.G.A.T. (Society of Graphical and Allied Trades)
    Drivers
    Warehousemen
    Press-men
S.L.A.D.E. (Society of Lithographic Artists, Designers, Engravers and Process Workers)
    Process camera operators
    Artists
    Etchers
    Routers
    Mounters
A.E.W. (Amalgamated Engineers and Foundry Workers)
    General Engineers
E.E.T.P.U. (Electrical, Electronic, Telecommunications and Plumbing Union)
    Electricians
    Plumbers
U.C.A.T.T. (Union of Constructional and Allied Trades and Technicians)
    Carpenters
    Painters
National Union of Sheet-Metal Workers, Coppersmiths and Heating and Domestic Engineers
    Heating Engineers

This means that in the Composing Room, alone, men of four different Unions are involved, as follows:
N.G.A.
    Compositors
    Linotype operators
    Perforator operators
S.O.G.A.T.
    Press-men
A.E.W.
    Linotype engineers
    General engineers

N.A.T.S.O.P.A.
Assistants
Electricians

TIMES NEWSPAPERS LTD. PUBLISHING DIVISION
AND TIMES SUPPLEMENTS

The Times Newspapers Ltd. Publishing Division has been headed since 1971 by Mr. Derek Jewell,[103] assisted by a staff of fifteen. Mr. Jewell is also in charge of publishing the three *Times* Supplements (Literary, Educational and Higher Education), an operation that he has headed since 1968. The Supplements take up a quarter of his time: the rest is devoted to the Publishing Division, which handles the Company's non-newspaper material, ranging from books to microfilm. The current list of books and pamphlets has 28 items: they run in price from 15 p (for facsimile reprints of historic issues of *The Times*) to £20 for *The Times Comprehensive Atlas of the World*. Another list—of posters, wall charts and prints—contains 47 items. There are also several series of booklets and folders—*Times Authors, Issues of Today,* and *The Times Topics.* A selection of film strip of *The Sunday Times* for 1972–73 is published at £10 a set.

The Publishing Division also handles Readers' Offers (for example, specially produced gramophone records at reduced prices) which bring in a profit of some £100,000 a year. The Division is free to undertake any entrepreneurial activity that will benefit Times Newspapers Ltd., and is in accord with the Company's reputation and image. It is at present planning several television programmes based on archival material. It also deals with Syndication (see later).

Two of the Division's publications specifically concern *The Times* daily issues. The first consists of photographic copies on 35-millimetre microfilm, of all five Times Newspapers Ltd. periodicals, including *The Times*. The films are arranged by annual volumes varying in size from a small number of pages for 1785 (for £8.00) to the much more bulky volume for 1972 (for £86.75). They are

---

[103] Born 1927: Oxford graduate; entered journalism in 1951 with the *Liverpool Daily Post:* Assistant Editor of *The Sunday Times* from 1962: still a 'pop' and jazz music critic for that paper.

manufactured by the Microfilm Corporation of America and sold by a Times Newspaper Ltd. subsidary—Newspaper Archive Development Ltd., of Reading (England).

The second publication is *The Times Index*, in bound volumes. For the years 1790 to 1905 there are 65 volumes at $22 a volume: for 1906 to 1960 at prices ranging from $44 to $110; and, from 1967 onwards (six volumes for each year), at a cost of £30.60 a year. They are bought by many reference libraries.

Syndication

A great deal of care is taken to see that *Times* reports and articles are objective, accurate and comprehensive. Hence they are much in demand by other periodicals and news services abroad. Nearly all *Times* material is, however, copyright; permission to use it, after it has once been printed, must be negotiated with *The Times* by each periodical or news agency separately. These negotiations are undertaken by the Times Newspapers Ltd. Syndication Department whose representative in *The Times* offices is Mr. Brian Packham,[104] with one Secretary.

Only one newspaper or news agency in each city or area is granted the right to reprint *Times* material. The amount paid for this right depends on the size of the circulation of the newspaper and its economic position. Each periodical and agency may re-syndicate the *Times* material within its own area and so recoup a percentage of the fee paid to *The Times*.

At present, *The Times* has syndication agreements with 31 foreign papers. These can be divided into three groups:
— Those with their own offices and staff within *The Times* building (Eighteen papers).
— Those with their own offices and staff elsewhere in London (Five).
— Those with no London offices of their own (Eight).

[104] One of the men with the longest service with *The Times* (41 years). Born in 1917, he joined *The Times* as a copy boy at the age of fifteen. Later Chief Telephonist and on the Night News Staff. Syndication Executive since 1970.

The geographical distribution of the place of publication of these papers overseas, or the head office of the news agencies, is as follows:

Europe	12
The Americas	8
Asia	7
Africa	2
Australia	2

The Times syndication agreement with each newspaper or agency gives exclusive rights of co-publication, within an agreed area, of material from all sections of *The Times except* the following:
— Letters to the Editor (the copyright remains with the authors).
— News Agency reports (unless agreed in advance).
— Special articles and feature articles with restricted copyright (indicated by a C in a circle at the end of each: but the right of first option is accorded).
— Photographs, maps, cartoons, diagrams, charts and crosswords (the rights are sold separately by *The Times* Picture Department: see earlier).
— Material from the three *Times* Supplements—Literary, Education and Higher Education (only the right of first option is accorded).

Material from *The Sunday Times* is handled by another executive of The Times Newspapers Ltd. Syndication Department.

For those foreign papers and news agencies with offices in *The Times* building, each syndication agreement provides that, for six days a week, the paper or agency will receive:
— By 4 pm daily, a schedule of the contents of the following morning's *Times*.
— Between 3 and 9 pm, a copy of all Telex material sent to *The Times* by all its foreign correspondents and by some of its home correspondents.
— Before 9 pm each day, proofs of all material appearing in the first edition of *The Times* the following morning.
— A copy of the first edition as soon as it comes off the presses.
— Background material.

— Copies of all other messages received by *The Times* Communications Centre (by special arrangement only).

All this material is delivered by hand to each client's office in *The Times* building by a *Times* messenger.[105]

In addition, all clients have the use of the services of a *Times* Syndication Liaison Officer to ensure that:

— all the arrangements set out above work smoothly;
— clients get advance notice of important news in which they are specially interested; and that
— clients are put in touch, if they wish, with *Times* editorial staff members or specialist writers.

The staff of clients with offices in *The Times* building are also entitled to use its:

reference library (open from 9 am to 5 am);
canteen, bar and editorial mess.

Each client with an office within *The Times* building pays rent per square foot and rates, as well as charges for lighting, heating, floor and window cleaning; and for the use of messenger service, library and canteen.

Each client is entitled to cable to his own head office whatever *Times* material is covered by syndication agreement. But *The Times* itself cables no material abroad: it supplies only a 'Lifting Service'; i.e., a copy of the printed newspaper for despatch by the client[106] by air mail to its head office abroad from which items may be lifted.

The Syndication Department entertains journalists visiting *The Times* and arranges interviews with the Editor and the editorial staff.

It also arranges the sale of copyright *Times* material to authors, publishers, schools, universities, societies and business houses for reproduction in book, magazines and pamphlets.

---

[105] By special arrangement, this material can be delivered by hand to the offices of clients elsewhere in London: alternatively it can be collected by them.
[106] For clients with no office in London, the copy is sent direct by *The Times*.